Leading the Way:
A Century of Service

*The Florida Federation of Women's Clubs,
1895-1995*

Library of Congress Catalog Number 94-71073
ISBN 0-9640869-0-5
Published by:
GFWC Florida Federation of Women's Clubs, Inc.
4444 Florida National Drive
Lakeland, Florida 33813
Copyright 1994 Jessie Hamm Meyer

Except for brief excerpts cited by reviewers, no part of this book may be reproduced in any form without express permission in writing from the publisher.

Leading the Way:
A Century of Service

*The Florida Federation of Women's Clubs,
1895-1995*

By
Jessie Hamm Meyer

To the Woman's Club of Ocala

Jessie Hamm Meyer

Dedication

Dedicated to all women of the Florida Federation of Women's Clubs who sought to preserve Florida's natural beauty and who gave their talents, energy, wisdom and time to the improvement of educational opportunities, health, and social conditions for all Floridians.

— *Jessie Hamm Meyer*

Contents

List of Illustrations	vi
Acknowledgements	viii
Introduction	xi
1 — Florida Background	1
2 — Glimpses of Early Clubs	4
3 — Organization of the Florida Federation of Women's Clubs	37
4 — The Second Decade, 1905-1915	56
5 — A Third Decade and World War I	82
6 — The "Bust" and Great Depression, 1925-1935	102
7 — Growth, Change, War	121
8 — Beginning Another Fifty Years	154
9 — The Fifties	167
10 — The Sixties	188
11 — The Seventies	207
12 — The Eighties	223
13 — The Nineties	242
14 — Conclusion	256
Bibliography	262
Appendix — List of Past Presidents and Junior Directors	269
About the Author	272

List of Illustrations

1. Green Cove Springs Club, 1888 — 9
2. Steamboat Manatee — 10
3. Horse and Buggy, 1900 — 10
4. Bessie Williams, pioneer clubwoman — 13
5. Melrose Woman's Club, 1893 — 14
6. Mrs. Pamela Borden Hamilton, First FFWC President — 32
7. Mrs. E. G. G. Munsell, "Mother of the Florida Federation" — 32
8. Pioneer Club delegates at Biltmore Hotel, 1928 — 33
9. Early ribbon badges — 80
10. "Lighter" crossing Intracoastal, Delray Beach — 81
11. Ft. Lauderdale Woman's Club, 1917 — 144
12. Coco Plum Woman's Club, South Miami, 1915 — 144
13. St, Petersburg Woman's Club, 1929 — 144
14. Sorosis of Lakeland Club, 1922 — 145
15. Lakeland Woman's Club, 1927 — 145
16. Jacksonville Woman's Club, 1927 — 146
17. Sorosis of Orlando — 146
18. Daytona Beach Palmetto Club, 1905 — 147
19. Daytona Beach Palmetto Club, 1925 — 147
20. Miami Woman's Club, 1913 — 148
21. Julia Tuttle House — 148
22. Delray Beach Woman's Club — 149
23. West Palm Beach Woman's Club, 1915 — 149
24. Tallahassee Woman's Club, 1926 — 150
25. Sarasota Woman's Club, 1940 — 150
26. Monticello Woman's Club, 1920 — 151
27. Wauchula Woman's Club, 1925 — 151
28. Madison Woman's Club, 1939 — 152
29. Key West Woman's Club, 1902 — 152

30. Colahatchee Woman's Club, Oakland Park, 1939	153
31. Vero Beach Woman's Club, 1917	153
32. Dedication Plaque, Everglades National Park	160
33. Park Lodge, built and maintained by FFWC	161
34. Carolyn Pearce (Mrs. E. D.), Past President of FFWC and GFWC	176
35. Original FFWC Headquarters, Lakeland, 1956	177
36. Jeannine Faubion (Mrs. Raymond A.), Past President of FFWC, GFWC	254
37. New FFWC Headquarters, Lakeland, 1990.	255
38. "Bert" Alberti (Mrs. Patrick), Centennial President	256
39. Map of the FFWC Districts	257
40. Jessie Hamm Meyer, Historian	272

Acknowledgments

First of all, I owe Jimmie Smith a debt of appreciation because she asked me to write a history of the Florida Federation of Women's Clubs. It has been a challenging and rewarding experience as I have attempted to write about what these women were doing during one hundred years of fast paced history in a unique place called Florida.

Without the constant and encouraging support of my husband, Dr. Harvey K. Meyer, I could not have done the detailed research necessary nor sacrificed the retired life style that most people in their late 70s and early 80s consider their due. He has accompanied me as I did research, gone to meetings, made friends of my friends from all over Florida, read the manuscript, and insisted that writing the history was worth doing when I became discouraged thinking it an exercise in futility. He has shown more than ordinary interest in the completion of this history giving his time and considerable talent to the design of the cover and the selection of illustrations.

Bert Alberti has edited every page using her journalistic expertise to change my plodding old fashioned prose into a more nearly 90s style. Sometimes she questioned; she always encouraged. *Leading the Way* has become "our book." Bert has been a tremendous help and FFWC is fortunate to start its second century with a president who has her intellectual ability, experience, energy and charm.

When our archives were in storage and I was first starting research, Karen Albert, FFWC headquarters secretary, was helpful and considerate as I carried cardboard boxes of archival material from its unairconditioned storage to her cool office and spread old records on tables which she made available.

Every member of FFWC owes a debt of gratitude to Vi Thornburg, Marcia Bright, June Sutton and Judy D. Martin, who unpacked the cardboard cartons of archives, sorted and placed FFWC records in the archives room of the new headquarters building.

Marie Bowers, FFWC headquarters office manager, was most helpful during the days I spent at headquarters. Marie was there to help whether it was making a typewriter available, copying a difficult document or telling me the best place to eat lunch.

I am indebted to Charlyne Carruth and Frances S. Widegren for their constant encouragement and contributions of their particular talents.

Dr. Robert Collins of Florida Atlantic University convinced me that I could use a computer. He has been a reporter, he is a writer, an English professor, an editor, a desk-top publisher and, best of all, a friend who agreed to get my efforts camera ready for the publisher. Without Bob, getting this history together would have been difficult, if not impossible.

Most important of all is the debt owed to all those who have written histories of their clubs and to those who have kept records. For most of recorded history, women have been left out. That is changing. Women in Florida made a difference and because Florida Federation women kept records, their story of one hundred years of service can be told.

Jessie Hamm Meyer
Melrose, Florida, 1993

Leading the Way: A Century of Service

Jessie Hamm Meyer

Introduction

AT the 1891 meeting of the newly-formed General Federation of Women's Clubs held in the home of Mr. and Mrs. Thomas A. Edison in West Orange, New Jersey, Jennie June Croly said:

> One thing that will strike you is the all-around character of club women.... Perhaps its central idea, unity in difference, attracts such women; but it is also because they come from the homes, because they have been wives and mothers and are ready for the human enlightenment that club life brings.
>
> The eagerness with which the women's clubs all over the country have taken up history, literature, and art studies, striving to make up for the absence of opportunity and the absorption in household cares of their young womanhood, has in it something almost pathetic.
>
> But the ground will soon have been covered. Is there not room in the clubs for outlook committees, whose business it should be to investigate township affairs, educational, sanitary, reformatory on lines of improvement, and report what is being done, might be done, or needs to be done for decency and order in the jails, in the schools, in the streets, in the planting of trees, in the disposition of refuse and the provisions for light which is the best protection for life and property?"

Mrs. Croly's ideas of what women could do were a call to action and were expressed only four years before the Florida Federation was organized. Such ideas were startlingly ambitious and almost brazen in a time when women had no vote, but Florida women working together in the Florida Federation or as members of their local clubs tackled enormous jobs. Their most visible contribution was the libraries which they founded and operated in towns and cities all over the state.

At the heart of much of their work were children. They petitioned the legislature for laws against child labor and for

Leading the Way: A Century of Service

compulsory education. Well equipped schools, trained teachers, kindergartens, playgrounds, juvenile courts, industrial schools for juvenile offenders, tonsil clinics, immunization programs, dental care and school lunch programs involved Florida Federation club women at every level.

Tree planting and bird protection marked their conservation efforts from the beginning. Later, endangered species and wetland preservation got their attention. The Florida Federation of Women's Clubs was the only woman's club in the country that owned and operated a park of several thousand acres for more than forty years — Royal Palm Park which became a part of Everglades National Park.

Safety was a high priority as they tried to convince the legislature to pass laws removing livestock from Florida's roads and highways. They worked for improved roads, bicycle paths, driver training, highway patrols, and for safety devices such as the reflective road markers that define travel lanes in the dark or in the rain.

Art, poetry, international relations, religion, literature, music, and history were not only subjects for study but inspiration for creative work. Indian Welfare, scholarship programs, citizenship training, patriotic support in times of war and strong stands against movies, television and comic books which they considered unsuitable for children occupied their minds, hearts and actions.

Agnes Gerlach, a charter member of the Fort Walton Beach Woman's Club organized in 1921, summed up the work of her club with a vigor of expression springing from first hand experience.

> This club has always stood for culture, charity, health and welfare including the study of Federal, State, County and City Laws and Ordinances. In the beginning of Camp Walton-Fort Walton, until the men's club was organized, the Woman's Club was the only law enforcement group that we had around the area. If persons, regardless of color or creed, were ill-treated, the women went to their rescue. If fleas were bad, we got rid of them. If cattle ran at large, we fenced them out. If children were in need of hot lunches, we furnished them with lunches — if they needed shoes or clothing, we saw that they were clothed — if babies needed layettes, we sewed and furnished them.... We furnished crutches and braces

for crippled children, had children fitted with glasses, held a clinic in town, had a doctor come out from Pensacola and remove tonsils, had a Christmas tree each year with toys and clothes for the underprivileged, sent baskets of food for their Christmas dinners, sent donations to the orphans' home, worked for better laws and better schools and founded a library, worked for mosquito eradication, too. In fact there wasn't much that we did not work for. We cleaned the town yearly and tried to beautify it in spite of the cows. We built a clinic. We had no doctor during the war — our clinic was all we had. We had to use it, help with it and stay well or die.

Most of the programs that women instituted required money and their funding projects varied with the times and the clubs. Suppers, bake sales and catering were the most common fund raisers. Trash and treasure, rummage, garage and yard sales could usually help the treasury. Fashion shows and card parties always seemed to be a dignified and reliable way to fund projects. One club rented a "patch" of ground, planted and tended a crop of sweet potatoes which they sold for a nice profit. Another club raised cabbages on their land and sold them to the townsfolk. The Crescent City Village Improvement Association held a two day fair in 1914 that netted $1000.00. Because their town had no movie theatre, they borrowed the money from a member's husband and built one. The entire theatre with seats, screen and machine cost $7,000.00 and they were able to pay back their loan within "a short time." Members believe that theirs is the only woman's club in the country that owned a movie theater from 1914 until the 1930s when "talking pictures" made their machine obsolete.

Several clubs sponsored or produced plays, follies and musicals, which were both money making projects and opportunities for talented people to express themselves while entertaining their audiences. In their early days, many clubs had rules against any projects that could be construed as gambling or "games of chance." As attitudes changed, raffles became a more acceptable way of raising money, although it was often advertised as "a drawing" and people "contributed" a set amount for each ticket. Usually the "prize" was fairly modest, but one club was given a saddle horse which the club could not keep but it made a popular prize for the club's raffle.

Leading the Way: A Century of Service

Ambitious clubs sometimes raffled a car or a television. Clubs seldom had funds to complete all of their projects but Florida communities are better for their one hundred years of service.

1 – Florida Background

WILLIAM Bartram wrote of the Florida which he visited in the 1760s and 1770s and John H. Audubon wrote of Florida as he saw it in the 1830's.

These books were significant and their descriptions of swamps, snakes, alligators, birds, insects, teeming wild life and heat appealed to naturalists but did not bring many new settlers to Florida. Harriet Beecher Stowe, who was a well known author because of the popularity of her book, *Uncle Tom's Cabin*, came to Mandarin, south of Jacksonville on the St. Johns River, as a winter visitor. While there she wrote a book, *Palmetto Leaves*, about her Florida experience, which was published in 1872.

Sidney Lanier, a popular poet in the last half of the 19th century, wrote *The Scenery, Climate and History of Florida* which was published in 1875. Lanier's primary purpose for writing the book was to promote the Great Atlantic Railway. George Barbour had toured Florida with General Grant in 1870. As a result of his trip, Barbour wrote a book, *Florida for Tourists, Invalids and Settlers*. Ledyard Bill in *A Winter in Florida* described a trip up the St. Johns from Jacksonville to Sanford and from Picolata to St. Augustine.

Interest in Florida was high. Dozens of articles about the state appeared in magazines and newspapers. Books and articles were widely read both in the United States and Europe. Florida winters were presented in such glowing terms that areas accessible by steamboat or railway became popular as winter residences for the affluent. With a winter home in Florida, they could escape the snow, ice and cold of their northern homes. The St. Johns River towns became the most popular winter resorts in the nation. Elegant hotels catered to wealthy tourists and winter homes became common along the banks of this wide north- flowing river. Comfortable and even palatial steamboats ran on regular schedules from Jacksonville, Mandarin, Orange Park, Palatka and Enterprise.

After the Civil War many of the small, pre-war railroads were in financial disarray as was the state government. When the state began recovering from the war and the corrupt "reconstruction" which followed that war, (known in the North as The War of the Rebellion and in the South as The War of Northern Aggression), Florida's government began a program to attract railroad building and immigration. The state had no money but it had millions of acres of land. To railroad builders, the state offered liberal land subsidies such as alternate sections of land six miles deep on either side of the railroad. The most important of those who were attracted by the state offers were Henry B. Plant, William D. Chipley and Henry M. Flagler. Under the leadership of these enterprising men, companies were incorporated, agricultural and immigration bureaus were set up, land sales organizations were formed, hotels, ports and warehouses were built, and brochures about the wonders of Florida were circulated. In 1883, mining of phosphate deposits started one of the state's major industries and two years later the cigar industry moved to Tampa. By the early 1880s Henry B. Plant had linked Jacksonville to Tampa by rail and William D. Chipley had joined Jacksonville to Pensacola. Flagler had extended his railroad from Jacksonville to St. Augustine where he built the famous Ponce de Leon Hotel. After the big freezes of 1894 and 1895 wiped out most of the citrus of North and Central Florida and left winter residents shivering, Flagler decided to extend his railroad to Miami. The residents of the little settlement of Miami were joyous to welcome the railroad in 1896.

All of these changes brought permanent settlers to Florida but growth was not spectacular. By 1900, there were still fewer than a million people in the entire state. Much of the state remained a frontier. Jacksonville was the largest city with only 28,249 persons, according to the 1900 census. The same year's census showed Chicago with nearly a million inhabitants. The census of 1880 indicated that 47% of Florida's population was black and illiterate. These people were available for work in the fields and woods, prompting many winter residents and tourists to invest in Florida land. Citrus groves were planted, winter vegetable crops were cultivated and some cotton was grown. Virgin forests with their wealth of timber beckoned investors who set up sawmills to turn the great cypress trees and yellow pines into lumber. A turpentine industry developed. All of this land activity needed supervision; therefore, some of these investors came earlier in the season and stayed later, so that Florida became their homes. If they could afford to leave during the summer heat, they went to the mountains or the northern states as summer residents. Flagler continued to build hotels, and by 1908 Flagler hotels alone could accommodate 40,000 guests. Tourism and homes for winter residents, Florida's biggest industry, justified the idea that climate was Florida's greatest asset. Florida had become a strange mix of somewhat sophisticated and affluent people clustering in the towns and small cities and of hardy pioneers living in a state that was still largely a frontier.

2 – Glimpses Of Early Clubs

THE history of the Florida Federation of Women's Clubs is a record of how its members reacted to their times. What they did in their communities and their state was determined by their purposes, goals and moral values. The minutes, treasurer's reports, oral histories, newspaper clippings, and copies of programs tell us not only about the clubs themselves but also about the economics, social attitudes, customs, religious beliefs and problems of society during the years when women took the lead to better themselves and the communities in which they lived.

Unfortunately, some of the minutes of the first clubs have been lost to fire, hurricanes, neglect or aging paper. However, there are enough left to give us a picture of the activities of those women who showed unique foresight and strength in tackling the jobs which they set for themselves. Self-improvement in the arts and sciences were primary goals of some of the early clubs but improvement of their villages, education of children, philanthropic work and general broadening of their interests eventually became a part of all the clubs.

The season for winter residents was from the last of November until the first of May. Minutes show that these were the months when meetings were scheduled. Women who were winter residents took the lead to form the first Florida clubs for women. They came from cities and towns of the northeast and midwest where the woman's club movement had taken hold. However, minutes also reveal that after a few years meetings started earlier in the fall and extended later into the spring.

Those who lived in Florida the year round began to be active in the clubs, because they, too, wanted to better themselves and their communities. Membership often had to be limited to the number of women who could be seated in the parlor of a member who was willing to have the meeting at her house. Most meetings were held in the afternoon, but at least one club held certain meetings open to the public and scheduled them on nights when the moon was full. Without street lights, this was a practical solution which allowed men who worked all day to accompany their wives and to benefit from lectures, concerts and debates or discussions about the needs of the community.

Public opinion was essentially the same in Florida as it was in the rest of the country: "Men had clubs — women should not — neither should they speak in public." Because of this, the very first clubs called themselves by such names as "The Village Improvement Association," "Reading Group," or "Literary and Debating Society."

Towns and villages grew in places accessible either by steamboat or railroads and it was in these communities where the first clubs were organized. Sand roads wound through rural Florida and travel by horse-drawn carriage or on horseback was possible, but long distance trips were not undertaken casually. Supplies were often freighted to rural communities in wagons pulled by oxen. Not many streams had bridges but there were ferries over the larger streams and rivers.

It is impossible to give the history of every club which eventually joined FFWC. However, the histories of the "PIONEER CLUBS", those formed before 1900 and still active 25 years later, give modern readers a glimpse of what club women of those early days set out to accomplish.

GREEN COVE SPRINGS
VILLAGE IMPROVEMENT ASSOCIATION

The oldest woman's club in the Florida Federation of Women's Clubs is The Village Improvement Association of Green Cove Springs, which was organized February 20, 1883, with Mrs. A. M. Rutledge elected as its first president. The history of the VIA records —

> "PURPOSE: To promote neatness and order in the village, improve and beautify the streets and public grounds and generally do whatever would lend to the improvement of the village as a place of residence."

The history of the VIA further states: "Any woman or girl could become a member by simply doing one or all three things, (1) pay five cents weekly, (2) plant and protect a tree, (3) give ten hours labor under the direction of the Executive Committee". They later changed one bylaw to read: "Any woman or girl who shall pay $1.00 per year instead of the five cents weekly may be a member." Their source of revenue being limited, they imposed fines on each member of the Executive Committee, "five cents for being fifteen minutes late for a meeting or ten for an absence." They made badges with the emblem "VIA" and fined a member five cents if she forgot to wear her badge.

The first year was an active one. Members petitioned the mayor and council to improve the streets and not to cut down the trees. They wrote to the U. S. Agricultural Department for advice on what kind of shade trees to plant and they spent $45.00 to have clay and sawdust spread on the streets. They dug out weeds, planted flowers and declared "sandspur grass is destroyed." They found that this was a premature and overly optimistic conclusion because that prolific and tenacious plant had to be dug out again and again.

For some unrecorded reason, no meetings were held from September 20th, 1884, until January 21, 1888. Mrs. E.G.G. Munsell came from New York in 1887 and she and Miss Penelope Borden became active in reviving the Village Improvement Association of Green Cove Springs. The renewed organization voted honorary membership for men and appointed a committee of three men, husbands of members, to supervise work on the cemetery. Fifty dollars was appropriated for cemetery work and $90.00 was appropriated for sanitary work during the summer. One barrel of copperas (iron sulphide) was bought wholesale at two cents a pound which was distributed to townspeople to disinfect "their outdoor vaults" better known today as "privies" or "outhouses". Carbolic acid was bought and poured into public drains and a man was hired to clean the streets twice a week for 75 cents a day. Later a "VISITOR'S GUIDE" had this to say: "The Association employs a man whose duty it is to go over the city daily with a wheelbarrow and tools, for the purpose of cleaning the streets of stray paper and trash of all sorts. This is buried out of sight or burned. A Committee of ONE lady takes charge of this man for one week, laying out and inspecting his work for the week. Thus all the ladies take a personal interest in the work, and because of this process, thoroughly posted as to the general cleanliness and sanitary conditions of the city."

John and Ellen Borden of the Borden Milk family gave a cottage to the VIA in 1888. A Mr. J. J. Merritt gave a single book to start a library and this prompted visitors and members to donate books — the beginning of a library which The Village Improvement Association of Green Cove Springs maintained from 1888 until December 1961 when their library became a part of the Clay County library system. This first club adopted a motto, "When the Matrons and the Maidens of a Nation are BUSY and VIRTUOUS that Nation is rising. When they are NOT SO, it is in rapid decline, for Wise and Virtuous women are God's Modelers on Earth of a Nation's Heroes and Sages." The VIA also formed "an auxiliary society for children called the Star Branch" which remained in existence for fifteen years and had an enrollment that "soared to one hundred and thirty children." Meetings were held weekly and their motto was "cleanliness is next to Godliness." They instilled in these children the "importance of the respect for property, wild life and cleanliness of body and soul."

Attention to neatness and order in the village continued to

be a prominent activity. "The streets were again saw-dusted and provided with good pine walks. Gayly painted barrels (14 in all) were placed on platforms on street corners with a bit of humorous verse, encouraging townspeople to throw their trash and particularly their orange peels into the barrels."

When money was needed to carry out projects of the association, direct solicitation resulted in some donations by interested citizens. For other needed funds the VIA gave receptions, teas and concerts and also sponsored moonlight excursions aboard THE MANATEE on the St. Johns.

According to information compiled by Mrs. Norma J. Rosakranse, "By 1890 the work of the VIA was so well publicized throughout the state and the country, similar organizations were now in existence, using Green Cove Springs as a model. The town was referred to as 'The Parlour of the South', and reference was made to the green and orange barrels with their humorous verses and the employing of men to clean the streets." This interesting feature was somehow printed in a newspaper in Germany and ridiculed by the editor, but the German Emperor happened to read the article about the work of the VIA and its barrels for trash. "He thought it a novel idea and full of originality and gave orders that the plan be carried out in the Empire."

In July of 1894, members of the VIA of Green Cove Springs, realizing that the women of several other towns and villages had organized, decided to invite these groups to think about joining together into a federation. One of the things that prompted them to do this was an action of the Florida Legislature allowing cattle to roam freely in towns of less than 1200. The women of Green Cove Springs had tried to keep their little town clean and had petitioned the legislature to pass a law against free- roaming cattle but to no avail. They thought that if groups over the state could join together they could be more effective. The following letter was sent to Crescent City Village Improvement Association. (That letter or a similar one was sent to other women's organizations in the small towns of Florida.)

Fig. 1. The VIA of Green Cove Springs celebrated its centennial in this clubhouse, built on the site of its oiginal clubhouse which was donated by John and Ellen Borden in 1888.

Green Cove Springs
July 17, 1894

To the President of the Crescent City V.I.A.

May I bring to your consideration the subject of State Federation? The ladies of the Village Improvement Association of Green Cove Springs have for the past year had a matter under discussion, and think that the Union of all the Societies would be the means of strengthening and encouraging the individual club. Although each society may have its distinctive lines of work, the bonding together of many, and coming into communion and heart touch the whole and give added zeal to our work. We would like some expression from you upon the subject, and if a sufficient number of clubs will co-operate, we propose to call a meeting of delegates from each society in the early winter, to discuss and frame a Constitution and Bylaws for the governing of said Federation.

After bringing this proposition before your members we will be glad to have you write us, and trust the plan of State Federation will be acceptable.

With greetings from the Village Improvement Association of Green Cove Springs, I am very sincerely,

Eliza A. Graves, Cor. Secretary

Leading the Way: A Century of Service

Fig. 2 (Top) The MANATEE, a steamboat used by the VIA of Green Cove Springs for "Moonlight Excursions" on the St. Johns River in early years. Fig. 3 (Bottom) Familiar land transportation before automobiles (from the FFWC *Clubwoman*).

All of the members of the committee on federation were from Green Cove Springs: Mrs. E. N. Burrows, president; Mrs. E. V. Low, corresponding secretary; and Mrs.E. G. G. Munsell. Many leaders of the VIA of Green Cove Springs were winter residents and were well aware that a General Federation of Women's Clubs had been formed on a national level in 1890. They were not far behind in attempting to form a Florida federation.

A brief history of the clubs which sent delegates to the organizational meeting in Green Cove Springs follows.

CRESCENT CITY
VILLAGE IMPROVEMENT ASSOCIATION

From a history of the Village Improvement Association of Crescent City written by its first secretary, Miss Bessie Williams, we find that:

> During the fall of 1889, a busy keeper of a small boarding house in Crescent City raised by subscription the munificent sum of twenty dollars with which to build a board walk along two blocks of the little business street where the sand was especially deep.
>
> Encouraged by her success in this great town improvement, this busy person then obtained in the same manner a sum of money for the purpose of placing at the railroad station a sign which would enlighten the traveling public as to the location and attractiveness of Crescent City. This sign stood on two long, slender legs in the middle of a mud puddle where pigs were usually wallowing. At the top was printed in small letters, 'Two Miles to'; and then in larger letters, 'CRESCENT CITY', and in much larger letters, 'A BEAUTIFUL LOCATION'. It hardly needs to be mentioned that the traveling public was more entertained than enlightened.
>
> This second adventure so heartened the lady that she decided to ask the women of the village to come together for the purpose of planning further improvements.

The lady was Mrs. W. D. Burton, the first president of the Village Improvement Association of Crescent City. Mrs. Williams wrote that twenty women responded and that they patterned their organization after that of Green Cove Springs. "At their first meeting they planned intensive work for town improvement, which included grubbing out dog fennel and coffee weed from the streets, making shell walks, crossings and

Leading the Way: A Century of Service

a few roads, trimming trees on the streets and care of the cemetery. A plot of land was given to the club and a building was donated provided that the association move it. This was done and the association set aside one room to be used as a library."

The library became the club's major project which they operated from 1890 until 1987 when the library became a part of the Putnam County library system. The Crescent City V.I.A. was the first woman's club in Florida to own its own club house. Unfortunately, their club house was destroyed by fire in November 1968. Miss Bessie Williams ends her history in this way:

> It was an interesting and disturbing fact that many of our best women did not venture to join this women's organization, fearing to lose the respect of their husbands and families if they became a part of such an audacious group of women, who dared to think they could do for a town what the men had not done. At the initial meeting, held for the purpose of forming the Village Improvement Association of Crescent City, eleven states, England and Canada were represented but no Floridian was present.

Minutes that are in existence for the Crescent City Club go back only to May 14, 1923. Histories of Crescent City written by Miss Williams and by George Miller plus court records and old newspaper clippings have enabled Marjorie Neal Nelson to piece together the history of the Woman's Club of Crescent City.

MELROSE LITERARY AND DEBATING SOCIETY

The Literary and Debating Society of Melrose did not get a delegate to the organizational meeting but answered the invitation showing interest and sent a delegate the next year. From the excellent history prepared by Maude Watkins we learn that the first meeting of what was to become the Melrose Woman's Club was held July 23, 1890. The nine women who met that day in the home of Mrs. Eliza King decided to call their group "The Literary and Debating Society." Their next meeting was on August 8th during which they elected officers and

Fig. 4. BESSIE WILLIAMS, Gold Medal Pioneer Clubwoman and historian of the V.I.A. of Crescent City. Feted at the Golden Jubilee Convention of the General Federation of Women's Clubs in Atlantic City, New Jersey, May 1941.

Leading the Way: A Century of Service

Fig. 5. Clubhouse of the Melrose Literary and Debating Society — Melrose Woman's Club. Used since November 10, 1893, making it Florida's oldest in continuous use by a woman's organization.

decided on the topic for debate at the next meeting.

On August 20th, the President, Mrs. King, read a prepared paper on "Equal Rights" which was discussed and the minutes show that all agreed that women should have the right to vote. Mrs. King was a strong believer in the suffrage movement and as president she may have influenced their choice of subject for their next meeting: "Equal Financial Rights between Husband and Wife."

At their fourth meeting on September 5th, the members discussed the topic chosen at their previous meeting and ambitiously chose three topics for their next discussions:

(1) Does a woman by marriage under existing laws of society and state benefit her condition?

(2) The relative influence of labor and capital;

(3) The equal standard of morality for men and women.

Melrose women began their organization in July which indicates that their homes were in Melrose and that they were not just winter residents. By April 3, 1891, the Literary and Debating Society was discussing ways to improve the community of Melrose including more houses for rent, manufacturing of some kind, a public well, a school-house well, sanitary rules and regulations and also shade trees for the streets. They did not stop with that list for they wanted to get the schoolhouse painted; they asked store-keepers not to throw their trash and rubbish into the street; and they definitely believed that the community needed a hall for meetings and entertainments.

Their desire for a building or hall began to be more than a dream as they discussed ways to raise and accumulate money for the purchase of land. Mrs. Eliza King and Miss Nellie Glen offered to donate land. To accept the land, the society had to take the steps necessary for a proper deed to be made while they continued to accumulate funds. By March 1892, members voted to put their accumulated funds in a "safe bank" and at their April meeting the treasurer reported that $215 had been placed in a bank in Connecticut which left them with $1.51 in their treasury. They voted at this meeting that the officer in whose name the money had been deposited should not be held responsible in case of bank failure.

The topic chosen for their next discussion was "Free Coinage of Silver." Both the action taken on finding a "safe bank" and the topic chosen reflected the uneasiness of the time, which was the preface to the Panic of 1893.

Much of the members' time during the next several months dealt with incorporation, plans for the hall and accumulating enough money to pay for it. They had voted to spend $400.00 for the building; but the carpenter whom they preferred to build their hall bid $489.00. However, he agreed to deduct $20.00 from his bid as a donation. By this time they had accumulated $351.00 and decided to go ahead with the building which would be 26 X 40 and 14 feet in height. There was to be a front porch and a chimney. Although they were occupied with getting their building, they still found time to write a letter protesting the behavior of Yale students (The minutes do not say what the Yale students were doing that members of the Melrose Club felt that they should write a letter of protest) and letters to Florida legislators against a bill which had been introduced permitting legal houses of prostitution. They also continued their discussions, amended their rules and managed an orderly exchange of books and magazines.

The clubhouse of the Melrose Literary and Debating Society was put into use November 10, 1893. This clubhouse is now on the Historic Register and is the oldest clubhouse in the state that has been in continuous use by a woman's club since it was first opened.

The minutes for the first seven years of the society's existence show many changes in the bylaws of the Melrose Literary and Debating Society, but by 1897 members must have felt that they were stabilized enough that they had them printed. The entry fee to the society was fifty cents and dues were twenty-five cents quarterly. Visitors to Melrose and relatives could become associate members. No money was to be raised for the society by lotteries. One of the bylaws states: "We shall always bear in mind that the aim of this Society in its public entertainment as well as its private meetings shall be moral, mental and social by nature."

Voted into membership of the Florida Federation of Women's Clubs at the meeting in Jacksonville, January 29, 1897, the Melrose Literary and Debating Society invited the newly formed FFWC to "hold the convention of 1898 in their place, the delegates to be guests of the Society."

The minutes also record the answer: "While fully appreciating the courtesies it was thought that some point nearer of access would insure fuller attendance and the Cor. Sec. was instructed to acknowledge the invitation with thanks expressing regrets at non-acceptance."

The Literary and Debating Society of Melrose dropped out of the Florida federation for a number of years. Some members may have felt rebuffed because their invitation was not accepted, but it is more likely that the inconvenience of travel to FFWC meetings was the reason for this club's lack of participation in the federation.

THE FAIRFIELD IMPROVEMENT ASSOCIATION — JACKSONVILLE

The Fairfield Town Improvement Association was organized in 1894 and was a charter member of the Florida Federation of Women's Clubs. Mrs. N.C. Wamboldt was the first president and she became the second president of FFWC in 1897. The Fairfield Club felt the need of a club house soon after it was organized and a lot was donated by H. B. Plant of the Plant Investment Company with the stipulation that the building placed on it should cost a certain amount and that the building should always be used for civic or educational purposes. Soon after it was built, the hall was opened as a recreational and reading room for soldiers who were encamped near-by as a result of being called to duty in the Spanish American War of 1898. Like many other clubs the Fairfield Club used its club house to start a library.

The second annual meeting of the FFWC was held in Jacksonville with the Fairfield Town Improvement Association as the hostess club. Among the outstanding leaders in the early history of FFWC were Mrs. L. E. Wamboldt and Dr. Ellen

Lowell-Stevens who were members of the Fairfield Town Improvement Association.

When Fairfield became a part of Jacksonville the word "town" was dropped from the club's name and it became the Fairfield Improvement Association. The report from this organization in the 1904-1905 yearbook states that the club had only eight members "all devoted to town improvement. A primary school is held in their building during the week and a Sunday School on Sundays.... The Association takes entire care of their property and is free of debt." In the 1909-1910 year book this club reported 18 members, while the Woman's Club of Jacksonville, federated in 1898, reported 270 members.

The Fairfield Club was continuing to work and by 1912 had 23 members. They continued to make yearly reports, but did not show much growth. In the intervening years more women's clubs were organized in Jacksonville and five clubs reported from that city in the 1928-1929 year book. It is regrettable that a club which furnished so much impetus to forming of the Florida Federation failed to furnish its history to the Convention of March 1928, when the Pioneer Clubs were honored and their histories were published in that year book.

THE PALMETTO CLUB OF DAYTONA BEACH

The Palmetto Club was not a charter member of the Florida Federation of Women's Clubs but soon became very active in the federation and joined the General Federation of Women's Clubs before FFWC joined.

In Daytona, a group of ladies met every week to play whist during the winters of 1892 and 1893. After a year of card playing, some of the group thought that they should be doing more worthwhile things; therefore, they decided to devote an afternoon every other week to serious reading. During the winter months of December 1894 and of 1895, the group met on alternate Thursdays and had varied discussions about their reading. By November 1895, the club had 36 members and the influence of the woman's club movement had reached

Daytona. Many members of the whist and reading group were winter residents and were cognizant of the effectiveness of the women's clubs that were being formed in the cities and towns of their northern homes. They decided that each member would invite a friend to the December meeting. A club was formed, officers were elected and "after free and full discussion, it was decided to call their organization 'The Palmetto Club', as being typical of Florida." At the following meeting, a draft of a constitution was submitted and after much discussion was adopted along with the bylaws. One of the bylaws limited the membership to 50 as that was the "limit of the accommodation of Mrs. Weeks' parlour."

Unlike some of the other early clubs, the history of The Palmetto Club records that its purpose was one of mutual improvement. They were mostly women of education and wealth. In fact it was said that The Palmetto Club "has the cream of the 400 from the different northern states."

For their club's declared mutual improvement members chose for consideration such subjects as Ethics of Literature; Peace and Arbitration; A Glance at Romanticism; Studies in Black and White; Ethical Forces of the Universe and Co-ordination Factor of Modern Life. Members were supposed to be prepared to discuss the subject of the afternoon when called upon.

However, by January 1897, The Palmetto Club had decided to enlarge the scope of its club work. One of its first projects was "to get the cows and pigs off the streets" — a tribute to practicality.

Miss Celia Doener suggested a motto for the club which was adopted and later used by the Florida Federation of Women's Clubs: *In great things unity, in small things liberty, and in all things charity.* (These words are credited to John Amos Comenius, a bishop of the Moravian Church in the mid 17th century. Bishop Comenius, a leading educator ahead of his time, is best known for being the first educator to put pictures in children's schoolbooks.)

The Palmetto Club continued to work for the improvement of their community by insisting on clean streets, better street lighting and abolishment of offensive billboards. They were concerned with the health of the community and made people aware that tuberculosis and other diseases could be spread through dairy products.

In the history written for publication in the 1928-1929 year book, we read: "The Philanthropic Department does splendid work amongst the colored people, maintaining two kindergartens, where the kiddies are taken care of while their mothers are away at work. Here the children learn better ways of living. The members have saved many little ones from physical and moral harm. The Public Welfare Department does great work through the schools and co-operates with the City Improvement Committee. This department started the school nurse, school luncheons, also Better Baby movement, holding clinics for examination of babies, both white and black. Through this department the Parent-Teacher Association was organized. This year (1928) they have taken over the Humane Society."

Soon after the Palmetto Club was organized its history indicates that its members felt a strong desire for a suitable meeting place of their own. They outgrew Mrs. Week's parlour and met in hotels, the yacht club, the opera house and finally built a beautiful clubhouse which was considered one of the most outstanding clubhouses in Florida.

THE WOMAN'S TOWN IMPROVEMENT ASSOCIATION OF TARPON SPRINGS

A history of the Woman's Town Improvement Association of Tarpon Springs printed in the FFWC Yearbook for 1928-1929 states that: "The Woman's Town Improvement Association of Tarpon Springs was organized February 8, 1892, by Miss Helen G. Warner (whose press name was Helen Harcourt). Mrs. Soledad Safford, wife of the former Governor of the Arizona Territory, was the first president and Mrs. J. C. Beekman the Chairman of the Executive Board. There were twenty-six members. The object was to keep the streets clean and to beautify the town and the little park of about five acres in the center of town. Yearly dues were a dollar and there was a fine of 10 cents for absence from any regular meeting. Business women, however, were exempt from fines.

The first year membership dues amounted to $35.00 and fines $4.50. All kinds of entertainment were continually in progress: "dances, plays, women's minstrels, historical tableaus, art figure tableaus, all day and moonlight boat picnics, wrapped auction sales, everything to turn a penny with which to plant one or two of the principal streets for long distances with cabbage palmetto and Grenvillea oaks." The women hired colored men to clean the streets and vacant lots, and committee members would stand by, directing the work. No time was lost by these men resting on their hoes and rakes or discussing "Brudder Jones' rally day de nex Sunday cummin." From row boats these men would even clean the beautiful bayou with rakes and long poled hooks. The bottom of the bayou was cleaned and no green moss or trash was allowed to accumulate. Wild ducks were encouraged and came in large numbers. In those days cattle roamed the streets and the Women's Town Improvement Association was obliged to fence the park where they had planted shrubs, valuable trees and grass.

In 1894, the Women's Town Improvement Association "placed many street lights in the most needed places, with kerosene lamps that went out automatically at mid-night, but had to be lighted by a boy or man; the town council paid for that service. The women bought three barrels of oil at a time and stored it in a large steel tank that they were fortunate in purchasing."

Mrs. Safford was a delegate to the meeting held in Green Cove Springs in 1895. It is to be assumed that she rode the train from Tampa to Jacksonville and then got down to Green Cove Springs on one of the boats that ran on a regular schedule on the St. Johns River. Mrs. Safford's presence at that meeting gave Tarpon Springs the honor of being a charter member club, and one of its members, Mrs. J. C. Beekman, was elected President of the FFWC for the years 1899-1900. However, due to ill health, Mrs. Beekman was never able to preside at a meeting; she sent reports and papers to be read by others

Leading the Way: A Century of Service

and "carried the Federation in her heart."

ORANGE CITY VILLAGE IMPROVEMENT ASSOCIATION

A group of women in Orange City began meeting in 1886 to sew for the poor. As they sewed, they discussed the needs of their community. Led by Mrs. Louise Morse of New Hampshire and Mrs. Frank Hooker of Chicago, the Village Improvement Association of Orange City was organized May 15, 1894. The club members met twice each month at the homes of members. By the end of the first year the club had grown from 12 to 28 members. They formed a library association, placed a water fountain "for man or beast" on the main street, laid the first sidewalk in Orange City, planted shade trees and urged merchants to keep their places of business tidy. Mrs. Hooker was president from the club's beginning in 1894 until she died in 1897. She left her mark and memories in her community:

> While she was President, the town council ordered many of the oak trees cut down. A man came to her and told her what he was ordered to do. She replied, with some emphasis, that no trees should be cut; that she would shoot any one who tried it. The trees still stand royal monarchs today (1928).

There was no electricity in those days so people carried lanterns at night. The VIA voted to place lamp posts at different corners of the streets. They bought thirteen lamps at $4.00 apiece, and hired a man at $2.50 a week to light and care for them.

In 1897, Miss Melissa Dickenson bought a building and gave a room in it for the use of a library for one dollar a year. The VIA was to have the use of one room with free use of the facilities and also the use of the hall for any entertainment purposes that was for the benefit of the VIA.

Not having to concern themselves with the work and expense of obtaining a club house, the club women during their early days directed their energies toward their principal purposes for organizing. Much credit is given by the Orange

City Village Improvement Association to Miss Melissa Dickenson for her gifts of time and money to her community.

On March 10, 1907, fire destroyed the records of the VIA, but a Miss Boyles had kept records and clippings from local papers and notes were taken from the papers of Miss Dickenson so that this club was able to write its history. They had increased from 12 members in 1894 to 80 in 1920.

VILLAGE IMPROVEMENT ASSOCIATION OF ORMOND BEACH

The VIA of Ormond Beach was organized in 1891. The club responded to the call by the VIA of Green Cove Springs to the meeting in February of 1895. It was the intention of the club to send a delegate but she became ill. It was not until 1898 that the Village Improvement Association of Ormond Beach was admitted to the Florida Federation of Women's Clubs.

This group of women started a library in 1891 and assumed the responsibility of keeping the streets clean. They purchased barrels so that the citizens of their town would be encouraged to deposit their trash in the barrels instead of throwing it on the street and they hired a man to keep the barrels emptied.

There were no bridges across the Halifax River during the early years when the VIA of Ormond Beach was working to "provide neatness and order in the village and do whatever may tend to improve and beautify our town as a place of residence and keep it in beautiful condition".

Feeling the need for a place to meet, the club bought a lot on North Beach Street for $1200 in 1894 and paid off the debt within five years. Members of the VIA of Ormond Beach were proud that they were able to build a club house before the village of Ormond Beach had a city hall.

The following clubs were not charter members but they were pioneer organizations of women active in their communities before the end of the 19th Century and later became a part of the Florida Federation of Women's Clubs.

Leading the Way: A Century of Service

APPALACHICOLA — THE PHILACO WOMAN'S CLUB

In 1896, 21 women organized the Woman's Reading Club of Appalachicola. This club was noted for its cultural interests but soon became involved in civic and educational affairs. They took on beautification projects and furnished supplies for the school. Later they were instrumental in forming an organization which eventually became the Parent Teacher Association.

A statement written in 1928 about things as they were when the club was organized states:

> Now when this club was organized, there was no railroad in Appalachicola. We had no telegraph line, no motor boats, no motorcycles, no electric lights, no telephones, no wrist watches, no vanity compacts, no Chamber of Commerce, no organization for civic betterment, no water works, no shell roads, no automobiles, no typewriters, no white canvas shoes, no X-Ray, no Parent-Teacher organization, no Cemetery Association and no appendicitis.

What a strange collection of things to mention that Appalachicola didn't have! There appears to be more than a little humor on the part of this writer.

(What could have been mentioned was that in Appalachicola, in 1848, Dr. John Gorrie, a physician, had demonstrated the process of making artificial ice! It was quite by accident. Remembering a lesson learned in physics that air becomes heated when compressed and cooled when released, Dr. Gorrie built a machine that he hoped would cool the room of a yellow fever patient. It did, but it also made ice. A machine that would make ice in 1848! A British patent for the process was issued in 1849 and a United States patent in 1851. Dr. Gorrie spent the next ten years trying to get someone to finance his invention but he died in 1855 unrecognized for what he had done. In fact his invention was written up in some northern papers as a hoax. "Only God can make Ice", they said. Dr. Gorrie's invention in Appalachicola did more to make Florida a livable place than any other single invention but even in 1928 the person writing the history of her club did not realize the importance of Dr. Gorrie's work; at least she did not mention it.)

Jessie Hamm Meyer

Mrs. Dwight Mitchell, in her history of the club states, "The club needed a new name that would better reflect the purpose of the organization. In 1903, Mrs. C.F. Buffam, then president, took the name Appalachicola and, using no letter twice, coined the name 'Philaco' from Greek words meaning love, hospitality and strength."

Like other women's clubs of Florida, the Philaco Club started a library and maintained it. They began a study of American history soon after organizing and then set themselves the task of learning the history of all the Americas.

The club's first charitable work provided a nurse for a poor woman, which, in 1898, they could do for the sum of three dollars a week. Throughout the years the Philaco Club has been sensitive to the civic, educational and cultural needs of the community. Much of the financing of their work has been done through sales of their cookbook, which they have revised several times.

THE HOUSEKEEPER'S CLUB OF COCONUT GROVE

In 1891, Miss Flora McFarlane, Mrs. Kirk Munroe, Mrs. Joseph Frow, Mrs. Charles John Peacock and Mrs. Benjamin Newbold-Gardner organized The Housekeeper's Club of Cocoanut Grove (note the spelling). Women lived in more or less isolation around Biscayne Bay and they wanted to know more of each other and wished to foster some of the ideals and characteristics of friends and homes that they had left in the North. The dues were to be ten cents each quarter and they decided to meet for two hours every Thursday afternoon. They met in a Sunday School building and sewed articles of clothing or useful household items which they planned to sell. They had their first sale in April and reported eight aprons, five towels, two waists, one shirt and one tie amounting to $3.80. Also, ten cents worth of sewing had been done for Mrs. Kirk Munroe. The money which they made was to benefit the Sunday School building where they met.

While the women were busy with needle and thread one of the members would read articles that were related to home making. Miss Flora McFarlane, who had come to Coconut Grove in 1886 to teach in the first school, was elected the first president of the Housekeepers' Club.

These women began to look forward to having a clubhouse but they continued to give their money to the Sunday School building. Finally, they declared that they had taken care of the spiritual needs of the community and, in 1897, built a club house on property donated by Commodore R. M. Munroe. "A fair stage was built" and the club began to have literary programs, plays, and musical productions as well as special event celebrations, such as the Fourth of July. The custom of devoting some meetings to domestic issues persisted. It also remained the custom that no children were allowed at regular meetings so that mothers could be free of care and home duties. The club arranged for child care on club days. Dues were set at fifty cents a year and the club continued to be fairly democratic. Money was raised for their special projects with fairs, the sale of items donated by people from the North, special programs and all the usual events of that day. The Housekeeper's Club of Coconut Grove was welcomed into The Florida Federation of Women's Clubs in 1901.

THE HIGH SPRINGS NEW CENTURY WOMAN'S CLUB

The High Springs New Century Woman's Club was organized in 1899 and was federated in 1900. In the history of this club, compiled by Mrs. Otto Kahlich, we find the following paragraph:

> High Springs at the time our club was organized did not have an enviable reputation, as many of the club members so well remember. I think our greatest desire for the success of our club was that we thought we would wield our influence for good. I hope and really think we did create a sentiment that was most helpful. In those days we were more of a literary and social club than are clubs these days, Yes, we studied Kipling, Shakespeare, Longfellow, Tennyson and current events. We had some in those early days who did not approve of a Woman's Club — a minister of one of our churches who knew what we were studying, on a Sunday morning,

Jessie Hamm Meyer

during his discourse, spoke of Shakespeare as being vile and said that he wished it was in his power to collect every volume of Shakespeare that was ever published and make of these a bonfire. — I think he did not like a woman's club and thought that he would show us how much he disapproved of our selection of such an author for our study. However, we continued our study of Shakespeare for many months."

These pioneer club women had several names suggested for their club and finally voted that the name should be The New Century Club of High Springs, a name which is again very appropriate as we are soon to enter the Twenty-first Century.

THE WOMAN'S CLUB OF PALATKA

This club was organized as the Woman's Fortnightly Club of Palatka in May 1897, and was admitted to FFWC at the annual meeting held in Daytona, January 1898. At this time the club had 40 active members and 18 honorary members. When the Palatka club was organized and federated its purpose was "intellectual improvement", but like many women's clubs it founded and supported a library.

The first year's work included "Studies in American History" and "Discussions of Current Events". According to the Palatka Club's history, "Professor Carson of Stetson University in Deland gave a series of lectures on 'Critical Events in American History'. Upon the afternoon set aside for the discussion of causes that led up to the Civil War, fearing this topic might result in a repetition of that event, a tea party was tactfully substituted for the literary program."

When the club voted to add "Philanthropics and Civics" to its program of endeavor, some of the members threatened to resign because they believed that only the home was "Women's Sphere," but the first work of the Civics Department brought the club some national attention, in *The Ladies Home Journal* under the heading "What Women's Clubs Are Doing":

> For fully twenty-five years an old boiler discarded by the railroad company lay half buried under debris, with rust and decay adding to the general unsightliness, in the town of Palatka, Florida. Mrs. George Gay is chairman of the Civic Department of the Florida State

Federation and her home is in Palatka. Her trained eye determined to rid her town of this eyesore, and one morning her neighbors saw her directing a gang of workmen who were digging a monster hole, into which the old boiler was tumbled and the ground was covered with grass and flowers planted thereon."

The Woman's Fortnightly Club of Palatka was incorporated in April 1910, as the Woman's Club of Palatka. A few years later this club had seven departments and supported the Legislative Program of The Florida Federation of Women's Clubs.

PALMETTO VILLAGE IMPROVEMENT ASSOCIATION

Because records have been lost, the Palmetto Village Improvement Association members are not sure whether their organizational meeting was in late 1899 or early 1900. Their first minutes were from April 20, 1900, and show that they had received a copy of the Constitution and Bylaws of the VIA of Green Cove Springs. The work of the Palmetto VIA seems to have followed fairly closely that of the VIA of Green Cove Springs.

One of the first projects of the women of this club was to buy barrels and paint them so that people would be encouraged to keep trash off the streets. They sent a committee to the Town Council with an offer to pay half the cost of "hitching posts" on a vacant lot to get some of the "parked" horses off the Main Street.

They invited the men to a clean-up day at the cemetery and fed them a picnic lunch. A reading room as well as recreational facilities got the attention of these club women. Since there was no ice cream or soft drink "stand" in the town the women were able to finance much of their work with "ice cream suppers."

After a few years, the club changed its name to Library Association and spent most of its energies building up a library and through the help of some of the town's citizens eventually obtained a Carnegie Library.

In 1915, the members of the old V.I.A., the Library Association and other women of the town met in the new library and became the Woman's Club of Palmetto which soon joined The Florida Federation of Women's Clubs. This club presented its history at the 1928 Convention as one of the pioneer clubs of Florida.

THE WOMAN'S CLUB OF JACKSONVILLE

The Woman's Club of Jacksonville was organized in 1897 and in 1898 joined the FFWC with a membership of 70. During their first year educational, philanthropic and cultural departments began to function.

The history of this club records no opposition to women having a club. In fact just the opposite is recorded:

> From the beginning, the club has had the sympathetic understanding and assistance of the press, pulpit, and the business and professional men of Jacksonville. Throughout its triumphant existence it could never have functioned so successfully but for the generous gifts of time and service from our generous men. Editors, lawyers, doctors, bankers, preachers, and plain citizens have most generously responded to our appeals for help, and have evidenced their confidence in us by asking our aid in matters of civic importance.

This club's influence in its city was felt through the club's contributions and assistance to many civic minded organizations. Other organizations developed from this club and charitable groups were helped as the Woman's Club of Jacksonville grew to 800 members during its first thirty years.

While by modern standards Jacksonville was not a large city, it was the largest city in Florida during those years, which might account for the more enlightened attitude toward women belonging to clubs. However, the leadership of the club showed a very positive attitude and was apparently adept at obtaining co-operation from the entire community.

OZONA VILLAGE IMPROVEMENT ASSOCIATION

The following history was submitted by Dr. Grace Whitford to the Florida Federation of Women's Clubs in 1928.

> A small group of women, some born in the neighborhood, others

who had moved from the North to Ozona, met May 17, 1897, and formed the Ozona Ladies' Village Improvement Society. At that time there were no paved roads in the entire section, transportation was by horse-drawn vehicle or oxen and limited to the few, at that; cattle and hogs roamed at large and social intercourse was largely restricted to the immediate vicinity. These women felt the need of an organization for village improvement and as a provision for wholesome amusement for old and young (especially with an eye to preventing juvenile delinquency), by promoting educational and inspirational life. Wanting to build a clubhouse to serve as a community center, the society incorporated in January 1900, and built and financed its own club house, the site having been donated by a member in March of that year.

Their clubhouse served as a community center as they had planned: "young and old have danced, played, listened to lectures, held commencement exercises, public meetings and even voted in election years." It also housed a circulating library.

ORLANDO SOROSIS

Orlando Sorosis Club was founded in 1893 by nine women as a reading and study club. Membership was limited to 25 and the women met in members' homes. Dues were sixty cents a year.

By 1899 the club had procured rooms in the Armory Building where they met and later started the first Circulating Library in Orlando. In 1901, the club was given the use and income from a business building in the heart of town, bought for this purpose by a member, Mrs. W. C. Comstock, of Chicago and Winter Park. Upon her death, this property was deeded to the club by Mr. Comstock.

The Orlando Sorosis Club grew and contributed to the cultural life of Orlando. It was not until 1912 that this club joined The Florida Federation of Women's Clubs and in 1915 the General Federation of Women's Clubs. Having united with the state and national organizations, Orlando Sorosis became less exclusive, opening its membership to all women desiring what this club had to offer. The members of the club also broadened the club's programs to include citizenship and community service, music, drama and literature.

THE MARRIED LADIES' AFTERNOON CLUB
(The Woman's Club of Miami)

Only four years after Miami was incorporated, the Married Ladies' Afternoon Club came into being. A group of friends who had been visiting and reading together decided on a summer afternoon in 1900 to form a club. Its purpose at that time was for mutual improvement and pleasure. They planned to use their ten cent weekly dues to buy books for their little circle. By 1902, the women voted to make their club more literary and placed a ban on elaborate refreshments except for very special occasions.

In 1903, the group had grown to 80 members and they had accumulated approximately 1000 volumes. In November of 1903 this club joined the Florida Federation of Women's Clubs and in 1905 it became affiliated with the General Federation of Women's clubs. In 1906, the name of the club was changed from the "Married Ladies' Afternoon Club" to the "Woman's Club of Miami."

Before the club acquired a building of its own, its library's large volume of books became a problem to handle. In one of those early years the books were moved six times from one temporary location to another. The ladies felt that the librarian's salary should be raised from six to eight dollars a month and that they should begin to plan for a real club house. An appeal was made to Henry M. Flagler for help in obtaining a club house and library. Flagler donated land on East Flagler Street and club members raised $13,000.00. The Woman's Club of Miami built its club house which could also serve as a library.

In 1923, the club sold the lot and clubhouse for $345,000. This money was used to buy a lot on Biscayne Bay where an elegant new clubhouse was built. The new building housed the library from 1926 until 1951. The Woman's Club of Miami also operated branch libraries including two branch libraries for black people. In 1951, Dade County assumed responsibility

Leading the Way: A Century of Service

Fig. 6. (Top) MRS. PAMELA BORDEN HAMILTON, first President of the Florida Federation of Women's Clubs. Fig. 7 (Below) MRS. E. G. G. MUNSELL — known as the "Mother of the Federation." (These are photographs of oil portraits displayed in the clubhouse of the V.I.A. of Green Cove Springs.)

Jessie Hamm Meyer

Fig. 8. Representatives of Pioneer Clubs honored at the 1928 convention in the Biltmore Hotel, Coral Gables.

Leading the Way: A Century of Service

for the libraries.

TAMPA WOMAN'S CLUB

The Tampa Woman's Club was born the very first month of the new century — January 1900. It had a limited membership with very literary tendencies and few philanthropic or civic intentions. "By 1914, it had studied the history of nineteen countries with other annual programs on Colonial History, American Literaure and Sociology."

When the club was only a year old it gave itself a birthday party, a "Gentleman's Night." Each gentleman was requested to bring a book — 40 books were donated and these books became the nucleus of a splendid library.

The club was thirteen years old before it decided to join FFWC, "but it soon realized the advantages this important step offered and a broader outlook on woman's work brought a corresponding incentive to greater achievement."

THE WOMAN'S CLUB OF FORT MYERS

This club was organized in 1900 and joined the Florida Federation of Women's Clubs in 1904. It also established a free reading room and a library in 1904. Mrs. Frank Stout was elected its first president but resigned after five months. No reason is given in the club's history for her resignation. Mrs. Julia Hanson was selected to take her place and in 1928, when the "pioneer clubs" were honored, Mrs. Hanson was still president of the club.

The Woman's Club of Fort Myers supported the legislative and conservation programs of FFWC. In fact, Mrs. Hanson served as state chairman of Bird Protection for five years and state chairman of Seminole Indian Welfare for six years.

TITUSVILLE PROGRESSIVE CULTURE CLUB

The first president of this club, Mrs. Blake Walker, wrote

that the early records of their club's beginnings had been lost, so she trusted her own memory and that of early members to gather information.

> The summer of 1900 in Titusville was very dull. A few of the girls in the town formed themselves into a club and called themselves 'The Bachelor Girls'.... Miss Susie Brown was our president. We met at different girls' houses once a month in the afternoon, talked, had light refreshments and so had a pleasant time. After a few months, Miss Susie Brown sent in her resignation and was married shortly afterwards. I was made President and as we wished to continue having Miss Susie Brown, now Mrs. Susie Brown Brady, with us in the club, we reorganized, took in married women, kept our officers and called ourselves the Progressive Culture Club. We met once a month and for our brain work read *Green's History of Florida*.

The club joined the state federation in 1905 and at that time the president was Mrs. William Mark Brown.

Every club has an interesting history; however, descriptions of the "early clubs" end with those formed through 1900. (Possibly other clubs could trace their histories to a time before 1900 but if so, these clubs failed to write their histories and present themselves to be included in the 1928-1929 yearbook.)

The purposes of the women forming clubs varied from cultural or intellectual improvement, improvement of their towns, philanthropy, social needs or escape from "dull summer" boredom. Whatever the reasons were for organizing, only those clubs that found broad-based purposes which answered deep needs within the women and their communities lasted and continued to grow. Elitism, making social status necessary for membership, a dearth of leadership, failure to train and welcome new members and allowing "keeping up the clubhouse" to become more important than being agents of change, doomed some clubs to becoming little more than card playing social clubs, and others to dissolving their organization.

Not all of the clubs that joined the Florida Federation of Women's Clubs before 1900 were honored as pioneer clubs in

Leading the Way: A Century of Service

1928. Some had disbanded and others had withdrawn from FFWC. However, 13 of the 16 clubs whose beginnings are described here continued to be active in FFWC in 1990.

Jessie Hamm Meyer

3 – Organization of the Florida Federation of Women's Clubs

CLUBS organized before 1900 were mostly in towns along waterways or railroads, but even in these towns and villages the approaches to club work were as varied as the towns. When the Village Improvement Association of Green Cove Springs invited clubs to meet for the purpose of uniting into a federation, delegates came from Crescent City, Tarpon Springs, Fairfield of Jacksonville and Orange City. The meeting was held on the 21st day of February, 1895, in Green Cove Springs. The committee for planning a federation was Mrs. E. N. Burrows, Mrs. E. V. Low and Mrs. E. G. Munsell, all of Green Cove Springs. These women had planned the meeting well and a constitution and bylaws were adopted by the delegates, Mrs. S. B. Safford of Tarpon Springs; Mrs. Emma C. Tebbetts, Crescent City; Mrs. T. L. Morse, Orange City; Mrs. L. E. Wamboldt, Fairfield; Mrs. E. A. Graves, Green Cove Springs.

The meeting resulted in a statement of purpose: "The Florida Federation of Women's Clubs has one object, namely; to bring the women's clubs into acquaintance and mutual helpfulness. Any club applying for membership must be free from sectarian or political bias, and must express the spirit of progress on broad and humane lines."

The constitution which these delegates adopted had only five articles and 13 bylaws. The term of office would be two years, each club would have two delegates, and the dues for each club would be two dollars per year. The election of officers followed: President, Miss P.A. Borden, Green Cove Springs; First Vice President, Mrs. E. C. Tebbetts, Crescent City; Second Vice-President, Mrs. L. E. Wambolt, Fairfield; Secretary-Treasurer, Mrs. E. V. Low, Green Cove Springs; Recording Secretary, Mrs. S. L. Morse, Orange City; Auditor, Mrs. S. B. Safford, Tarpon Springs. Each club represented thus had an officer to represent it on the state federation board of directors.

The next morning, Washington's birthday, February 22, 1895, at ten o'clock, the newly formed Florida State Federation of Women's Clubs convened with Mrs. Tebbetts, first vice-president, presiding. The records show that after the approval of the minutes of the day before, the first business presented was a motion by Mrs. Burrows: "that each society on the return of its delegates, hold a meeting for the purpose of drawing up a petition to the Legislature of Florida, praying it to rescind the act allowing cattle to run at large in towns of less than twelve hundred inhabitants." The motion carried. Since the problem of cattle running at large was the original and chief reason for attempting to get the united action of women's clubs, the history of FFWC is interrupted here to explain some of the difficulties these women faced in achieving their goals.

Fighting the "Sacred Cow"

In 1939, Mrs. Lucy Washington Blackman wrote a history of FFWC. Concerning the action of that first meeting and continuing attempts to get rid of cattle roaming the town streets and country roads of Florida, Mrs. Blackman wrote:

> Thus it has been for more than thirty years, that between the Federation of Women's Clubs and the Legislature of Florida, the sacred cow has been an ever present bone of contention — skin and bone literally — It looks as though there might be thirty more years of contention ahead of us before this ticky and emaciated beast shall be sufficiently immersed and groomed, and made fit for society. Well, I think I can promise the legislators of those coming days that the Federation of Women will still be on hand with their resolutions and persuasions!

However much the women's clubs of Florida wanted to get rid of the cattle roaming their streets and grazing on their lawns, shrubbery and gardens, it was not easy. Cattle had been important to Florida for many years. During the Civil war, the Confederate Army had depended on the cattle drives from Florida for its meat. The Union Army also bought or confiscated Florida cattle, shipping them from South Florida ports which they controlled. These range cattle may have been skinny and tough, but they were better than no meat at all. Cowboys rounded up and drove them to market or port. At Punta Rassa and Tampa cattle were loaded on ships and sent to Cuba. Cowboys and cattle drives were not only factors of western life but also of much of Florida. Long-horned cattle roamed free, living on whatever they could find to eat. In 1898, three years after the FFWC took action by passing a resolution against free roaming cattle, not only cattle would be leaving the port of Tampa for Cuba. Teddy Roosevelt and his "Rough Riders" and many other American soldiers would embark for Cuba to fight in the Spanish American War.

It was impossible for the women meeting in Green Cove Springs to understand the life of backwoods Floridians whose livelihood often depended on an open range. These club women had little contact with cowboys and rural dwellers of the interior of the state. As late as 1939, when Mrs. Blackman was writing her history of FFWC, Floridians who could afford it ate western corn-fed beef, but poorer Floridians had to be content with meat from the range cattle. Many poor families depended on selling their few "woods cattle" for their only cash each year and had no money to buy the barbed wire for fences. Florida cattlemen were so powerful politically that for many years they prevented the legislature from passing a law compelling them to fence in their cattle.

The Florida Federation of Women's Clubs did not give up but circumstances brought change where petition failed. With the ever increasing number of cars on the roads, the citizens of Florida became more and more concerned about accidents involving cars and cows. In 1948, Fuller Warren ran for Governor and was elected on a promise to get the cows off the roads of Florida. Soon thereafter the Legislature passed a fence law which was then implemented. It took over 50 years to get the cows off the highways and streets and out of the yards and

Leading the Way: A Century of Service

gardens of Florida citizens. Mrs. Blackman was not far wrong in her estimate of the time that it would take to get rid of the "sacred cow."

Had the cattlemen of Florida listened to the women's clubs of Florida, they might have been more prosperous, because with the building of fences, improved stock was introduced and pasture grasses were improved resulting in Florida becoming a truly great cattle state.

Before the first meeting of FFWC in Green Cove Springs was adjourned, the conventioneers gave the secretary-treasurer "discretionary powers to use the money in the treasury for all necessary expenses pertaining to the office." She had ten dollars — five clubs — two dollars each.

The Great Freeze

Plans were made for the next annual meeting in January 1896. The newly formed Florida State Federation was not yet a member of the General Federation of Women's Clubs but Miss Borden announced her intention to invite Mrs. Henrotin, General Federation President, to be present to address the next convention. Due to previous engagements Mrs. Henrotin had to decline. This was fortunate because when the 1896 annual meeting of the FFWC convened only four delegates were in attendance. There were two from Green Cove Springs and two from the Fairfield Club of Jacksonville. The president, first vice-president and the recording secretary were all absent. The minutes refer to the "hard times" that kept delegates from attending. A financial "panic" had hit the country in 1893 and its effect was accentuated by the disastrous freezes in December 1894 and February 1895, the worst since 1835. Orange groves had thrived near Deland, Ocala, Melrose and Orlando. Citrus groves were wiped out in all of Florida except in the southern tip. Devastation of the citrus industry added to the financial problems already troubling the country caused failure of banks, stores, hotels, boarding houses, and newspapers, which resulted in overwhelming discouragement to many inhabitants who had hoped to find a new life in Florida. Those who depended on tourists and winter residents for their living were bankrupt. Many whose hopes were dashed by what became known as "The Great Freeze" gave up and returned to their northern homes. Abandoned homes were common throughout Florida. These were, indeed, "hard times."

Amid all the depression and discouragement that had settled over Florida, the four delegates at Green Cove Springs held to their agenda. Miss Borden had moved to New York City and sent in her resignation as state president, but it was not accepted. The delegates must have believed that she would return to Florida at least for part of the winters. Mrs. Wamboldt, second vice- president from the Fairfield club, presided and Mrs. Burrows acted as recording secretary. Mrs. Low, secretary-treasurer, reported that there were known to be seventeen clubs of women in the state at that time. An effort should be made to bring these clubs into the federation. Her financial report showed that the "discretionary powers" given to her at the meeting in 1895 had been used wisely. She reported that after paying for 200 copies of the constitution, 250 letter heads and envelopes, a secretary's book, a treasurer's book and postage stamps and postal cards, she still had fifty cents on hand out of the ten dollars which had been the total receipts. Mrs. Low also reported that she had written to clubs in San Mateo, Clermont, Silver Springs, Avon Park, Lawtey, Starke, Merritt Island, Gainesville, Pensacola, Deland and Key West inviting them to become members of the Florida Federation of Women's Clubs.

Reporting on the action to petition the legislature to prohibit free roaming cattle, the minutes record, "On May 6, 1895, Mr. Fleming introduced in the senate, Bill 284, amending the act defining what cities shall impound live cattle. The bill passed the Senate on May 17th, but was not successful in the House."

The afternoon session of this meeting was given over to "interesting historical reports from six societies." Apparently, in spite of the hard times and not sending delegates, the clubs were interested enough to send reports. "The program was enlivened with music, instrumental and vocal," would indicate that women from the VIA of Green Cove Springs and some from the Fairfield Club in Jacksonville were in attendance. Before the convention closed the Fairfield Club extended an invitation to hold the next meeting in Jacksonville. The invitation was accepted.

On the 29th day of January 1897, the Florida Federation of Women's Clubs met in Jacksonville for a one day session. Again the president and first vice-president as well as the recording secretary were absent. Mrs. Wamboldt presided and Mrs. E.A. Graves of Green Cove Springs took the minutes. Three new clubs were admitted to membership: The Palmetto Club of Daytona, the Literary and Debating Society of Melrose and the Avilah of Rockledge. Nomination of officers were announced during the morning session and election of officers in the afternoon. The elected officers were: President, Mrs. L. E. Wamboldt, Fairfield; first vice-president, Mrs. M. A. Ruger, Daytona; second vice-president, Mrs. M. Thompson, Merritt Island; recording secretary, Mrs. Viola P. Beekman, Tarpon Springs; corresponding secretary, Dr. M. Rickard, Fairfield; treasurer, Mrs. Ella N. Burrows, Green Cove Springs; auditor, Mrs. Scudder, Crescent City.

The Age of Consent

At this session the women became more serious in their petitions to the legislature. The matter of roaming live stock was a constant aggravation and kept them from reaching their goals of keeping their communities clean and beautiful but their petition at this session was a serious moral matter. The resolution was offered by the Palmetto Club of Daytona. Those women wrote in very straightforward plain English about a matter that was considered to be a very delicate one. It was as follows:

> Whereas, the life of a nation depends on the sturdy morality of its people; when men so far forget morality and justice as to place the age when a girl may legally consent to her own ruin far below the age when she can legally dispose of a few paltry dollars; when our law makers deliberately shield vicious men in the perpetration of the heinous crime of destroying womanly virtue by making it legal for a girl of ten years to consent to such destruction, and also to place herself for life outside the protection of the law, as one not of a previously chaste life and conversation, it remains

for us who love justice and mercy to move in the matter and do what we can to bring Florida's law to a higher moral tone.

Therefore be it resolved, that we do earnestly protest against any legal difference in age between moral and financial responsibility, and that we petition the legislature to raise the age when a girl may legally consent to her legal, social and moral ruin, to the same age as that at which they are willing to allow their boys to take financial responsibility — twenty-one years.

Organized womanhood could petition but individual women could not vote. However, they were able to get 500 signatures on a petition in which the age of consent was put at 18 years. This was not the age they had hoped for but was better than the age of ten. A bill reflecting the petition was tabled on the third reading "on account of the capital punishment features." The petition had had nothing to do with capital punishment. It would appear that this feature was added for the express purpose of keeping the bill from passing. The federation kept the issue alive and a later legislature placed the age of consent at eighteen.

The next meeting was held in Daytona, January 25 and 26, 1898. Mrs. Wamboldt, having presided previously for an absent president, now presided in her own right. It appears that getting the elected recording secretary to an annual meeting was a real problem. Miss Amelia Potter of the Palmetto Club agreed to act as recording secretary pro tem.

Invitation from the General Federation

Three clubs were received into membership: The Woman's Club of Jacksonville, the Woman's Fortnightly Club of Palatka and the Village Improvement Association of Ormond. Eleven clubs were now members of FFWC. The Florida Federation of Women's Clubs was not yet a member of the General Federation of Women's Clubs, but it was a matter to discuss at this meeting. A letter from the president of GFWC to Mrs. Ruger of the Palmetto Club dated March 25th, 1896, states:

There exists a State Federation of Women's Clubs in Florida, not, however, a member of the General Federation. I think it is largely a matter of expense with the Florida Federation; they would like to join but are not well off. In fact, they are quite straitened as the clubs are small and few.

Leading the Way: A Century of Service

> The President of the Florida Federation is Miss P. A. Borden, Green Cove Springs, Fla.
>
> I wish you would join the State Federation and strengthen its hands. I trust, another year, the Florida Federation will belong to the General.
>
> I am going to send you the head of a letter on which is the Florida State Federation. I enclose, also, a circular on General Federation, which, I trust, will interest you and also a blank to be filled out provided you decide to join the General Federation.
>
> I am very much interested in the State Federation and glad to help them in any way possible.
>
> I enclose, also, a circular letter telling of the programme for the Biennial meeting in Louisville this coming May.
>
> Trusting I have given you all the information you desire, I am
>
> Truly yours,
> (signed) Ellen M. Henrotin

Another letter to Mrs. Ruger from Mrs. Henrotin dated April 18th, 1896, showed that her previous letter met with success so far as the Palmetto Club joining the General Federation was concerned:

> I have just received your application for membership into the General Federation, and have forwarded Ten Dollars ($10.00) (the Biennial dues) to Mrs. Cooper in California.
>
> Many thanks for the enclosed copy of the constitution and also for the programme.
>
> The first club joining the Federation from a state has the right to appoint one of its members State Chairman of Correspondence for the State. Will your club kindly make a selection and send me the name and address of the lady selected, that I may communicate with her and request her to receive this appointment?"

Mrs. Henrotin was a persistent person. Another letter from her was dated December 17, 1896, and addressed to Mrs. Ruger:

> I am more than anxious to bring Florida State Federation into the General Federation, and I am sure that if Florida joins, sooner or later Alabama will be forced into the same notion. If it is a question of money, I know someone who will pay the Biennial dues of the Florida Federation. It is nearly two years before the dues must be paid and I want the moral influence of Florida in the Federation. Will you not help me in this and above all give me the address of the President of the Florida Federation? I wish to write to her and endeavor to secure her co-operation.

I remember with pleasure our visit together at Louisville and I am sure you enjoyed that great meeting. Please let me hear from you on this subject, and believe me,

Yours fraternally,
(signed) Ellen M. Henrotin

At the Daytona convention January 25 and 26, 1898, a committee of three, appointed to look into the matter of joining the General Federation, came up with a solution which was approved: "We recommend the acceptance of the liberal offer which has been made by a friend of the federation to pay the fees required to join the General Federation." In this way the Florida Federation of Women's Clubs became a member of the national organization. Mrs. Wamboldt of the Fairfield TIA and Mrs. Scudder of the Crescent City VIA were chosen as delegates to the GFWC convention to be held in Denver in June of the same year.

Near the end of the twentieth century, it is almost beyond the imagination that the delegates meeting in Daytona would not have been willing to pay, nor would they have had $10 to pay, state dues to the General Federation. Keep in mind that individuals were paying fifty cents or one dollar dues to their individual clubs and each club was obligated to pay two dollars annually to the Florida Federation. That amount kept some clubs from joining the federation. Many of the women in these clubs represented families of considerable wealth, but the money was not often theirs to manage. An inspection of old photographs of women's club groups taken toward the end of the nineteenth century shows that they carried reticules — very small purses — no room for check books, credit cards, folding money — only very small change.

Variety of Interests

The minutes of this meeting report that a "reciprocity committee" was appointed, whose duty it was to gather and preserve papers read before the federation and to add them to others from local clubs. These papers were for circulation among the federated clubs, and "this exchange of papers became a very conspicuous and helpful feature of state work" according to Mrs. Blackman in her history of FFWC published in 1939. Among other papers read at the 1898 meeting was one on Social Purity by Mrs. Duncan U. Fletcher, which led to the appointment of a Committee on Social Purity.

The Jacksonville Club invited the federation to meet in Jacksonville in 1899. This meeting was held in the elegant Windsor Hotel and according to the records, the delegates to this meeting had a most enjoyable time giving and listening to the reports of the seven clubs that sent delegates. Always the first business of the meeting was paying dues — two dollars for each club represented. President Wamboldt presided but for the fourth time the recording secretary was absent. Mrs. J. H. Durkee of Jacksonville took the minutes which resulted in thirteen large and closely written pages.

Such minutes, that describe and include not just actions taken, but also discussions and comments, may not reflect the most efficient way of record keeping but they give pictures of people, times, and places that allows a research historian to interpret the how's and why's of the actions taken.

The variety of the reports given at that meeting is amazing. Beautification of towns, formation of forestry clubs, tree planting, discussions of current topics, organizations for children (later sponsoring Scout Troops) and clubs for young girls (the equivalent of present day Juniorettes), support of public libraries, studies in various literary and historical subjects, philanthropic work that furnished nurses, medicine and food for the poor and a Mother's Club to teach negro mothers how "to nurse, teach and amuse their children" were only a few of the many projects undertaken by the women of the towns and villages where women's clubs had been organized. The foundations for the many departments and projects of FFWC clubs working 95 years later were laid by these enterprising women.

Mrs. Rebecca Douglas Lowe, President of GFWC, was a guest at the 1899 meeting. The topic of her address was education and in the discussions during the meeting, the minutes record that when the women strayed from the topic, "Mrs. Lowe carried the thought back to the discussion and theme of education." (In the late 1980's, Phyllis Wood made a tape, "Let Me Tell You about My Club," which humorously and delightfully points out how club members stray from their topic. Mrs. Wood had long experience both in her own club and on the Board of Directors of the Florida Federation.)

"Old Adam's War Cry"

In the late 1930's, when Mrs. Blackman was writing her history of the Florida Federation of Women's Clubs, she interviewed some of the early leaders such as Mrs. Wamboldt, Mrs. Beekman and Mrs. Cummer. Apparently one of the greatest obstacles that the women encountered in trying to build their federation was the opposition that men had to their club work. Mrs. Blackman wrote:

> I have it from Mrs. Wamboldt, from Mrs. Beekman and from Mrs. Cummer, presidents of those early days, that the men of the towns and the state at large were bitter in their denunciation of Women's Clubs. The old Adam war-cry, 'Woman's place is in the home' reverberated through the pines and over the rivers and lakes and the ocean from Pensacola to Key West. Mrs. Cummer told me that she was often reviled to her face for having anything to do with such an iniquitous movement. Her noble husband, however, was one of the earliest 'best club husbands,' of whom today we have such a fine company."

Mrs. Blackman added:

> Thanks be, there were enough women with spinal cords starched stiff, who raised their undaunted eyebrows and said, 'Ah! Indeed!' to this masculine mandate — and then went forth and did as they saw fit.

In spite of the long distances, poor traveling conditions, poverty following the "Great Freeze" and opposition in their own homes, women founded and maintained the organization, its sole purpose being to improve themselves and the places where they lived. Getting to know women from other communities, being able to socialize with like-minded members and working for common goals throughout the state strengthened their resolves "to make a difference".

Not all was work at the 1899 meeting. The minutes also record that on the last day of the meeting it was announced that the Woman's Club of Jacksonville would escort the ladies to the Ostrich Farm, one of Jacksonville's most popular tourist attractions, at three o'clock in the afternoon,

Leading the Way: A Century of Service

Mrs. William Ruger of the Palmetto Club was elected president and Mrs. W. W. Cummer of Jacksonville first vice-president. Mrs. Ruger soon resigned and at a called meeting held in Jacksonville, Mrs. Beekman of Tarpon Springs was elected president. However, Mrs. Beekman was never able to serve because of ill health. Mrs. Wamboldt had presided at four annual meetings and Mrs. Cummer presided in Mrs. Beekman's place at the meeting held in Palatka in 1900, at Daytona in 1901, as the elected president at Crescent City in 1902 and at Ormond Beach in 1903. Mrs. E. G. G. Munsell of Green Cove Springs was a leader in the formation of the Florida Federation of Womens Clubs and refused the presidency many times, preferring to serve in other ways. However, because of her work and dedication she became known as the "Mother of the Federation."

The Housekeeper's Club of Coconut Grove was admitted to FFWC at the Daytona meeting in 1901 and the VIA of San Mateo was admitted in 1903 at the Ormond Beach meeting. There were reports of increased membership in many of the clubs and much was accomplished during these years. Many clubs felt that a clubhouse was a necessity and much time and effort went into raising money to buy land and build club houses. The houses which these clubs built often became much needed community centers.

Improving Education

Education and the public schools got more and more attention from these club women. Money was easier to raise as citrus groves, truck farming and businesses that had been destroyed by the Great Freeze were again thriving. The economy of the entire country had also improved so that tourists as well as new citizens were entering the state in increasing numbers.

Minutes record also that the reciprocity committee was busy gathering and exchanging papers on many subjects. For the first time a state chairman of household economics and a state historian were appointed.

The Palmetto Club drew attention to the controversial subject of women on school boards at the 1901 meeting in

Daytona. When a woman had tried to run for the school board in Daytona, it was decided that since she was not eligible to vote, she could not be eligible to run for office. The women felt that the public needed to be educated on the subject of the need for women to be represented on school boards, but others felt that "if we continue, we can force the men to take some action." It was finally decided that they should go to the legislature about allowing women to serve on school boards.

With the general economy becoming much better, the question of raising the dues to FFWC was debated. At the meeting in 1900, it was decided that instead of two dollars per club, the dues would be ten cents per capita. Clubs formed locally were not always willing to join the Florida Federation, because they felt that there were no benefits to be gained by joining the state organization. Visitors from other clubs whose members would not agree to federation came to annual meetings to give their regrets and to explain their disappointments.

Food and Drugs

The president of the state Women's Temperance Union came to an annual meeting in 1903 to ask the federation's cooperation in an appeal to the legislature to pass a bill requiring that the effects of narcotics and stimulants be taught in the lower grades of the public schools; the federation agreed to send a delegate to a conference that was to be called to consider the matter. The union president also mentioned the Domestic Science departments in Stetson University and Rollins College. It appears that she was trying to get clubs interested in giving illustrated cooking lessons as part of their work. There is no record of wide acceptance of this idea. Most of the club members had organized and joined together to improve their communities or their minds — not their cooking.

At Ormond Beach, in 1903, Mrs. Lawrence Haynes was elected president and Mrs. E. G. G. Munsell of Green Cove Springs was elected first vice-president. In 1904, the annual meeting was held in Jacksonville in the "handsome new club house of the Woman's Club." Every officer was there except the auditor! The clubs admitted to the FFWC at this meeting were: Woman's Current Events Club of Live Oak, Twentieth Century Club of Gainesville, New Century Club of High Springs, Village Improvement Association of Lake Como, Woman's Club of Fort Myers, Club of Current Events of Tampa and the Married Ladies' Afternoon Club of Miami.

At the 1904 meeting the board of directors voted to print fifty copies of the reports given. Because of the cost of printing, the length of minutes had to be considered; therefore, the minutes for that meeting were much shorter than the hand written minutes of previous meetings. However, their minutes were long enough that one concludes that the meeting was a huge success. An invitation from the Married Ladies Afternoon Club of Miami was accepted for the 1905 meeting. This was a significant change from the rather limited geographic area that had been the location of all the previous meetings.

Meeting in Miami

In spite of the distance to Miami, delegates were present from Green Cove Springs, Orange City, Fairfield, Jacksonville, Daytona, Palatka, Ormond and San Mateo. Coconut Grove and Miami were not only well represented but also active in entertaining the delegates. The Ladies Afternoon Club of Miami was hostess to the convention but the afternoon session of the first day was at the Housekeeper's Club of Coconut Grove, and a reception took place there that evening. The twenty-two delegates to the 10th annual convention were met at the station on the night of January 24th and "immediately driven to the palatial hotel, The Royal Palm, where, through the courtesy of the hostess club they were right royally entertained. A short walk through the magnificent grounds of the hotel led to the Fair building on Biscayne Bay where the Married Ladies' Afternoon Club holds its meetings, and here the Federation convened. The hall was decorated with coconut leaves, crimson hibiscus and other tropical plants." (Early minutes and reports of the various clubs and of the federation are full of descriptive adjectives and adverbs reflecting the somewhat ornate writing of the period. Decades later these details breathe life into the pages of what could otherwise be rather dull reading. They took time to give an elegance to their lives which under many circumstances were harsh and demanding. Addresses and responses were always "graciously" given, refreshments were "delicious", and decorations were "beautiful". Later minutes and reports tend to report only the facts because as the clubs became more numerous and extended the areas of their work, there were more reports to be written. Publishing costs had to be kept down; therefore, secretaries and chairmen had to make every word count. Finally secretaries were instructed to report only facts and actions taken.

The President of the Ladies' Afternoon Club of Miami in welcoming the delegates said in part:

> We, the Ladies' Afternoon Club of Miami, bid you a most hearty welcome to our far Southern home, and trust your sojourn among us may be so pleasant that ever after the name 'Miami' may fill your minds with pleasant memories..... Five short years ago I came to the banks of the Miami River in a small boat; the place where we now stand was a mangrove thicket. There were but two families living here. I tell this in no boastful spirit, but to merely ask for your indulgence, for if our club falls short in many ways we plead our youth and inexperience; what we lack in experience we will try to make up for in earnestness of purpose and true fraternal feeling.

The Corresponding Secretary reported that the federation had grown by the addition of two new clubs, The Progressive Culture Club of Titusville and the Cycadia Cemetery Association of Tarpon Springs, which was, in fact, a reorganization and rechartering of one of the oldest clubs — The Woman's Town and Cemetery Improvement Association of Tarpon Springs. She also reported, "Year Books have been issued at a cost of $5.00 giving something of the history of our federation, and copies mailed to all clubs in our state and many in other states. Over a hundred letters and postals have been written."

Mrs. Lawrence Haynes of Jacksonville was president and in her address reported on the Biennial Convention of the General Federation of Women's Clubs. Florida had one of the largest representations attending the convention and Florida's

Reciprocity Bureau was one of the largest in the GFWC. Interest in traveling libraries had been expressed throughout the state. Mrs. Haynes thought that some funds might well be invested in a "traveling library or two". She expressed belief that the federation's hope for kindergartens in the public schools might be realized at the next meeting of the legislature, but suggested that each club appoint a committee to contact senators and representatives in their districts to interest them in a bill to provide kindergartens in the schools.

Self-Improvement vs. Domestic Science

After the president's address a Mrs. Ewing from Chicago gave a talk on "The American Kitchen." Mrs. Ewing had been giving lectures for twenty years under the auspices of various clubs and societies. At first little interest was shown in her subject of domestic science. It was thought that women did not need instruction in how to cook and keep house since they were supposedly born with such knowledge but thinking had changed and now many colleges had such courses. Mrs. Ewing shared this bit of logic: "Society is the heart of civilization; the home is the heart of society; the kitchen is the heart of the home, therefore the kitchen is the heart of civilization. Then let us improve them; the average kitchen is a disgrace to intelligent women." In conclusion she said, "Woman's noblest ambition is to make and keep a pleasant, healthful and happy home." There is no record of how her address was received. Certainly many of the women listening to her were members of clubs that stressed self improvement. The study of Browning and Shakespeare, appreciation of art and music, and the writing of papers on such topics as "Women as Equal Partners in Marriage" was quite different from the study of domestic science.

After this meeting was adjourned the women were taken by launch at one o'clock across "the beautiful sunlit waters of Biscayne Bay to The Housekeeper's Club of Coconut Grove" where they had an afternoon business meeting and listened to committee reports.

The education and industrial committee reported that great advances had been made in many states in compulsory educa-

tion laws:
> That is our need and our work in Florida, and now is our opportunity. Let the Federation stand as one unit for this worthy purpose that the time may be hastened when no child in our state shall grow up in ignorance. Shall we go forward? You as individual clubs must decide.

The reciprocity committee reported that its bureau now had ninety-four papers; ten had been added the past year. Educational topics were the ones most often requested. There was "a need for papers on Village Improvement Work; copies of work already accomplished would be most helpful." Individual club members often worked at researching and writing papers on topics of interest to their club members. These papers were for circulation among the various clubs of the federation. When a club wanted a program on a certain topic, it could write to the chairman of the reciprocity committee and if she had a paper on that topic she would mail it to the club that requested it. When the club was finished with the paper it was mailed back to the reciprocity chairman so that it would be available for other clubs. Getting the papers typed was not easy. Writing scholarly papers was a challenge and reading them or listening to them was educational. These papers were instruments of adult education for club members before public institutions made correspondence courses available, before community colleges reached out with their myriad courses, and before public radio and television furnished educational opportunities for adults all over Florida.

Forest Preservation

The report of the forestry committee was a strong argument for the necessity for forest preservation. It embodied many extracts from addresses made before the American Forestry Congress recently held in Washington, D.C. President Theodore Roosevelt said: "If the present rate of forest destruction is allowed to continue, a timber famine is obviously inevitable. What such a famine would mean to each of the industries of the United States is scarcely possible to imagine. And the period of recovery from the injuries which a timber famine would entail would be measured by the slow growth of the trees themselves." This report urged that the women of Florida work together for the passage of a national forestry law.

After some discussion, it was moved by Mrs. Gifford of Coconut Grove that the federation endorse the proposal to name a Federal Forest Reservation of Paradise Key in the Everglades to preserve the unique groups of royal palms, since this was the only spot in the United States where these palms were found growing naturally. This motion carried and the result of this action created a series of actions which led to the establishment of Everglades National Park. (Much more about this later.)

The report of the bird preservation committee urged clubs to encourage their members to put out food and water for birds and boxes for martins, bluebirds and wrens. The chairman read a letter from the Audubon Society asking for greater cooperation from the federated clubs.

Membership in the federation had grown from 400 to 800 members and there were now twenty-one clubs in the federation. Reports from nineteen of these clubs were read at the 1905 convention.

After the business meeting, the delegates were entertained in the home of Mrs. Kirk Monroe. Along the way to her home they had enjoyed visiting the Biscayne Bay Yacht Club and the Kirk-Monroe Library, and walking along the shore of the bay. It was dark by the time they got back to the Housekeepers of Coconut Grove clubhouse where they were served a banquet. Before the banquet was over a storm came up which prevented them from returning to their Miami hotel in the launch which had brought them across the bay. Because there were not sufficient carriages to take all of the delegates back to Miami in one trip, it was quite late before all of the ladies returned to their hotel rooms. Meetings the next day were again in Miami, where, in spite of the adventures of the previous night, the delegates were ready for more reports and more business at the scheduled time. There had been some apprehension as to whether delegates would attend the meeting which was so far from the area where they usually met, but the Miami meeting was well attended and declared one of the best that the federation had enjoyed during its entire ten years.

Early Newsletters

Few things are perfect and there were still problems to be solved. The "Florida Bulletin" and "The Keystone" were the early newsletters that kept members of the federation informed. The success of this endeavor apparently left much to be desired since in her report the State Correspondent said, "To make your official organ truly helpful you must not only send it news of your work, but you must also read it yourselves." This statement is as timely in 1995 as it was in 1905.

This first decade of the clubs of the Florida Federation of Women's Clubs shows amazing results. Records give a vivid picture of what then was demanding the thoughts and energies of Florida club women. The varieties of their enterprises laid the foundation of many departments and divisions of the late 20th century FFWC. The names may not be the same but the seeds were sown. Community beautification, observation of Arbor Day, forest preservation, philanthropy, clean-up days for cemeteries, formation of mothers' clubs as well as auxiliary societies for children and, above all, support of libraries. They studied English and American literature, current events, history, and Greek mythology showing an ever broadening intellectual interest. They tried through petition and education to persuade legislators to vote for laws that would result in better educational opportunities for the children of the state and also laws for the preservation of forests and birds. With the close of the convention in Miami in January 1905, the curtain came down on the first decade of the Florida Federation of Women's Clubs.

Leading the Way: A Century of Service

4 – The Second Decade, 1905-1915

By now there were luxurious hotels in many of the coastal cities and a network of railroads connected smaller towns to the principal cities of Jacksonville, Tampa and Pensacola. Key West was also a major city with a population of over 17,000. In 1904, Henry Flagler began work on "the railroad that went to sea" from Miami to Key West, a distance of 155 miles, 70 of which would be over water. To complete this daring engineering job took eight years, approximately $20,000,000 and thousands of workmen, 300 of whom lost their lives. An inaugural train of five private cars carrying 82 year old Flagler, and many United States and South American dignitaries arrived in Key West on January 22, 1912. The train was met by a crowd of about ten thousand enthusiastic people who considered this remarkable feat of engineering as the eighth "wonder of the world". The railroad's completion brought rail service ninety miles from Havana and much closer to the great Panama Canal project where work was accelerating and anticipation for its completion was high. The extension of the railroad from Miami to Key West and the digging of the Panama Canal reflected the optimism of a country that believed that there was no "impossible dream."

Sawmills dotted the state manufacturing lumber from the magnificent virgin forests that had covered much of Florida. Timbering was big business. Greek sponge fishers had moved to Tarpon Springs making it the biggest sponge market in the world. The principal streets of larger towns were being paved as more and more motor driven vehicles began to appear. Pictures of outings at the beaches taken in 1905 show more carriages than cars, yet motor driven vehicles had become so common in most towns that horses no longer became frightened when one of these noisy things came along. Daytona had become known as a testing place for automobiles and speed records were constantly being made and broken on its wide beach. It is interesting to note that Henry Ford came to Daytona in the winter of 1904 to demonstrate his "flivver" but lacking the price of a hotel room he slept in his car.

Baseball was the popular sport in rural communities and golf was the society sport. It was the custom to dress in one's Sunday best before going out for a game of golf; however, a 1905 picture of a group playing the game shows that the "green" was not green at all but hard packed soil.

Exploitation Destroys Natural beauty

Steamboats still plied the waters of every stream where they could navigate, but pleasure trips on the St. Johns and Oklawaha rivers were no longer popular with winter visitors. So-called sportsmen shooting from the decks of steamboats had killed out the wealth of birds that had once added to the beauty of a trip on the St. Johns. They had killed not for food or even for the feathers of these birds but just to prove their marksmanship or for the fun of seeing live birds fall dead. Many of the great cypress trees that had lined the banks of rivers or stood in majestic stands in the lowlands had been cut for timber. The Oklawaha was being used for rafting logs to saw mills more than for travel to enjoy the scenery and the abundant riches of Florida's flora and fauna.

The reader might well question why these details of life in Florida are recorded in a history of FFWC. There were not a great many environmentally minded people working in organizations during those years. However, the response of the women of the Florida Federation of Women's Clubs to their rapidly changing environment was strong and effective. In fact, in some communities these changes were reason enough for women to organize and after some local meetings, they saw the advantages of joining the federation. The women of Florida began campaigns for the preservation of birds, the conservation of forests and the planting of trees in their towns and

Leading the Way: A Century of Service

cities. Their efforts intensified as they witnessed the further degradation of Florida's natural beauty and resources.

In 1905, the Florida Federation voted to adopt as its colors jasmine yellow and palmetto green. Later at a GFWC Convention, the Florida delegates wore their Florida badge, a green ribbon with a narrow yellow ribbon and the word "FLORIDA" printed on the yellow ribbon. Some of the delegates heard a group of women talking and one of them asked "Who are the greenhorns with the yellow streak?" It was an unkind remark and the Florida delegates vowed to change the Florida badge. In 1926 Miss Maude E. Knight was asked to plan a new badge. The state flower which was the orange blossom and the state bird which was the mocking bird were chosen. Mrs. E. G. Harris of the Palmetto Club in Daytona Beach designed and painted a badge in 1928. That year several federation members painted fifty badges and sold them to delegates planning to attend the GFWC Convention. In 1930, FFWC had a set of three color blocks made to facilitate production of badges.

In April of 1906, twenty-eight FFWC officers and delegates met in convention as guests of the Current Events Club of Tampa. The corresponding secretary reported that two new clubs had been added to the federation, The Woman's Club of Tallahassee and the Ladies' Friday Musical Club of Arcadia. The treasurer's report was brief: the sum of $145.26 had been in the account, and expenses had been $134.25, leaving a balance on hand of $11.03. There was always a need for more funds to carry on the work of the federation but no discouragement was reported. They were gratified by the report that the legislature had passed the kindergarten bill which they had supported. That bill had actually been written and submitted by the Woman's Club of Tallahassee. The FFWC saw the need to train teachers for this work and began soliciting donations to endow a scholarship in the Kindergarten Department of the Woman's College at Tallahassee. Fourteen clubs pledged five dollars each toward the kindergarten scholarship fund. They were disappointed that their attempts to get a law passed for compulsory education had met with defeat, but they looked upon it as only a temporary setback.

Jessie Hamm Meyer

Better Pay for Teachers

The keynote address to officers and delegates was given by Mrs. Frances Clayton, assistant principal of Tampa High School, who spoke of the necessity of equal opportunities for all children. Most of all she urged the women to work for better trained and better paid teachers. Mrs. Clayton pointed out that the average salary of "lady teachers in Florida, reckoning from primary grades through college classes, is only $206.00 per year". She questioned, "Have you ever reflected that the cook who prepares your children's meal receives, when we include the important item of her board, fifty per cent more per year than the common school teacher in Florida? That the carpenter who builds the shell in which your boy or girl shall pass a few short years is paid three times as much as she to whom you have entrusted a large share of the training of that part of your child which shall outlive all time? That the colored 'odd jobs' gentleman who cultivates turnips in your back yard receives considerably more than the instructor who is cultivating the triple nature of your child, the physical, mental and moral?"

Such forthright speaking intensified the determination of women listening to Mrs. Clayton to improve the educational opportunities of the children of Florida. Some of their work bore fruit and women of FFWC have continued their struggle for good schools. Seventy-five years later a speaker could still truthfully say, "Did you know that the star football player on the college team may get a million dollar contract as soon as he has graduated while the student who has graduated as a trained teacher will get a contract with pay equal to that of the city worker who picks up your garbage?"

While education was the principal interest of the women assembled at the 1906 convention, other department chairmen also made important reports. The reciprocity committee reported that it had 60 papers in the bureau and that new ones were being added. These papers were available for clubs to use either as programs or as the basis for discussion groups. The bird preservation committee was proud of programs that many clubs had given on ways and means to prevent the destruction of birds and that the federation was a sustaining member of the Florida Audubon Society. The forestry committee reported that need existed for immediate legislation dealing with forest preservation, "Let us explain to the legislators that if the turpentine men and lumbermen are allowed to use every tree that soon our 'Land of Flowers' will become a second Sahara."

The library extension committee reported that almost every club had good news of numbers of libraries supported by individual clubs.

The social purity committee had circulated a petition to have the "polygamist, Reed Smoot," removed from Congress, but nothing else is recorded about Congressman Smoot or this petition. After this report, a question was raised as to whether there was an institution in Florida for the "rescue of fallen girls." The president of the Current Events Club of Tampa answered that there was such an institution in their city called "The Door of Hope." She also said that the women of Tampa had raised $3,600 for this home. At this time a collection was taken and the reports read, "A voluntary offering of $14.16 was collected for this noble cause."

The only other standing committee was household economics, which apparently made no report at the 1906 Convention.

Individual club reports were made by delegates, which revealed a mind-boggling variety of projects in philanthropy, literature, music, art, civic improvement and a few clubs admitted devoting some programs to just plain fun. Day care for black children of working mothers, equipping and hiring a teacher for a school, buying properties and building club houses, planting trees, cleaning cemeteries, donating books and volunteering as librarians, trying to influence legislation by petition and persuasion, giving concerts and myriads of fund raising events were reported by these clubs.

Mrs. Richard Adams of Palatka was president of FFWC and her address to the convention reflected the oratorical style that was expected of public speakers of that era. A brief quotation illustrates this better than any description. "We meet to bring our individual lives with the best that they contain, into a harmonious union that our convention may be, as one of our foremost club women has said, 'a centrifugal as well as a centripetal power,' that they may be the concentrate of experience and the dynamic of experiment that shall lift humanity up the heavenly ladder whose topmost rung is peace on earth, good will to men." This lofty language was the style for public speakers of that day but it also reflected the high ideals and aims that motivated women to meet and work together.

The "Keystone" correspondent urged clubs to send in interesting items and accounts of "their doings". She also reported that since the last convention the "Keystone" had published 12,650 words. Almost 90 years later, we are bombarded by millions of words through various media, and counting the number of words written during a year would never occur to a chairman.

It was at this convention that the matter of juvenile courts was brought up and Mrs. Clara Raynor of the Palmetto Club of Daytona Beach urged that the federation take up this work which had such splendid results in states where these courts were established. It was decided that all clubs inform themselves on this subject and instruct their delegates how to vote at the next convention.

The idea of a Florida Federation of Women's Clubs emblem was adopted at the Tampa Convention. "An orange leaf in green enamel with an orange in yellow upon it, with F.F.W.C. and the date of organization, 1895" was agreed upon. The state motto also was adopted that year, and was the the same as that of the Palmetto Club of Daytona Beach:

> In great things, Unity
> In small things, Liberty
> In all things, Charity

It was in 1905 and 1906 that a new constitution was adopted, because the old one was inadequate for the growing organization.

In 1906, the management of the State Fair held annually in Tampa asked the federation to select ten subjects for prize essays, which would be awarded at the fair to students in Florida schools. The selected list follows:

> What the Woman's Club means to Mankind
> What shall be done with juvenile offenders?
> The City Beautiful
> What of the trees of Florida?
> Our feathered friends
> Compulsory education
> Traveling libraries
> Child labor
> The value of music in the development of character
> Traveling art galleries

The women who selected these topics knew what they wanted the young people of Florida to research and to know.

Delegates decided that November rather than April would be a better time for the annual meeting because they could take back reports and suggestions for action to their individual clubs in time for the clubs to incorporate the federation's ideas into their own programs during the current year. Because of this change, there were two conventions in 1906, the second one was in Tallahassee. This also resulted in Mrs. Adams holding the presidency for only eighteen months. Mrs. Clara H. Raynor of the Palmetto Club was elected President for 1907 and 1908 and Mrs. T. M. Shackleford, Vice President. The Twentieth Century Club of Gainesville was hostess for the 1907 Convention and most of the meetings were held in the Elks Club. Delegates as well as officers and chairmen were entertained in the homes of the hostess club.

Child Welfare

Child welfare became an area of interest early in Mrs. Raynor's administration. It had become increasingly evident that a compulsory education law would be difficult if not impossible to pass as long as children could be legally exploited because of a lack of any laws controlling the hours or conditions under which children were forced to work. A law to limit the hours that children would be allowed to work was needed.

In 1907, Mrs. Raynor reported that civics, art, civil service reform, child labor and club extension had been added to the departments which were active during the previous administration.

Clubs were asked to donate books or money for traveling libraries. Mrs. Raynor reported that four traveling libraries, containing 268 books, were being used. Two of those four libraries, including their cases, were donated to the Florida Federation of Women's Clubs by the Massachusetts State Federation of Women's Clubs. These libraries were in great demand by communities that had no libraries. Mrs. Raynor also reported that about five hundred magazines had been sent to the Railroad Extension Camp for the men who were working on the extension of the East Coast Railroad from Miami to Key West.

In 1906, a petition was drafted and sent to Governor Napoleon B. Broward and the Florida Legislature asking that a committee be appointed to draft a Child Labor Law that would approach a Standard Child Labor Law which was affixed to the petition. This petition had been signed by members of five other organizations as well as by many individuals across the state. The bill was drafted, almost entirely by Mrs. Raynor, and after much discussion and letter writing it passed the Senate unchanged, but the age of a child that could be legally employed was changed from 14 to 12 in the House. Governor Broward urged the passage of the bill which stated that children under 12 would no longer be allowed legally to toil in the cigar factories of Tampa or elsewhere before six o'clock in the morning nor after nine o'clock at night. This does not seem to be any great victory from the viewpoint of modern-day club women; yet only a few years had passed since a manufacturer in the Northeast who had grown wealthy on the work of child labor protested any law being passed to limit his practice. He had said, "So the children die young! We are a prolific people. They will be replaced." A public expression of such an attitude indicated that much had to be done to change the thinking about children in the industrial world with its social and economic adjustments. Women had much work to do!

The Child Labor Committee had a real sense of accomplishment when it reported that the Child Labor Law had been passed, but they did not rest with the passage of the law. The chairman of the Child Labor Committee wrote to the sheriffs of the counties where child labor was most rampant asking them what they intended to do about enforcing the law. When any reply was unsatisfactory this hard working chairman saw to it that petitions were circulated and signed by enough leaders, concerned citizens and organizations that the sheriff would decide to enforce the new law as he bowed to the weight of public opinion.

Compulsory Education

At the November 1908 Board of Directors' meeting in Live Oak, delegates were challenged to keep working with their legislators for a compulsory attendance law. Since the legislature met only every two years, this was an off year. The women had tried through three legislative sessions to get this law passed but had had no success. Mrs. Raynor in her address to the convention in Live Oak said:

> In Florida we have 217,000 children of school age; seventeen thousand only above the fifth grade, and thirteen counties in the state having more black than white. Eighty-seven thousand children of school age do not attend school. A little less than half of these are presumably males, future citizens who will make laws, and conduct government. Florida ranks eighth in illiteracy of the States. Thirty-five of the States are under compulsory attendance laws, also eighty per cent of the civilized people of the world have compulsory school attendance laws in their countries. Through the press and by all legitimate means we are now working for a local option compulsory education law, hoping to educate the legislators of 1909 that they may see the necessity of compelling parents or guardians to give the children under their care at least sixteen weeks' schooling per annum.

The compulsory education bill had failed previously because of the expense of providing sufficient schools in the so-called black belt. A local option law would have a much better chance of passing. The schools for blacks and whites at that time were not only separate but there was little thought of "separate but equal." It would be many years before real efforts would be made to bring the schools for blacks equal to those of whites, and this would be done only in the hope that Florida could avoid integrating its schools.

School attendance had doubled in some areas of Florida as a result of the enactment and enforcement of the Child Labor Law. In Tampa and Hillsboro county seven new schools had to be built to accommodate the increased enrollment. Since children could still legally work during the day, it seemed that public opinion had changed significantly with the passage of this law. The citizenry in general began to believe in the value of an education and as a result the people could see that a compulsory school law was needed.

Several clubs had maintained private kindergartens in their towns before the enactment of the law to make free kindergartens available in the public school system. The federated clubs had done well paying their pledges to the scholarship fund to train young teachers in kindergarten work. Clubs were urged to continue to give five dollars per year to the fund. Eighty-five dollars was more than enough to take care of a student for a semester at the College for Women in Tallahassee.

Mrs. Raynor's administration was noted for the beginnings of other work which would be continued for some years to come. One of the topics brought before the board meeting in Live Oak was the plan to abolish the convict lease system. Also mentioned was the hope that "execution by the electric chair would be substituted for execution by hanging."

Public Health

A health crusade was begun. Tuberculosis was a dreaded disease that was taking the lives of the young as well as the old. Because of information which indicated that tuberculosis could be spread through the milk of diseased cows, many clubs had been working to make sure that dairies did not sell milk from tubercular cows. The FFWC supported the sale of Red Cross Christmas Seals for the benefit of tuberculosis work in the state. Work was begun to persuade the Superintendent of Public Instruction to declare a Health Day in all schools when sanitation, hygiene, prevention of tuberculosis and other health measures would be presented to all members of the communities.

The meeting at Live Oak was held in the new Court House with various social functions given by the Live Oak Woman's Club. Reports of committees and clubs at this meeting again showed a wide variety of projects undertaken. Each administration was having more and more difficulty making ends meet. The publication of the reports, minutes, and speeches resulted in books of almost 100 pages. Since other state federations, the Florida clubs and the chairmen of standing committees wanted copies of the reports, it was necessary to print at least 200 copies. This was done at the unbelievably low cost of between fifty and sixty dollars, but it was still a large part of the Federation's budget. Receipts from membership fees for 1908 amounted to only $127.70, collected from twenty-eight clubs with a total membership of 1,331. Early the next year, clubs were asked to donate ten cents per capita to help meet the expenses of the FFWC and most of the clubs responded thus enabling two hundred fifty copies of the manual to be printed at a cost of $60.00.

Mrs. Lena W. Shackleford of Tallahassee, President 1909 to 1910, built upon foundations laid in the previous years. Lucy W. Blackman sums up this administration in her history, *The Florida Federation of Women's Clubs, 1895 to 1939·*

> Mrs. Shacklesford's administration was marked not so much by new enterprises undertaken as by a polishing and refining of what was already established or in process of building. The standing committees were organized into departments in which work was more carefully correlated, and the chairmen of departments were made members of the board of directors. A department of music was created and a legislative committee was appointed. Seven new traveling libraries were added.
>
> Dr. Ellen Lowell-Stevens of the State Board of Health was sent over the state by the federation, to speak to clubs and schools on 'Health and Hygiene'. The clubs used their share of the Christmas Seal proceeds to install drinking fountains in school buildings and in sanitary enterprises for schools and towns.

Individual club reports at the conventions held in Palatka and the following year in Ocala indicate that they were doing splendid service to their communities. Most of the clubs raised money to help their schools. One club paid the salary of a music teacher. Nearly all the clubs helped buy school supplies such as maps and books. One club managed to get a playground built on the site of a former livery stable. They helped keep the streets clean, provided for garbage and trash disposal, urged school boards to add rooms to school buildings or to build new buildings. They planted trees to shade their streets and placed benches in parks for the enjoyment of the citizens. Some clubs installed street lamps in their towns and hired a man to light them and keep them trimmed. Three clubs reported establishing rest rooms for women who came to town to shop or for the use of working girls. One club also reported hiring a maid to keep the rest room clean.

The Town Improvement Association of Ormond Beach maintained a library and reading room which was never locked. The last person to leave after nine o'clock turned out the light. Visitors and citizens enjoyed this facility and the club reported neither abuse nor vandalism.

Before the convening of the State Legislature in 1909 the FFWC legislative chairman had a lawyer draft three bills for the federation. One was concerned with the certification of teachers; another, the requirements for principals of primary schools and a third, required fire protection for teachers and pupils in the public schools.

There had been attempts to allow women to serve on school boards but since they were not yet allowed to vote, they had not been allowed to serve. A petition was presented to allow women to serve but since this would require changes in some laws the petition was withdrawn as not being timely. Another petition pleaded for better care of convicts but since the state had leased the prisoners for four years previous to the convening of the Legislature nothing could be done at that time. (Convicts were leased to businesses requiring unskilled manual labor. It was a cheap way of getting work done since the payment to the state was minimal. The cost to the state of keeping prisoners was decreased. Often the conditions under which the prisoners worked were inhumane according to information held by those who were in favor of prison reform.)

Domestic Change of Heart

The FFWC also campaigned for Domestic Science in the

schools. It had been generally believed that a woman was either born knowing how to run a household or that her mother would teach her. However, knowledge of nutrition, the necessity of sanitation in the prevention of disease and the management of household finances were taught in some of the colleges. The thinking of federation women had now changed from indifference to a definite belief that these subjects should be a part of the curriculum in the public schools.

Concerted efforts around the state to improve welfare, education, and conservation were gradually taking effect. Some laws passed showed progress. Also needed were programs to make citizens aware of the need to conserve the natural resources of the state, to educate all of Florida's children and to protect the health of the people.

Mrs. J. Stanley Frederick of Miami was elected President of FFWC at the Ocala meeting in 1910. She resisted the presidency saying that she lived too far south from the center of club life since only three clubs were on the lower East Coast, The Housekeepers' Club of Coconut Grove, the Woman's Club of Miami and the Entre Nous Club of West Palm Beach. However, she accepted the presidency and was an outstanding leader. In 1911, the annual meeting was held with the Women's Club of Jacksonville and with the Entre Nous Club in West Palm Beach in 1912.

Reforming the Reformatory

Lucy W. Blackman records in glowing terms the work of two legislative chairmen who worked during Mrs. Frederick's administration:

> The accomplishment of the legislative committee of this period is especially noteworthy. Mrs. Henry Wight of Sanford, formerly of Jacksonville, for the first year of this regime, and Mrs. Frank E. Jennings of Jacksonville, for the second year, displayed a leadership unequaled up to that time and unsurpassed in any later period. A pamphlet entitled 'Some Laws of Interest to Florida Women' was compiled by Mrs. Wight and distributed at the Jacksonville meeting in 1911. It was widely mentioned in the press of the country; which, led by *The Delineator*, was conducting a more or less vigorous campaign on behalf of the rights of women.

Mrs. Blackman praised the FFWC legislative committee:

> The legislative committee devoted the year 1911-1912 to a study of the state institutions of Florida, concentrating its attention on the State Reformatory at Marianna. Rumors of the 'impoverished and unsanitary conditions existing in that institution and the obsolete methods of correction obtaining there' came to the attention of the committee.... The legislature sent its own committee to investigate the reports. The visit of the committee of the lawmakers was arranged long in advance and when the distinguished gentlemen from Tallahassee arrived in Marianna, all was 'spic and span' with a chicken dinner in their honor awaiting them. A decent case of legislative white-washing followed their report.
>
> Two members of the federation's legislative committee, Mrs. Henry Wight and Mrs. W. B. Young, put on their hats one morning and, uninvited, unannounced, unexpected and evidently unwanted, arrived at the reformatory for a spend-the-day visit. Although no criticism of the management was made by this committee, its report was a sensation. The institution was the only refuge in Florida at that time for delinquent boys and girls —white and black—and the appropriation for maintenance was disgracefully meager.

The Federation's legislative committee published a small pamphlet entitled 'A Plea for the Marianna Reform School', which went to all candidates for the legislature, to women's clubs and to the press. Speakers went throughout the state on behalf of the reforms which were needed at the Marianna school and asked for support of the bills which the committee was preparing to present to the next legislature. These bills would provide for the betterment for women and children as well as reforms at the reformatory and other state institutions.

It was the work of this committee that laid the ground work which later resulted in the Florida Industrial School for Boys at Marianna and and the Florida Industrial School for Girls at Ocala. The FFWC kept working for improvement in the care of these boys and girls, many of whom were not delinquent but simply were victims of circumstances over which they had no control.

The various chairmen of standing committees and women involved in their club's work were becoming educated about the ways in which change in society could best be brought about. They learned from their mistakes. For example: twenty-seven states had passed laws allowing women to serve on school boards. A premature petition to the Florida legislature was ineffective because a constitutional amendment was necessary before such a law could be passed in Florida. In her annual report of 1911, Mrs. Wight advised:

> This point brings me to a matter that seems to me of great moment—viz: the importance of our club women studying conditions, knowing exactly what they are about, and then striving to create public sentiment in their own communities. If the women really feel that a woman on the school board would be an advantage, thinking and talking about the idea right at home, and in connection with local conditions, will do more to bring it about than anything any legislative committee can do in two months of the session. If we see reforms that are needed, let us devote ourselves to the creation of a favorable public opinion. This is something that the legislature cannot take as a joke—if they are sure that their constituency is favorable to a measure, they will not ignore it.

When Mrs. Jennings became chairman of the legislative committee after Mrs. Wight resigned, she presented a list of reforms and changes that were needed in the state. She gave stern advice: "Accurate knowledge of any subject must precede judgment and judgment must precede action." With such advice from the legislative chairman, the club women of Florida became better prepared to deal with the state legislature. There had been a time when agitation and "sandspur" tactics had caused legislators to look upon some of these women as pests who should "shut up and go home."

Mrs. Fredricks visited many clubs that were not members of the federation while she was president and as a result twenty-one clubs were added to the federation during her administration.

Traveling Libraries

The extension librarian reported that there were ten traveling libraries. In order for these books to be used to maximum benefit she had instituted some new rules: A library could stay in one place six months; a fee of one dollar was to be paid to the library fund; the the club receiving the incoming library was to pay the freight charges; and a bill of lading was to be requested when starting a shipment.

Mrs. Fredericks wished to distribute the books over the state at approximately equal intervals and she felt that these libraries must be periodically overhauled, removing old books and adding more recent works of fiction.

The number of traveling libraries was increased from time to time, and they traveled back and forth across the state, being kept in the homes of club women who acted as librarians. There was a good selection of books with plenty of interesting fiction and always a children's shelf. The cases in which the books were shipped were shelved and opened on hinges, so that they served as book cases with no need to pack and unpack them. The books were usually shipped by train and continued to reach communities where there would be no libraries for another decade. The women who acted as librarians for these traveling libraries performed a notable service but they also worked to obtain local libraries. In 1926, these books and cases were thoroughly repaired and donated by the federation to the newly appointed Florida Library Commission as a nucleus for their proposed circulating libraries. They were sent to the commission's headquarters in Tallahassee. Two hundred volumes which had been donated to the federation by Mrs. William Jennings Bryan from Mr. Bryan's library were also sent. These books had never before been in the traveling library circulation.

Sex Education?

The 1912-1913 manual does not list a Reciprocity Chairman because a Bureau of Information has taken its place. Listed also is a Social Conditions Committee whose chairman reported going to several high schools where she gave talks to groups of girls and groups of boys. It is a bit difficult to figure out what she talked to them about. She states:

> The chief difficulty encountered in this work is the enlightenment of the public—along the lines of this work—has been and is—the social sentiment which masquerading under the guise of modesty and, has resolutely refused to recognize the need for knowledge. The apathetic indifference is changing to one of active interest as shown by the effort of several clubs to give this subject more attention and study.

Through two finely printed pages of her report the subject is never named but since she talked to the girls and boys separately, one gathers that her unmentioned subject was SEX. One cannot help but wonder whether the boys and girls to whom she talked understood her message. In May 1914, the topic for discussion at a meeting of the Ladies' Improvement Association of Delray was "Should sex hygiene be taught in public schools"? The minutes of that meeting record that several articles were read and after much discussion the consensus was that it should not. "Should students be informed about sex?" was a topic for discussion in many clubs at that time and 90 years later, parents, citizens and school personnel continued to discuss this same topic without agreement.

The chairman of the Social Conditions Committee also wrote that the use of cigarettes and alcohol by young women must be opposed. (Was it perfectly all right for young men to use these drugs?) Such a question is based on a wrong assumption. This was a time when daring young women were beginning to smoke and even drink publicly. This was shocking and cause for concern. Women were accustomed to men using tobacco and alcohol and they understood the problems of such use. They hoped to keep women from succumbing to harmful habits.

Charlotte Lockwood in *If These Walls Could Talk*, a history of the Vero Beach Woman's Club (organized in 1915), observed:

> To men, during the first two decades, Florida was a place to be alive, to do things, to take advantage of intermittent prosperity, to pioneer with all the romance and advantage of ox teams, mules, sail boats, steam boats, lumber wagons, trains, automobiles and electric generators run by gasoline motors.
>
> To women, it meant keeping house without the daily milkman, the iceman, the mailman, the paper boy, the garbage man — perhaps miles from the grocery store with little or no transportation.
>
> To women, it meant bending over a washboard and tub, perhaps heating water in a kettle over an open fire in the yard.
>
> It meant that the house might have termites, the kitchen probably had roaches, the cat had fleas, the dog had ticks, the baby had red bugs and everybody had mosquito bites.

By 1916, the Woman's Club of Vero Beach had a clubhouse

Jessie Hamm Meyer

and three hundred books to move into it for a town library. The lumber for the building had been delivered by ox cart. To help pay off the $400 mortgage on the club building three members borrowed an acre of ground and planted cabbages to sell in the community. The history of the Vero Beach Woman's Club is like that of most of the early clubs in that the women did what needed doing.

> When in the early days, the baker's daughter died of diptheria, the woman's club members cleaned the bakery, disinfected it to the satisfaction of the health officials and announced the bakery safe. When somebody wanted the school floors scrubbed, woman's club members volunteered.

One of the first women elected to Congress, Ruth Bryan Owen, visited the Vero Beach Woman's Club in 1924. "The luncheon in her honor was catered at 35 cents a plate."

A List for the Legislature

Clubwomen individually and collectively were influenced by a strong motivating force to make their communities, their state, their nation and the world a better place. This desire has driven club women to spend their talents, time and energies in volunteer service, not always effectively, sometimes making mistakes, but informing themselves and gradually, persistently and patiently bringing about changes. They learned that big as well as small problems are not readily solved andthat partial and multiple solutions must be tried.

The legislative committee offered the following list to FFWC for the Florida Legislature to consider:

> To make wife-desertion a felony
>
> To remove a married woman's disability in the matter of making contracts and controlling her individual property
>
> To place women on the school boards
>
> To amend the Juvenile Court Law
>
> To restrict child labor more stringently

The 1912-1913 manual is the last one where detailed reports of individual clubs appear. Thereafter reports were filed with the bureau of information because of the federation's rapid growth. For historians or anyone interested in the variety of projects being done all over Florida, the manual contained a wealth of information. It was distributed to every club so that women in Miami could know the projects of the club women of Pensacola. Small clubs could know what the big clubs were doing and vice versa. Growth has its price as well as its rewards. District directors wrote fairly comprehensive reports describing the activities of the clubs in their districts and these continued to be printed in the yearbooks and supply valuable information about the accomplishments of various clubs. These reports glow with positive deeds done — a reader might conclude that there were never any unsurmountable problems. Few if any board members wrote of the problems which they faced. However, historians of individual clubs often told all. Women disagreed on many things but generally they were the "little things of life" such as whether to serve refreshments or not, whether to paint the clubhouse or buy dishes for the kitchen.

The 1913-1914 manual lists seventy clubs in the federation, eighteen of which were new, and no withdrawals. One of those clubs organized in 1913 was the Woman's Civic League later renamed the Woman's Club of Winter Haven. The club's first president, Dr. Mary Jewett, insisted that blacks receive an education equal to that of whites and convinced the school board to erect a building for blacks.

Jewell Ulery in a history of her club reported 1913 as a busy year for the new club. There were thousands of house flies, caused by mule stables located in the city. City fathers ignored citizens' request to outlaw the stables. "The Civic League got the school children to enter an essay contest entitled 'The Dangers of the House Fly.' The essays were publicized, and pressure was put on city officials. Immediately a law was enacted to eliminate mule stables."

In the same year, "The club women toured the schools' outhouses. The poor conditions horrified the members. Dr. Jewett and members met parents and the school board. The outhouses were updated. The ladies planted vines outside to grace the structures. Sanitation and community improvement resulted."

Mrs. William Hocker of Ocala was President for the 1912-

1913 administration. In addition to the standing committees, Mrs. Hocker had appointed the following special committees:

Constitutional Revision
Industrial School
Tuberculosis Sanitorium
Seminole Indians

The convention of 1913 was held in Orlando. The departments of civil service reform, legislation, education, club extension, art, music, bird protection, literary and library extension, and health gave detailed reports which were published in the FFWC biennial book of 1913-1914.

Health and Sanitation

One of the jobs of the chairman of the health committee was selling Christmas seals for the benefit of work with "The White Plague" or tuberculosis. Distributing these to the many clubs over the state, trying to get them to sell as many as they possibly could and collecting the money for seals was no small job. However, the work was important. Further education, prevention, study and research were desperately needed. Some clubs managed to get "no spitting" ordinances passed. Common drinking cups in schools and on trains appeared to be one of the ways by which the disease was passed from one to another. An education campaign was launched to stop people from drinking from common cups. People began carrying their own special metal cups that collapsed into a small space. School children quickly learned to fold their tablet paper into drinking cups. Teachers took time to teach children that they should not eat or drink "after each other". There was a lack of definite knowledge about how tuberculosis was spread and there was no cure. Rest, good food and fresh air seemed sometimes to allow the body's own immune system to conquer the disease but it was increasingly clear that people who had it needed to be isolated from the general citizenry. To make matters worse, Florida's warm climate had attracted many northerners who came to the state in the hope that their tuberculosis could be cured or that their lives would at least be prolonged. The state legislature had passed a law in 1909 empowering the State Board of Health to establish a state sanitorium but nothing had been done. The FFWC in session sent a strongly worded resolution to the Secretary of the State Board of Health asking that something be done about the situation and offering the aid of the women of FFWC.

The Health Department Committee had a further resolution with clauses that explained the dangerous diseases of syphilis and gonorrhea as well as the burden on society of the defective offspring of mentally and morally defective parents.

> Resolved, that the Legislature of the State of Florida hereby, and it is, requested by the Federated Women's Clubs of Florida to add to the present laws governing marriage a clause prohibiting the marriage of idiots, habitual criminals, and all other mental and moral irresponsibles, and demanding from both parties seeking to marry, statements signed by reputable physicians certifying to their freedom from those conditions and from dangerous contagious diseases; in the absence of which no marriage shall be valid.

Not all petitions and resolutions that the women drafted would stand up under law. Such social engineering as would develop from their well meant petition could not have been implemented without violating the privacy and individual rights of Florida's citizens; but they raised awareness of the problems. Some of the resolutions developed into bills that became laws and much progress was made on many of the suggested bills. Appropriations for running the newly-named Florida Industrial School for Boys were almost doubled and an accounting system begun to assure that the funds were used correctly. The Child Labor law was amended and elaborated making the exploitation of children more difficult. Certification laws for teachers recognized the need of more training. Family desertion was made a felony but the legislature also recognized that imprisonment would leave the family with no income. No really satisfactory law resulted at this session nor would future sessions be able to legislate this moral dilemma.

The federation's legislative committee urged every club to appoint a committee to hold study classes to learn more about parliamentary law, mothers' pensions, compulsory education, need of a state board for charities, election of women to serve on school boards and continuing watch over conditions in the state industrial schools.

Resolutions were presented by various clubs, such as: a pension law that would give teachers a pension of ten dollars a month after they had taught for twenty years and that the state pay part of the salary of home demonstration agents and county farm agents as there were several counties in Florida that did not have the advantage of these agents. Some clubs were helping to fund the salaries of home demonstration agents while urging their counties to budget these positions.

The federation encouraged boys and girls in their farm work by giving prizes to winners in "Tomato Clubs", "Corn Clubs" and "Pig Clubs." Many of the federation's clubs were in small towns and represented Florida's population which was more rural than urban. Interest in the Seminole Indians continued but in the future clubs would have to clear their Indian work projects through the Indian Agent. The Fort Lauderdale Woman's Club "adopted" a Seminole Indian boy and sent him to the Carlisle Indian School in Pennsylvania. The school was successful for many western Indians but winter cold and separation from home were too much for this Indian boy reared in semi-tropical Florida. His letters were so pitiful that the club brought him back home.

Later the agent reported that the boy was attending school in Fort Lauderdale, which was a most satisfactory solution for training this bright boy to become a leader of his people. The Seminoles lived mostly to themselves; attempts were being made to integrate them into the general population but without a great deal of success.

The need for a training school for epileptics and the feeble minded was another subject that was brought up at the meeting in 1914. At that time epileptics and feeble minded were lumped together for there was as yet no treatment that would permit epileptics to lead normal lives.

A look at the wide ranging interests of Florida club women shows that the various committees had been doing their work in preparation for their annual meeting.

In 1914, the convention was held at the Lakeland public auditorium. Mrs. Hocker reported that membership in the Florida Federation of Women's Clubs had almost doubled during the previous two years. Eighteen new clubs had been added. Thirty women from Florida attended the Biennial Convention in Chicago in 1914 and Mrs. William B. Young of Jacksonville was elected to the General Federation Board of Directors. The Florida Federation of Women's Clubs was being recognized as an influential and mature organization. After the legislative efforts of Mrs. Wight and Mrs. Jennings, women's clubs were no longer considered a joke, not even by the Florida Legislature. Many husbands were supportive of their wives' federation work and most men had given up on the idea that clubs were "for men only."

Finances and economics are basic to all history. Mrs. Hocker made an enlightening statement to the 1914 convention regarding the finances of FFWC. She said, "Do you realize that this organization has only an income of fifteen cents per member with which to carry on its various activities? Out of this must come the dues to the General Federation, membership in several affiliated organizations, expenses of conventions, such as invitations, programs, entertainment of visitors, stationery and the year book. No other organization in the world operates on so small a capital, and in no other organization is there so seldom a call for money."

It was at the 1914 meeting that the revision of the charter and by-laws and the dividing of the state into five districts, each having its own vice-president, were brought to a conclusion and presented to the federation. Dividing the state into districts brought new impetus to club work and the growing membership could more adequately be absorbed into the machinery of the federation.

A memorial service for Mrs. E. G. G. Munsell was held at the 1914 convention. She was known as "Mother of the Federation" although she had often modestly declared that she was "only a member of the Mother Club" meaning the Green Cove Springs VIA. Part of the tribute paid to Mrs. Munsell credited her with bringing "into existence the most powerful body of women workers in the state. She was offered the presidency many times, but always refused on account of home business, although she held many other less burdensome offices in the

Federation, and it was while she was chairman of Education that the Federation Kindergarten Scholarship Fund was established. It was Mrs. Munsell's proud boast that she never missed but one meeting of the Federation."

First Woman on the School Board

April 18, 1916, Mrs. William Hocker was elected to serve on the Ocala School Board. Before woman suffrage was enacted nationally, some states (not Florida) and some towns had passed laws allowing women to serve in certain offices. Mrs. Hocker was the first woman in Florida to be elected to public office.

Mrs. William S. Jennings of Jacksonville was elected president under the new charter and by-laws giving her three years of service, 1914-1917.

Leading the Way: A Century of Service

Fig. 9. Early Federation Membership ribbons displayed at the FFWC Archives in Lakeland.

Fig. 10. Delray Beach Clubwomen cross the Intracoastal Waterway to the Beach on a "Lighter" propelled by woman-power. (From the History of the Women's Club of Delray Beach).

5 – A Third Decade And World War I

WHILE there had been tremendous growth during the second decade, much was changing. Mrs. Jennings began her administration as the war in Europe caused rumblings throughout the country and disturbed the "peace" meetings being held in America. Red Cross workers were busy making surgical dressings and sewing machines buzzed making supplies to be shipped to war-torn Europe. It has been said that practically every woman in the federation wore the "veil of Red Cross service" during these years. Even with the burden of the extra Red Cross service the regular work of the Florida Federation continued. Some new standing committees were added so that the complete list included: art, civics, civil service reform, education, music, public health, home economics, legislation, industrial and social conditions, conservation, bird protection, forestry, waterways, good roads, Seminole Indians, and parks.

A State Park

The Woman's Club of Homestead was organized and joined FFWC in 1914. The members realized that Paradise Key was unique and that its beauty should not be exploited. The Homestead Club assisted in procuring 1920 acres including Royal Palm Hammock on Paradise Key for park purposes.

In *History of Royal Palm State Park*, 1940, Mrs. Jennings wrote:

> For years there came from the lower Everglades to the Florida Federation of Women's Clubs reports of a beautiful hammock with towering royal palms on what was called Paradise Key. The Federation was asked to urge the legislature to 'do something about it'.

Mrs. John Gifford and Mrs Kirk Monroe, living on the rim of the Everglades, were especially solicitous that some action be taken.

As President of the Federation, 1914-1917, I conceived the idea of having the Federation take over the protection and maintenance of this very unique area. It required a vast deal of persuasion and manipulation to bring the Legislature of 1915 to the point of presenting 960 acres for a park to a group of women and to help finance their project as well, but the improbable came to pass.

Mrs. Henry Flagler met the Legislature's gift with a similar donation of rich land (960 acres) and the women looked out upon a dooryard of 1,920 acres for their great conservation project.

ROYAL PALM STATE PARK was the only possible name for their enterprise and as such it was dedicated on November 23, 1916, and the Federation has successfully managed the Park for the past 24 years.

Correspondence and records concerning the park indicate that the "success" of managing the park required work and patience. When the legislature gave the acreage to the FFWC to be preserved the state was to contribute $1000 annually toward the protection and improvement of the park. However, the bill giving the park to the federation did not include the $1000. There could be no early return on the land to help with the responsibilities which the federation had incurred. The park needed many things such as a keeper, care for the trees and protection of the plants. Walkways and roads needed to be constructed and "a tea room for visitors should be built." Appeals were made to the National Audubon Society and other organizations for help. Individuals made contributions and all clubs were asked to make contributions to help out at least until the legislature met again in two years. Those going to the dedication November 23, 1916, "jounced over almost impassable roads and palmetto roots and bridges built over night for the occasion." A contract was soon made for a hard surfaced road to be built from Miami to Cape Sable, thus making the park more accessible to people once the road was finished. The women of FFWC would find that taking care of Royal Palm State Park would be both a burden and a joy.

The Federation's twenty-first annual meeting was held in DeLand in November 1915 where Mrs. Jennings announced that an endowment fund of $25,000 would be started, the income from which could be used for federation work. This was an ambitious but necessary undertaking and while it was difficult to raise the money, it was the beginning of financial support for FFWC. Mrs. Jennings had spoken to 41 clubs and traveled 5,164 miles by railway to explain this. She was not asking for reimbursement, since this was her gift, but she did point out, "It is hardly fair to the federation to cast about for presidential timber just among those who are able to stand the expense. It will likely always be the case that a president furnish some of the expense of her office, but capability of the candidate to furnish same, should not be a paramount issue, and the same should apply to other officers and chairmen, hence the great necessity for the suggested endowment." (The Putnam Inn in DeLand charged $2.50 per day for a room without bath and $3.00 per day with bath — American plan. In 1915, most delegates stayed in the homes of members of the hostess club.)

The chairman of club extension reported that 29 clubs had been added with an increased membership of 1,380 women. Only three clubs had withdrawn. There were now 109 clubs in the federation with a total of 6,391 members. Clubs continued to be formed for various reasons. Good schools were high on the list of most women. Auburndale women organized because one of the trustees of the school refused to furnish a new broom for the teacher to sweep her room. That refusal was probably the proverbial "straw" but it was enough to get the women organized.

Life in Florida was not easy. It was in 1914 that Delray got its first electricity. On week nights the townspeople could have electric lights from six until eleven and on Saturday from six until twelve. One day a week the electricity was on during the day so that those who had electric irons could use them. A colony of Japanese raised pineapples on the outskirts of Delray. Members of the woman's club sewed canvas mittens and leggings for the workers in the pineapple fields.

Dixie Highway

There was a great deal of excitement to report from the good roads chairman. The Dixie Highway was coming to

Florida! An attempt was being made "to get 100 foot rights of way which would give room for planting of trees and beautification". Plans were on the boards to build a road across the peninsula to connect Tampa to Miami where it would link up with the road being built from Miami to Cape Sable. This road across the peninsula would also join the Dixie Highway, the great North-South Highway, which everyone hoped would soon reach Miami. Rapidly increasing numbers of cars in Florida made paved highways a necessity so the good roads chairman had plenty to do.

The federation met in Miami in 1916 and in her president's report Mrs. Jennings wrote that her duties had necessitated her traveling 10,210 railway miles and 596 car miles. She had given her full time to her duties. The new Royal Palm Park had required a great deal of work. Clubs were building club houses and she was often invited to lay a cornerstone or dedicate a building.

Through FFWC, three sites for an Industrial School for Delinquent Girls had been offered and one near Ocala had been chosen. The 1915 legislature had appropriated $30,000 for building and equipping the school but when Mrs. Jennings visited the site, no work had been done. In the meantime the girls who were to live there were turned back on the streets. She entreated the state officials to provide some temporary shelter for these girls. The FFWC through its committee on industrial and social conditions and special committees studied how other states handled the problems of delinquent boys and girls and influenced state officials to consider building the industrial schools on the cottage plan which afforded a more homelike atmosphere for the occupants than large dormitory-like buildings. However, these recommendations were not followed much to the disappointment of this hard working committee.

The industrial and social conditions committee also reported on conditions at the State Prison Farm at Raiford:

> We have it on good authority that the Prison Farm at Raiford is being run on very humane lines. They have the ten- hour day, good food and work in the open air.

The committee continued with a report on the use of drugs:

> The Harrison Anti-Narcotic Law, with its subsequent rulings handles the drug habit thoroughly. It is a national law and is being rigidly enforced. Many confirmed users have been obliged, for the lack of dope, to take the cure. An organization was formed in Jacksonville to help these unfortunates.

Such optimism! Or were they just naive? Yet there is some mention in social histories that at that time there was an epidemic of drug use and then it apparently decreased. The problems of alcohol and drug abuse were not permanently solved nor have the industrial schools kept up with the problems of delinquency. However, there is little doubt that the raising of public awareness by the women of pre-World War I years held in abeyance for a time these disturbing social ills. The 1915 Legislature passed "An Act Requiring the Teaching of the Evils of Alcoholic Beverages and Narcotics to Children in the Primary Grades of the Public Schools."

Between 1914 and 1916, the Florida Federation of Women's Clubs grew by 11 clubs and 380 members. Three county federations had been formed, which sprang somewhat simultaneously among clubs along the Dixie Highway for there is, "among women, a marked enthusiasm for the ornamentation and planting of the great thoroughfare."

Draining the Swamps

The waterways chairman advised strongly that the waterways must not be polluted and that pure drinking water must not be threatened. In 1916 the function of wetlands was not understood. This chairman joyfully reported the drainage of many areas:

> The Florida Drainage Association is doing a wonderful work and I have asked that they help us in our endeavors to do something for Florida. There are now thousands of acres of land in this state that through drainage, have become thrifty communities, and the land of wonderful value. There is work going on not only in the draining of the Everglades, but the Hammock Lands for several miles above Daytona.

Ignorance of the ecology of wetlands, their place in the food chain, their capacity to store water and to clean it, caused so many swamps to be drained that the burgeoning population of Florida would have cause for great concern before the end of the 20th Century.

The New Smyrna Beach Woman's Club reported that the club paid all of the expenses of its delegate to the convention in Miami — the amount was $17.00 which covered transportation, hotel and meals.

The time for holding the annual meeting had been changed from the even numbered years to the odd numbered years to conform to the General Federation of Women's Clubs conventions. Presiding at the convention of 1917 in Tampa, Mrs. Jennings announced that the FFWC had a membership close to 10,000 members, but the plan for an endowment of $25,000.00 made in 1915 had resulted in only $2,755.77.

W HEN the 1917 Convention met in Tampa, The United States was on a war footing.

Since 1914, GFWC had encouraged all of its federated clubs to take a strong stand for peace. Many programs during these years emphasized the necessity for the United States to stay out of the war in Europe. In spite of Germany's announcement that United States ships traveling to Europe would be sunk by German submarines, the United States attempted to negotiate a peace. This failed and German submarines continued to sink United States ships. In April 1917, the United States entered into an Alliance with European nations against Germany.

The war work of FFWC and of the many other organizations in the state could hardly be separated. The need for increased food production and preservation caused the national government to furnish county agents and home demonstration agents to every county that could use them. Roads were improved to transport food to ports for shipment to our military and that of our allies.

War Work

FFWC was not unmindful of the welfare and safety of the many women who had gone to work in munition factories. Safety for industrial workers had been of little concern in most work places. Accidental death and crippling of hundreds of thousands was accepted as the price that had to be paid to reap the benefits of the industrial revolution. Shorter working hours were urged by women's clubs because many accidents occurred due to extreme fatigue of the workers. Employers often expected their workers to work twelve to fourteen hours a day. There were few laws requiring management to install safety devices around dangerous machinery. Women's clubs pointed to France and England as having already recognized the need of legislation to protect workers in industry.

Club members sold Liberty Bonds, worked with the Red Cross, planted and cultivated vegetable gardens, gave canning demonstrations, sewed and devoted themselves to patriotic service.

Delegates heard reports concerning other projects. A lodge had been completed at Royal Palm State Park. They kept an eye on the industrial schools and sought additional appropriations for them. They tried to get the legislature to furnish free text books to public school children but failed. They were also disappointed that the funds for public health nurses had been cut so that the valuable health education work was greatly diminished. They wanted a tuberculosis sanatorium for each county but would have been happy to get even one in the state The waterways chairmen reported that there was an idea for an Inside Passage from Key West to New York and in that war time atmosphere there was wide recognition of the benefits which such a waterway, safe from enemy submarines, would bring to the country.

Mrs. Edgar Lewis of Fort Pierce was elected President for 1917-1918 and presided at the twenty-fourth annual convention at Daytona Beach, held in November 1918. Only eight days had passed since an Armistice had been declared and there was little said about it in the reports at the convention. Club members were urged to hold to the high level of patriotism that they had shown during the war and to act in ways which would best bring about reconstruction during the period of readjustment and peace. Reports to that convention had been prepared previous to the declaration of the Armistice and they showed how the federation president and Florida clubs had clubs had been totally absorbed in war work. Mrs. Lewis had met and served the federation at meetings of the State Council of Defense, Florida Division of the Woman's Committee, Council of National Defense, state executive committee of the Woman's Liberty Loan Committee, Food Administration and the United War Work Campaign. She had urged every club member to become a working member of the Red Cross.

Plans for Peace

The addresses at this convention were directed toward peace and were quite timely. Some titles were: "The League of Nations", "Plans for Colonization After the War", "U.S. Food Administration", "The War Victory Commission", "Education and Reconstruction" and "Equal Suffrage". "Equal Suffrage" was given by the Secretary of the National Woman Suffrage Association. The General Federation of Women's Clubs had not taken any active part in the Suffrage Movement since it was looked upon as a political subject. The GFWC preferred to allow other organizations to work in that area. From its beginning the GFWC was determined to refrain from being militant but for women to get the right to vote a certain amount of militancy appeared to be required. The Suffrage Movement had gained momentum as more and more women took jobs in munition factories and worked in many areas dominated by male workers before the war.

While the FFWC convention was being held after the Armistice was signed, reports told of the work that had been done during the previous year and the problems encountered. It was recommended that publication of the federation magazine be suspended. A paper shortage had made it difficult to get paper even for year books. There was not much demand for the traveling libraries as people said that they were too busy to read anything other than newspaper accounts of the war. A major drive for money to provide a recreation or rest place for our soldiers in France or Switzerland was made by the Red Cross and every club woman was asked to contribute a dollar. They gathered clothes for the destitute of Belgium and France and helped with entertainment and care of soldiers. In the midst of all the war effort and just before the Armistice a devastating epidemic of influenza swept through the United States. Women who were well enough to help, found themselves nursing, feeding and visiting the sick.

The press of war work had not kept FFWC committee chairmen from doing their work and preparing resolutions for passage at the convention in Daytona. Some of these subjects had been addressed before but without any action or implementation by the legislature. Feeble minded, idiots, retarded, epileptics, and the insane were still being kept in an asylum for the insane. Many of these were children of school age who could be trained to live useful lives, so the FFWC resolved to ask that a separate facility be built for those who were not insane. They also continued to press for good roads and bridges not only across Florida but for the entire country. They suggested, too, that alien prisoners be put to work building a system of highways. (With the armistice, international treaties would deal with these persons.)

The Vice-Presidents of the five districts made reports which showed that their contacts with the clubs in their districts were making the entire Florida Federation stronger. In spite of all her war work, Mrs. Lewis had found time to visit each district.

Postwar Disillusionment

The Silver Anniversary marked the Convention of 1919 which was held in St. Petersburg. Past Presidents, Mrs. Beekman (1899-1901) and Mrs. Shackleford (1908-1910), gave addresses as did others who had served as officers and chairmen during the last twenty-five years. While they celebrated twenty-five years of service, there was cause for concern because a period of reaction had set in nationwide. Sacrifice and patriotism were replaced with greed and selfishness, or so it appeared to some of the women meeting in St. Petersburg. Mrs. Lewis in her address at the convention warned, "All that we had of strength and courage and faith we need now, with yet more added. In this period of treacherous reaction what are we going to do? Weaken under the relaxation of a great strain, or brace ourselves that we may prove a safe anchorage to those less able to weather the storm?"

She had spent three weeks in Tallahassee while the legislature was in session. The compulsory education bill that FFWC had favored for so long passed but Mrs. Lewis expressed her discouragement with the legislative process:

> After watching the kaleidoscopic shifting of legislators and legislation, she would be a sanguine and confident person who could locate with any satisfaction the real reason for the success or failure of anything. There was the thrill which came with a knowledge of the backing and the confidence of a senate almost unanimous in the belief that women should be citizens — to be followed by quite a different thrill along the same line, but produced by treatment administered at the other end of the capitol building. After this it was disconcerting, to say the least, to have your warm and tender sympathy for the Seminoles crash against the senatorial opinion, later upheld by the requisite number of votes, that the Indians are a 'dirty, disease-breeding lot,' only fit for drowning; or your positive knowledge of the scientific value of Royal Palm State Park overwhelmed by characterization as a "local promotion scheme merely."

Equal Suffrage

The legislative chairman had worked to get equal suffrage passed in the state. Sixteen towns in Florida had passed laws granting equal suffrage to women, but Florida did not pass the Equal Suffrage Act. She reported:

> This passed the Senate but failed in the House. Primary suffrage was not a popular issue and the vote was for submission and lost by four votes. Would that I had time to go into some of the arguments used against this measure. They both were amusing and without 'rhyme or reason'. They still used the old argument that women were the inferiors of men both physically and mentally.

In 1919, clubs were so hopeful that women would be given the right to vote by an amendment to the Constitution that they asked men to come to their club meetings to give them "voting lessons."

Dr. Mary B. Jewett, chairman of the Political Equality Department, reported that by the end of 1918 twenty countries had enfranchised their women. She was encouraged that the 66th Congress of the United States "finally did what every Congress since 1878 has been appealed to do, passed the amendment granting suffrage to women." She was concerned that many states would not have legislative sessions in time for the amendment to be ratified before the presidential election in 1920. Special legislative sessions should be called. She said in her report:

> If our two Florida senators could have been brought to see the light during the 65th Congress, when we needed just their two votes, we would have a different story to tell, for at that time many legislatures were in session, or soon to be in session, and ratification would have made great progress. As it is it will drag along probably for some time, and it is quite likely that women of Florida and other states of the 'Solid South' will owe their enfranchisement to the greater enlightenment, and more real chivalry, of the other sections of the country.

Mrs. Jewett called the attention of the women at the 25th convention to progress made and she also questioned Florida's position.

> In 28 states women will vote for presidential electors next year irrespective of the ratification of the amendment, and those states can carry the election. How about Florida? Of course you know the answer as far as our Senators last June is concerned. They did their best to keep the women of Florida from securing justice, as they have persistently done whenever the subject has come up for decision. The women of Florida and the women of the country owe no thanks to our two reactionaries, Senator Duncan U. Fletcher and Senator Park Trammell.

The Political Equality Department had been formed only two years previous to this convention. No longer were members of GFWC or FFWC willing to stand by and let others work for equal suffrage. Dr. Jewett ended her report with an appeal:

> If our Governor would call a special session, and if our Legislature would do justice to the women of Florida by ratifying the federal amendment, I believe that the patriotic response of our women would be immediate. Can we, as a Federation, not do something to bring this about? Shall we not at least make an effort by making an appeal to the Governor to call a special session? I would rather make that effort and fail at ratification than not to make the effort at all."

(The governor refused to call a special session of the legislature, believing that ratification of the suffrage amendment would not receive the necessary support. The amendment became the law of the entire country in August of 1920. The Florida Legislature saw no need to ratify it. Not until the 1969 session did the Florida Legislature choose to go through the formality of approval.)

Mrs. Lewis had very positive feelings about the club women of Florida. She summed up her thoughts on the war years at the 1919 meeting:

> The clubs have been universally loyal; in fact, the fervency of their patriotic zeal blinded their clearer vision somewhat in the beginning of the year. Then it seemed in order to do their best in war work, they must give up the club. Later they found out that, in order to accomplish the greatest amount of war work, they must back it up by the strongest possible club. Plans for club work have shifted as everything in our lives has changed—been reorganized, readapted. But the vital thing is that the clubs have held. They have given their leaders; they have given their money; they have given their labor, their discipline, the results of their years of training and organization; but they have not committed the fatal error of disintegration. The work of twenty-five years is not wasted; the strength, the courage, the faith of those who builded the foundation on which we stand, is not to perish. The clubs of the Florida Federation have held, are holding and (please God) will hold to do yet greater work.

In spite of the many changes at work both on the national and local levels, the 1919 Convention established a Department of History for the purpose of collecting and preserving the "Local History and Romances" of each county in the state. Old settlers' stories of pioneer days, information from old letters and family records were desired by Mrs. Kirk Munroe who was chairman of this new department.

On the national level, Dr. Anna Shaw worked for Equal Suffrage and wrote:

> When I think of Florida club women having to do things like fixing up parks, cleaning streets, and setting out trees by your own club contributions and donations, it makes me furious, when, if you were a part of the government, it could be done and kept done. It is maddening and we have got to make men see it, and women see it, but neither men nor women will see it until we can vote.

Of the 4,121,000 U.S. men who had served in the military during World War I, 126,000 were dead. Approximately 50,000 of them had been killed in battle and others had died of disease. Poison gas had been used by the Germans against the Allied soldiers fighting in the war and these soldiers returned disabled by their experiences. The country was once again trying to work out a way to keep out of war. The League of Nations was widely discussed but the United States leaned toward isolationism.

For many years the Women's Christian Temperance Union (WCTU) had waged another kind of war. This was against the use of alcohol. The GFWC had been passing resolutions in favor of prohibition for years and in 1916 had sent a message to Congress which said, "When both food and manpower are at such a premium, we believe it folly to indulge in the waste of one and the dissipation of the other. We, the women of the land, pledge our sons, our money, our labor and our all, and we beseech the United States Congress to strike from our land the greatest despoiler of food and the greatest wrecker of manpower."

Little is recorded about the fight for prohibition in the FFWC archives. The Eighteenth Amendment or the Prohibition Amendment was ratified in 1920. This amendment prohibited the sale and manufacture of alcoholic beverages. The history of the Woman's Club of St. Cloud made a simple statement: "At our meeting we sang the Doxology when Prohibition won."

Mrs. J. W. McCollum of Gainesville who had been a section vice-president and had worked with Mrs. Lewis during the war years was elected president. Again the clubs of the state were divided first into eleven and then twelve districts, giving Mrs. McCollum 12 sectional vice-presidents with whom to serve. In 1920 the convention was held in Tallahassee and in 1921 in Gainesville. A new official publication, the Florida Bulletin, was begun at this time with Mrs. W. M. Pepper as business manager and Mrs. McCollum editor-in-chief. Mrs. Pepper had increased publicity for GFWC through increasing the number of Florida newspapers which printed what was referred to as Federation Pages. She urged clubs to use these pages and as press chairman she sent GFWC news to the newspapers of Jacksonville, Tampa, St. Petersburg, Miami and Orlando. It was a time of growth, and pulling those clubs that had strayed back into the federation. New efforts were made along old lines and new projects were developed, one of which saw a committee formed that was devoted to work on behalf of business and professional women.

Managing the Park

A lodge had been built to accommodate scientists working at the park as well as a few visitors who might want to stay longer than one day. The federation was still trying to get the legislature to contribute money toward the upkeep of Royal Palm State Park. Naturalists classified trees and plants, birds and wild life and all agreed that Paradise Key was a gem of natural beauty as well as being the only place in the United States where tropical plants grew in such abundance and variety. The number of visitors to the park increased and they wanted meals. The chairman of the park committee reported that more help was needed. When the women interested in conservation worked to get the state to turn over the land to them, they had not foreseen getting into the restaurant and hotel business. Apparently the visitors also wanted to be able to entertain themselves, because the park chairman reported that a piano was needed. Donations to a piano fund were taken and almost $100 was raised. Treasurer's reports for the next two years showed no expenditure for a piano, but furniture, forks and spoons were listed as expenses. No cook was hired. The warden was paid a salary of $1200 per year. The Florida Federation of Women's Clubs was the only state federation in the country that owned and supported a park.

Since the United States Treasury had instituted a campaign to promote thrift, the General Federation had adopted a resolution, "That we offer assistance to our government in promoting a campaign to make our country a thrifty nation." The Florida Federation had a director of a thrift committee and she reported that every club was asked to form a thrift circle and that every woman should have a thrift circle in her own family. This was not just to help the government by buying thrift stamps but "to stamp the habit of thrift on every citizen."

In April 1920, a Florida history department was formed with Mrs. Kirk Munroe of Coconut Grove, Chairman, and Mrs.J.C. Beekman of Tarpon Springs, Vice Chairman. The Times Union of Jacksonville, January 1920, printed an extensive article about this department part of which stated:

> The chairman of the department plans to have a working com-

mittee, each member of which will do all possible to collect stories, facts, legends and pictures of incidents connected with the settlement of places.

One member invited all the old settlers, white and black, to a "history gathering" and got each one to tell something of the place. She had a capable shorthand writer present who lost nothing. The notes of each county are kept separate, and the name of the person giving the information and the person recording it are carefully kept. Mrs. Beekman of Tarpon Springs has already contributed valuable informations and promises more. The department has also received a valuable newspaper clipping on the Abanaki Indians and prehistoric relics found near Yamate, southern Florida from Mrs. W. S. Jennings.

Mrs. J.M. Taylor of Gainesville sent in a most beautiful account of a plantation in 1861 and a thrilling story of a soldier of the Confederate Army.

Patriotism and Prohibition

A post war activity called AMERCANIZATION had claimed the attention of the public. Before the war, aliens entering the United States were usually ignored as long as they created no disturbances. However, when the draft for the war began, it was discovered that there were four million native-born illiterates living in miserable circumstances who would be easy prey of propagandists trying to disrupt our government. Many of these were offspring of immigrants who had not been integrated into the mainstream of life in the United States. Each wave of immigrants had huddled into groups speaking the same language and had adhered to the customs of the "old country" until these second generation children had children of their own. Because of increased immigration from southern European nations, restrictions were put on the numbers of people allowed to enter this country.

The Eighteenth Amendment had caused quite an industry to grow up around the illegal production and sale of alcoholic beverages. Florida's long coastline and its many inlets furnished ideal opportunities for smuggling. "Rumrunners" brought liquor from the Bahamas or Cuba and off-loaded it into small boats which came ashore at countless places. Bootlegging was big business in Florida and in most of the rest of the country. Newspapers headlined news of gangsters operating in the big cities of the north. Gangs operating outside the law were competitive with other gangs, quickly rising to prominence with fortunes made and methods of operating devised which continued long after the 18th amendment was revoked in 1933.

Reports of the twenties show a frustration at not being able to solve the multitudinous problems of society, but at the same time this was a period of growth in the Florida Federation. Bird protection, conservation of forests, more financial support for educational institutions, support for health and hygiene work, and education for women, both black and white, to use their franchise wisely were a part of the program that the FFWC set for itself.

The 1921 convention in Gainesville stressed a great deal of study and interest in prison reform. FFWC was working with the Extension Division of the University of Florida and with its Dean, B. C. Riley, to survey the conditions in jails. Although not completed, Dean Riley said, "the work of our clubs in making this survey, made it possible for him to present a report of this phase of work at the National Prison Reform Association Convention."

Censorship of movies had been discussed for some time in committees of FFWC. A bill was proposed but withdrawn when it was learned that censorship of movies had taken on national importance and a support of that movement might be more effective than their original proposal.

Miss Elizabeth Skinner (Jackson) was elected president at the Gainesville Convention and her first annual meeting was held in Green Cove Springs and the second in West Palm Beach. Delegates to the convention in Green Cove Springs were advised that they could get from railroads "a rate of one and a half for round trip from points in Florida to Jacksonville and the Independent Boat Line runs a steamer at ten o'clock each morning from the pier at the foot of Main Street, Jacksonville, round trip to Green Cove Springs $2.00. Parties of ten or more will be given a round trip rate of $1.50. The trip takes about three hours."

During Miss Skinner's administration, a reorganization

resulted in seven main departments and eighty or more divisions. This was an effort to bring the Florida Federation in line with the General Federation. Previously every club member felt morally obligated to be interested in every phase of her federation's work. Such an array of divisions had been confusing to the larger clubs as well as the smaller ones. Now no club was asked to do a project in every division and in every department.

Junior Membership

From the earliest days of the federation, various senior clubs had fostered clubs for young women, but in 1921, during Miss Skinner's administration, a junior department was formed which grew steadily and became the pride of the Florida Federation. In 1922, the General Federation added Junior Membership as a special committee, the aim being a training school for future clubwomen between the ages of 16 and 25 years.

The State of Florida had not continued its support of the Royal Palm State Park as had been promised but in 1920 the legislature appropriated $2500 for the park and ceded 2080 acres of land making a total of 4000 acres in Royal Palm State Park. In 1921 FFWC still depended on donations and money made from various projects but the park was becoming better known with 6000 visitors reported for that year. The lodge was described as "well equipped with hot and cold water and electric lights and at reasonable rates. All visitors to the park are requested to register at the Lodge to avail themselves of its hospitalities."

Miss Skinner named the following special committees: Children's Code Committee, Cooperation in Interest of Ex-Service Men, Near East Relief Committee, Royal Palm State Park "Entrance" Committee, Committee to Cooperate for "State Flower Show" and the Committee on Inter-Racial Relations. The Departments were: Applied Education, American Citizenship, Fine Arts, Public Welfare, Legislation, and Press and Publicity. Each of these committees had many divisions. Standing Committees were: Federation Endowment Fund, Royal Palm State Park, Bureau of Information, Library, History,

Transportation, Junior Department.

The meeting in Green Cove Springs in November of 1922 was like a homecoming since it was there that FFWC had its first organizational meeting. However, members were saddened as they listened to tributes to Mrs. Kirk Munroe who had died on September 8th of that year. Mrs. Munroe was one of the founders of the Housekeeper's Club of Coconut Grove, one of the oldest clubs in the federation. It was in the Folio Club of Coconut Grove and as chairman of the FFWC history department that she had worked to collect historical material from all over Florida. Because of her many contributions to club work she was known as The Dean of the Florida Federation of Women's Clubs. The state of Florida suffered a loss as well as the Florida Federation because she died before she wrote the history using the wealth of unique material which she had collected.

FFWC lost another much loved and respected member who died in June of 1922. Antoinette Elizabeth Frederick had the unusual distinction of having served as President of FFWC and also had been president of Coconut Grove Woman's Club, the Miami Woman's Club and the Moore Haven Woman's Club.

County federations had grown from eight to twenty-one and the aim was to have a federation in every county.

In 1922 the chairman of the Highway Improvement Committee had questioned county commissioners concerning what type of road improvement was going on in their counties. Many counties did not reply and there were some that replied that nothing was being done about roads in their counties. The reply from Alachua County was more complete than some and gives an idea of what was being done in 1922 to enable cars to travel from one one place to another without getting stuck in the sand.

> Roads completed; from Columbia county line to Burnett's Lake asphalt-macadam, a distance of 14 miles. From Gainesville to the Archer District, lime rock to be treated with oil, a distance of 8 miles. From Rochelle to the Putnam County line, pebble road, distance of 12 miles.
>
> Under construction: Gainesville to Rochelle, pebble road, a distance of eight miles, Gainesville to Waldo, lime rock, a distance

of 13 miles. Gainesville to Burnett's Lake, asphalt-macadam, a distance of 12 1/2 miles. Gainesville to Micanopy, lime rock, a distance of 18 miles. Gainesville to Newberry District, lime rock, a distance of 8 miles. All of these roads have sixteen feet of hard surface and a beautiful right of way sixty feet wide. They will be maintained and beautified.

An announcement in the 1923-1924 year book states that the federation had established a permanent headquarters at the Sorosis House, Orlando. The Bureau of Information and the Historical Bureau collected by Mrs. Kirk Munroe would be moved there. Year books, papers and other material would be on file and available for any club member requesting information.

Twenty-three county federations are listed in this year book. Forty-nine new clubs were added but 19 had either disbanded or withdrawn from the federation making a gain of 30 clubs with 1,180 new members. The 1923-1924 year book contains reports of the section vice-presidents and the chairmen of various departments, thus giving the reader an excellent record for those years.

Mrs. William F. Blackman was elected president of the federation at the annual meeting held in November at West Palm Beach. Her first year was marked by a change of the date for holding annual meetings from the fall to the spring of the year, resulting in Mrs. Blackman having a three year administration (1923-1926). Mrs. Blackman appointed Mrs. E. M. Galloway as the first chairman of the junior membership for Florida.

Spin-Offs

Clubs had extended and broadened their scope during the period after World War I. In the twenties, some of the groups nurtured by women's clubs began to move out and form their own organizations. The Federation of Garden Clubs was formed in 1922, the Parent Teacher Association was formed out of the Mother's Clubs in 1926. The League of Women Voters was formed at about the same time. The Business and Professional Women, Art and Music Federations also moved out making the functions of the FFWC somewhat more limited. This was a maturing process and each group had the blessing of the FFWC.

The years of the early twenties were incredible years in Florida. They would later be referred to as the "boom" years and 1926 was the year of the "bust." Subdivisions appeared in the Miami and Palm Beach areas and on the Tampa and St. Petersburg west coast areas. Later they were to spring up all over the central and southern part of the state. Buyers feverishly bought and sold options on land and were becoming "paper millionaires." Much of the building was flimsy with little thought of stability. People bought land without ever seeing it, giving credence to the joke, "He didn't know whether he was buying by the acre or by the gallon." Swamps were subdivided and sold without thought of how the land could be used.

Between 1922 and 1925, the skyline of Miami was completely changed as hotels were built to take care of affluent people who swarmed to South Florida to spend winters. Building went on as if the entire population of the United States was expected to move to Florida. Ships bringing building materials to Miami often had to anchor outside the harbour to wait their turn to unload. Miami and Tampa experienced their first traffic jams when thousands of people were brought to Florida on buses free of charge by companies selling land.

6 – The "Bust" and Great Depression, 1925-1935

THE decade began promisingly. Lucy Blackman (Mrs. William) held a called meeting at Daytona in March of 1925 to carefully smooth out the technicalities required to change the annual meeting date to spring. Chairmen brought their records and reports up-to-date, so that the chairmen and programs were ready for the clubs as they began their meetings in the fall. At the fall board meeting in Fort Lauderdale, Mrs. Blackman recommended that plans be made to increase the Endowment Fund and appointed Mrs. W. S. Jennings as chairman. With a goal of raising $25,000 an Endowment Fund had been started in 1915 when Mrs. Jennings was President and in the intervening ten years it had grown to only $10,048.67. A new goal of $100,000 was set. Mrs. Jennings formed a committee and began a campaign to get pledges of ten dollars per member from every club during a three year period. The annual spring meeting was held in March 1926 with the Woman's Club of Jacksonville hosting the meeting. The amount pledged to the Endowment Fund at the Jacksonville meeting was $24,916.

It was also a time of growth for the federation. Thirty-five clubs were added during Mrs. Blackman's administration with 1569 new members and fourteen county federations. An office of county federation chairman was created. A division of recreation and playgrounds was added and "A Gift of Land Is a Gift Eternal" became the slogan to encourage people to donate land for parks and playgrounds. FFWC published two booklets during the years between 1924 and 1926, "Florida Laws Pertaining to Children" and "The Natural Resources of

Florida."

Work of all the departments continued. The department of health was concerned with trying to get a public health nurse for each county. The elimination of hookworms in children and mosquito control were on-going problems. Not much progress was reported about work among the Seminole Indians. The Royal Palm Park committee reported that more than one person was needed to police the park because many of the royal palm trees that had been planted along the Ingraham Highway had been stolen. Also rare specimens were being removed from the park without permits. Park use had grown remarkably. From March of 1925 until March of 1926, 17,880 persons registered and 11,920 additional visitors who did not register were counted. A nursery was planned as a source of revenue for the park. More than 24,000 postal cards showing scenes of the park had been ordered at a cost of $135.25, and it was hoped that the resale of these cards would not only advertise the park but would also produce some revenue.

Resolutions were presented at the 1926 Jacksonville meeting protesting a bill introduced into Congress known as "The Lucretia Mott Amendment," a simple statement "that men and women have equal rights throughout the United States." Such a law would "strike at the delicate balance of protection that many states throw about women, imperil mother's pension laws, laws punishing non-support of a wife and laws to keep women out of dangerous occupations."

Convention delegates voted to work with other organizations of the state to get a sanatorium where tubercular people could be isolated from the general citizenry.

They also resolved to go on record "endorsing the Better Films Program of the National Board of Review as administered by the Committee for Better Films." Censorship of films was acceptable and there were regulations that prohibited many things which became common in films after censorship was forbidden. The women at this convention believed in strict censorship.

Because the number of delinquent girls had increased, more dormitory rooms and educational facilities were needed at the Florida Industrial School for Girls. The Florida Federation would try to get the next legislature to appropriate funds to build another building at the school.

Another resolution was: "That the Florida Federation of Women's Clubs send letters to Florida Senators and Representatives, reaffirming their continued stand for prohibition and absolute approval of the laws as they now stand, and urging that they use their influence to strengthen same and secure more thorough enforcement by the Federal Government of such laws."

Hurricane Disaster

Mrs. Katherine B. Tibbetts was elected president at the annual meeting in Jacksonville (1926). Mrs. Tibbets appointed Miss Daisy Belle John of St. Petersburg chairman of Junior Membership. But President Tibbetts had only a few months to organize her work because on the morning of September 18, 1926, a devasting hurricane hit southeast Florida. It took more than 300 lives, injured thousands and resulted in ruinous property damage, much of it due to poor construction. There was a tremendous cry for help among the clubwomen of the devastated area.

Many libraries that had been the pride of individual clubs were completely destroyed but some could be partially salvaged by diligent and careful work. Club archives were destroyed as were several club houses. Club members too had suffered losses from the violent storm. Mrs. Tibbetts called upon the clubwomen of Florida and they generously responded. In fact, offers of help came from clubwomen all over the country.

The lodge at Royal Palm Park was damaged by the hurricane's wind and water and before that damage had been fully assessed, fire swept through over fifty acres of Paradise Key threatening the lodge itself. The damage from the fire would have been greater had it not been for fire fighters from Coral Gables, Coconut Grove, Miami and Homestead who came to fight the fire. Members of the Park Committee who lived in the area rushed to defend the lodge by setting backfires to the terrain around it. Since their own homes had been

Jessie Hamm Meyer

damaged by the hurricane, Mrs. W. S. Jennings took the responsibility for getting repair work done to the structures in the park and for replanting palms. In her report, she gave credit to Mr. and Mrs. Wheelock, the warden and his wife:

> With less competent people in charge the loss at the lodge and the surrounding houses and equipment would have been much greater. Many of you know that when a portion of the lodge roof was blown away, that Mr. Wheelock immediately got more roofing and when he could not secure help, Mrs. Wheelock assisted him by holding him in place with a rope on the steep roof, while he did the repair work.

There was little income to the park from visitors during the next several months. The Florida legislature voted an appropriation of $5,000 to help the park. The park committee collected some rent from tomato growers who used a portion of the park land. They gave chicken dinners, sold potted plants and gratefully received donations from FFWC clubs and various individuals.

Florida's "Bust" Precedes the Nation's

The real estate boom had already begun to weaken before the hurricane hit. Of course, such unrestrained land speculation as took place in Florida in the early twenties had happened in other places and other times, though seldom on such a large scale. But the hurricane disaster hastened the "bust." Many who gambled on "sure things" lost, and many "paper millionaires" were left with nothing. Others had land that they could not sell at any price. Towns and cities that had over-expanded their budgets could not meet their obligations. Sidewalks and streets leading to nowhere soon were overgrown with weeds. The depression that was to hit the entire country in October 1929 had already started in Florida.

Happiness about the pledges for the Endowment Fund faded. Mrs. Tippett knew that it would not be wise to press for payment of those pledges. However, enough of the pledges were paid that the federation was in better financial shape than it had ever been. The annual meeting was held in St. Petersburg March 22-25, 1927, where it was reported that sectional meetings had been held as usual. The club women of Florida went about their business of raising money for the rehabilitation of the Royal Palm Park, of planning how they might influence legislation in the session to begin in April and held firm in whatever work they had planned. They changed the name of their publication from "The Florida Bulletin" to "The Florida Club Woman".

Mrs. Tippetts held the annual meeting of March 20-23, 1928, at the Biltmore Hotel in Coral Gables. On Thursday evening, March 22, the clubs formed between 1883 and 1900 were honored and they were referred to as "the distinguished dozen." In reality the number swelled to 18 in the 1928-1929 year book which contains brief histories of those clubs that pioneered woman's club work in Florida and must be treasured as a part of FFWC Archives. The following clubs wrote their histories: Ladies' Village Improvement Association of Green Cove Springs, The Village Improvement Association of Crescent City, The Ormond Village Improvement Association, The Housekeeepers' Club of Coconut Grove, The Woman's Town Improvement Association of Tarpon Springs, Orlando Sorosis, Orange City Village Improvement Association, The Palmetto Club of Daytona Beach, The Philaco Club of Appalachicola, The Woman's Club of Jacksonville, Ozona Village Improvement Association, Palatka Woman's Club, Palmetto Village Improvement Association, The New Century Club of High Springs, Titusville Progressive Culture Club, The Woman's Club of Fort Myers, The Married Ladies' Afternoon Club (now Miami Woman's Club), and Tampa Woman's Club.

Twelve section vice-presidents gave written reports which summarized what clubs in each section had attempted and accomplished. These reports are of inestimable value to a historian trying to reconstruct how club women responded to the problems of their communities as well as those of the state and nation. Each chairman wrote reports which were also published in the year book. A list of these reports gives us a clear idea of the subjects that concerned the women of Florida at a time when the state itself was in economic decline but before the Great Depression had settled over the rest of the country.

American Citizenship

- Indian Welfare
- Division of Visual Education
- American Homes
- Home Demonstration
- Home Economics
- Family Finance
- Education
- Division of Public Instruction
- Division of Rural Schools (fully one half of Florida children were in one room schools)
- Better American Speech
- Division of Community Service
- Highway Safety
- Conservation
- Forestry
- Division of Parks and Natural Scenery
- Bird Protection
- Flower Conservation
- State Beautification
- Chairman of Garden and Flower Shows
- Department of Fine Arts
- Division of Art
- Division of Literature
- Division of Drama
- International Relationship
- Department of Public Welfare
- Department of Institutional Relations
- Department of Public Health
- Division of Recreation and Playground
- Chairman of Junior Membership

The standing committees also had reports. The State Headquarters Committee reported that valuable FFWC papers were being cared for at the Sorosis Club of Orlando while some others had been placed in a vault of the First National Bank of Orlando. The report of the Royal Palm State Park took more than eight pages of this year book. The endowment fund reported a total of $22,095.86. Mrs. Jennings, the chairman of the fund, still had her goal set for $100,000.

Mrs. Murray L. Stanley was elected President at the Coral Gables meeting (1928) and her first annual meeting was held with the Palmetto Club of Daytona Beach. From that meeting came a firm resolution to keep the Florida forestry department from being submerged by the Fish and Game Commission. For a long time FFWC had been advocating protection of Florida's forests, and had helped to introduce forestry education into public schools. This meeting also advocated changes in the laws concerning education, such as: equal education regardless of race or sex, changes in the text book selection law, an appropriation for a survey to determine the cost of a sound and adequate teacher retirement system. It was determined, too, that FFWC request the legislature to appoint an Illiteracy Commission and a State Director of Adult Education.

Another resolution was passed deploring the use of pictures of young women on billboards advertising cigarettes or other tobaccos.

Another Blow

In 1928, a second hurricane damaged the lodge in Royal Palm State Park more severely than the one of 1926. This may have caused the committee that had most of the responsibility of dealing with the park to look favorably at another option. The Tropic Everglades National Park Association headed by Dr. David Fairchild and Mr. Ernest Coe had been instrumental in getting Horace M. Allbright, the Director of the National Park Service, and a group of distinguished scientists to come to Florida to survey as a possible national park site areas of Dade, Collier, and Monroe Counties and particularly the Cape Sable area which spans much of the southern tip of Florida. There was no other place in the United States where a tropical area was available, and none which was richer in wild life. If set aside by Congress, it would be the only national park that could be used throughout the winter months with comfort and enjoyment.

The possibility of their Royal Palm State Park becoming a part of the national park system would insure preservation of the area as well as remove the burden of care from the federation. A resolution was introduced and the delegates voted to endorse the creation of The Tropic Everglades National Park of Florida. The resolution also stated that the entire 4000 acres of the Royal Palm Park should be incorporated into the park and that those acres would be deeded to the federal government when the "plans and arrangements are definite, assured and deemed satisfactory." Copies of the resolution were to be sent to the Secretary of the Interior and other authorities.

The thirty-sixth annual meeting of the Florida Federation of Women's Clubs was held in Winter Haven, March 25-29, 1930. Much of this convention was occupied with club business and in reiterating stands taken in previous conventions.

The Tuberculosis Sanitorium Committee reported the situation unchanged. The bill providing for the sanitorium had passed but no funds had been provided for building and equipping it. The convention attendees resolved to ask Governor Carlton to try to get the legislature to proceed with funding the bill which it had passed.

A group of FFWC members had made a Federation Good Will Mission to Cuba during Mrs. Stanley's administration. Mrs. Stanley was ill and could not go but those who went were royally treated. Because "Her Excellency, Senora Machado, wife of the President of the Cuban Republic, has demonstrated her interest in improved understanding and friendliness between the womanhood of the United States and Cuba," this convention voted her an honorary membership in FFWC.

An Empty Treasury

During Mrs. Stanley's two years, 19 new clubs were added to the federation, five of them Junior clubs, but 10 clubs had withdrawn. Mrs. William A. Wilson was elected president at this convention and faced not only the long term effects of the "boom and bust" years and the aftermath of two disastrous hurricanes, but also the effects of the crash of the Wall Street Stock Market in October of 1929, which were beginning to be felt all over the country.

At Mrs. Wilson's board meeting in Tallahassee on November 5, 1930, serious financial problems were discussed. Bills had not been paid. Dues to GFWC had not been paid. There was not enough money in the treasury for officers' desk expenses. The FFWC's funds had been in the failed Bay of Biscayne Bank. As no deposits were insured, their money was gone. The board decided to divert the interest on the endowment fund to the general treasury. Later it was suggested that the endowment funds be used as collateral for a loan, but Mrs. Blackman, who was well aware of the history of the fund, moved that at no time should the endowment fund be used in this way. Her motion carried. Fortunately the endowment fund had been invested in Liberty Bonds which were still good. At this time there was no Federal Deposit Insurance to insure bank accounts. FFWC had an empty treasury and so did many businesses, individuals and other organizations. It was decided to ask GFWC if the Florida Federation could be late paying its dues.

The Club Woman was in arrears on bills but Mrs. Stanley took over all of the outstanding notes connected with her administration's responsibility for the journal. There were outstanding debts owed to the *Club Woman* by advertisers, but it was voted that these financial affairs be left to the *Club Woman* committee. Officers complained that it was difficult to communicate with members over the state because the "condition of our publication is in too unsettled a state to function" and newspapers had cut back on "the pages" (space allotted to FFWC clubs to report their news) due to their own financial difficulties.

At the convention an appeal was made to clubs to pay their dues early but not much was expected from this appeal because the individual clubs were also in poor financial condition.

Digging in Their Heels

The annual meeting of March 10-13, 1931, was held at Pensacola. While there was recognition of the "financial catastrophe" facing the federation, these women met it head-on with strength born of long years of club work training plus diligence and loyalty to the things which they believed important. They would eliminate all unnecessary expenses; they would offer a note for the amount of the dues owed to GFWC paying 4% interest and they would go about their business of trying to protect the gains that they had made. Their resolutions covered a wide range of subjects: from what the effect would be of constructing a dam on the Cumberland River in Kentucky, to national forests, to the welfare of Florida's children, to the recent educational survey made in Florida.

Health and education got the greater part of their attention and that attention was important because as state revenues fell, cut-backs in almost all areas were anticipated. The federal government appeared to be unable to deal with the mounting problems of hunger and unemployment. This convention went on record as being against further build-up of the U.S. Navy. FFWC voted to withdraw from the Florida Legislative Council. The belief was that this would better position FFWC in its stands before the legislature.

A number of clubs unable to pay their dues to the federation asked to withdraw but Mrs. Wilson assured these clubs that clubs meant more to the federation than just dues and most of the clubs were glad to stay in FFWC. However, without dues, the work of FFWC was severely limited. Officers had to spend their own money for desk expenses and travel to carry on the necessary business of the organzation.

The thirty-eighth annual meeting was held in Gainesville, March 29th through April 1, 1932. One of the first things discussed at the board meeting was concern about clubs that had not paid their dues to FFWC. Opinions differed from "if a club can't pay, it is better for that club to drop out" to allowing clubs to pay on the installment plan. The matter was referred to the sectional vice-presidents with a request that they report to convention. Many clubs throughout the state had lost their funds and families had seen their savings wiped out through bank failures. The Depression affected all phases of life, yet the records show that the club women continued to devise ways by which they could carry their work forward.

There had been references, motions, discussions, and much talk about the "Junior Problem" during the previous administration. Mrs. Wilson summed it up in her annual report:

Leading the Way: A Century of Service

> A minority group of Junior Department Clubs of the State Federation was organized into a separate Junior organization, calling themselves the Florida Federation of Junior Women's Clubs. It was an occurrence that threatened to strike at the foundation of our organization. Two apparent state federations might possibly be foreseen. Distinct lines would have to be drawn between this new organization and our own state and national organization. Distinct lines were established, the confusion and disruption gradually subsided, as did the new Junior movement and our Junior membership is again a harmonious and growing one.

Income from dues was cut by one third, but a determination to live within income was effective though restrictive. The lessened FFWC funds were placed in three different banks and obligations were met. Mrs. Wilson did not come to her office in the best of times but she did her best and that saw FFWC through those years of 1931 and 1932.

Mrs. Meade A. Love was elected President at the Gainesville meeting in 1932. She was from Quincy and federation members decided that FFWC Headquarters would be in Quincy. (The Sorosis Club of Orlando no longer had enough space for all of the documents that had been stored there. It is not clear from year books whether archives were moved.) Headquarters were wherever the FFWC president lived, a matter of convenience that saved the president travel expenses.

In spite of economic depression, there was great excitement in the country about an exposition which was to be built in Chicago. "A CENTURY OF PROGRESS" was, in reality, a World Fair and FFWC was asked to participate in the planning of Florida's part in this exposition.

Bank Holiday Threatens Convention

Mrs. Meade A. Love began her administration near the end of what Mrs. Blackman in her history of the Florida Federation referred to as the "Tragic Decade." The federation had managed to continue its scheduled meetings throughout this time of financial disaster — conventions, board meetings, and sectional meetings had met and carried on business. Mrs. Meade's first convention was to be held in Avon Park, March 14-17, 1933. On the morning of March 4, 1933, the day when Franklin D. Roosevelt was inaugurated President of the United

States, every bank in the country had closed its doors. The entire country was afraid as it had never been before. Roosevelt declared a "Banking Holiday." Florida women did not know whether they could get the money needed to travel to Avon Park. All plans had been made. Calling off the convention would cost the federation money and there was no cash even for postage. The Avon Park club had spent its money in preparation for the convention. Mrs. Meade called the Comptroller of Florida for advice and found that Florida banks would open two days before the convention. She had her doubts as to whether a quorum would be able to attend but 300 members registered and it was declared one of the best conventions ever.

Roosevelt had called a special session of Congress the day after he took office and presented an Emergency Banking Bill which the House passed in just 38 minutes. Most banks re-opened four days after they closed and the immediate financial panic was over.

Relief Work

The principal emphasis was again on the educational and health needs of the state. However, in the Avon Park meeting records there is a statement in the report of the Vice-President, Mrs. Robert M. Shearer, that addresses a topic previously not mentioned:

> The one over-shadowing activity of every club has, of necessity, been welfare work. In many communities the Woman's Club was the only organized group which could meet the requirements for undertaking the relief work made possible through Federal Aid.

Falling farm prices, another hurricane in 1932, dust storms in the mid-west, floods and continued unemployment had resulted in bread lines in the cities and while the Federal Government had been reluctant to resort to what it referred to as the "dole" there had finally been some effort to feed the hungry. The women's clubs had used their organizations to help those in need. Reports of the sectional vice-presidents mention that various clubs served lunches at schools, provided shoes and clothes for the needy, helped with soup kitchens and cooperated with churches and the Red Cross to meet the growing needs of society. There were few even in the private sector who were not also suffering privation.

Mrs. Love was not able to attend the board meeting in Winter Park in November 1933 because she had been in an automobile accident earlier in the month. She was confined to her home for the next several months but she continued to keep in touch with the federation work. Mrs. Robert Shearer presided at the board meeting, and followed a normal planning schedule for the federation.

The minutes of the FFWC meetings do not show whether the women realized that their times were watershed years. Such rapid changes as those that had occurred may not have yet "sunk in." There had been a revolution in the way government approached society's problems. When Congress adjourned on June 15, 1933, new laws showed a government in action: Employ the jobless, support crop prices, repeal prohibition, stop home foreclosures, insure bank deposits, build dams and more. The Civilian Conservation Corps was formed. It took unemployed young men, put them in uniforms, gave them food and thirty dollars a month (most of which was sent home), set up camps and put them to work planting trees, building roads, cutting paths or whatever needed doing. Many of the Florida state parks had their beginnings with the work of the CCC.

Mrs. Love still had not recovered from her injuries and could not attend the Convention March 20th to 24, 1934, in Tallahassee. Delegates to this convention resolved to appeal again to those in authority to carry out legislation passed in 1927 calling for an appropriation of $200,000.00 to build a sanitorium for the treatment of tuberculosis. They also resolved to urge the State Highway Department to forbid advertising signs placed upon highway right-of-ways. (Women are still working to beautify our highways by planting trees and shrubbery, picking up litter, and urging their law-making bodies to pass effective legislation to rid the highways of the signs which "uglify" the scenery.)

Because of their financial problems, delegates voted to change all gift scholarships to loan scholarships.

Defending "Frills"

During the years of the "bust", the bank failures, and the financial depression, many rural schools in Florida had remained closed. An effort was made to eliminate all the so-called "fads and frills" from the schools — meaning art, music and home economics. The FFWC took a firm stand against this and in some cases funded part of the salaries of art and music teachers. There was not an equal opportunity for children in Florida. Some counties were richer than others. An inadequate tax base kept money from being available for an even distribution among schools. The women were urged to study the situation in each of their communities. (Studies continue to show that children in many states do not have equal opportunities to learn and attempts are still being made to solve this problem.)

The Royal Palm State Park had been the site of a CCC Camp and a great deal of work had been accomplished in the park. However, it was not thought wise to keep the CCC boys in the park during the summer because of the possibilty of their getting malaria from the swarms of mosquitoes which were a pest of the Everglades during the summer months. The young men would return for another six months in October of 1934. There was hope that the next Congress would pass a bill creating a national park in the Everglades.

Mrs. Robert Shearer had been elected President at the annual meeting in Tallahassee, 1934. As Vice-President at Large she had traveled around the state attending sectional meetings and was well prepared to lead the state federation for the next two years. However, her tragic death in July after her March election left the federation devastated. Vice President, Mrs. T. V. Moore, was in Europe and would not be home until October. Mrs. Charles E. Hawkins, who had been the recording secretary for twenty years, took charge and with the executive committee managed the necessary business chores until Mrs. Moore returned and was advanced to the presidency. In October the Board of Directors elected Mrs. John Kellum vice-president.

Mrs. Moore's first annual meeting was at Melbourne. No

year book had been published in 1933 but reports for that year from the sectional vice-presidents were combined, condensed and published in 1934. The annual dues to FFWC from individual members were still fifty cents per capita and annual dues for county or city federations were one dollar per club. These combined reports stressed the value of teaching home economics in the schools to boys as well as girls. Department and division chairmen wrote what amounted to essays on their areas of concern: Safety in the Home, Safety and Fire Protection, Law Observance, American Citizenship, Indian Welfare, Conservation of Forests, Birds, Wildflowers, and Wild Life, Protection of Roadside Beauty, and Waterways. (The proposed Cross State Ship Canal is mentioned in this report as well as the completion of the Atlantic Seaboard Canal to Jacksonville. The reports also state that the stretch from Jacksonville to Miami "will be completed soon." Hope for a canal from Fort Myers to Pensacola Bay was also expressed.)

The Department of Education coordinated work with the Florida Educational Association and the Parent Teacher Association with the object of obtaining nine months of school through high school for every child as well as a salary schedule which would state a teacher's minimum wage. Surveys were conducted to find out why Florida did not rank higher educationally. Some of the money from the sale of automobile license tags and a tax on beer went to support education. The education chairman questioned this type of funding for schools as being totally inadequate.

The chairman for libraries wrote of many clubs that either had founded and supported local libraries or had sponsored traveling libraries.

Scholarships Resumed

The FFWC had no scholarships to give in 1930-1932 because of the bank failure but the scholarship chairman was able to report the receipt of $356.13 from girls who had been given scholarship loans by FFWC. Delegates to the 1932 annual meeting voted to re-establish the scholarship fund by allotting five per cent of the dues to this fund. With enough money to pay for three semesters of training, the scholarship committee felt safe in selecting a girl for a four year scholarship beginning in September 1932 and another beginning in February 1933. These scholarships were given as interest free loans. Eleven of the individual clubs reported giving scholarships ranging in amounts from $200.00 to $625.00.

Because many citizens could not pay their taxes, state, county and local governments could not meet all of their obligations. Many teachers had received only part of their salaries for two or three years. When teachers had to have their money, the state issued warrants which some banks would accept by discounting them a certain per cent. It was estimated that as many as 2,000 rural schools in the United States did not open their doors in 1932. Some of those schools were in Florida, thus denying some Florida children an opportunity for an education. Better funding, more teacher training and school consolidation was recommended by the FFWC Education Chairman.

The International Relations chairman was ill and gave no report but Mrs. Meade Love reported as acting chairman. She emphasized the importance of adherence to the Pact of Paris and expressed her conviction that Congress should forbid the shipment of arms or ammunition to any country which had broken that Pact. Educating people that war was not the way to settle international problems would go a long way toward peace. She wrote that there should be no more talk of the NEXT WAR. If all nations honored the Pact of Paris, there would be NO MORE WAR.

Written reports from various chairmen mention the Bible as literature, drama, Florida history, poetry and the arts in general as subjects chosen for study during the preceding year.

The department of legislation worked hard trying to get FFWC resolutions placed into bills which would have some hope of becoming laws. Most of the resolutions required additional funding and when the Florida Legislature met in April of 1933 the whole country was in an acute economic situation bordering on collapse. However, in her report this chairman stated:

> since that time (April 1933) the National Recovery Act of the

Leading the Way: A Century of Service

> President of the United States, Franklin D. Roosevelt, is working out its great plan of economic adjustment and rehabilitation and for a new social order in our own state and other states, to which the women of our Federation have given their best help to carry out in interpreting it and supporting it.

David Sholtz had been elected Governor of Florida in 1932 on promises to improve roads, schools and the general welfare of Florida citizens. The Congress of the United States on July 21, 1932, had passed an Emergency Relief and Construction Act which authorized the Reconstruction Finance Corporation to lend $300 million to states to help them in their relief efforts. This program was expanded and became the Federal Emergency Relief Administration (FERA) which granted more than $600 million nationally to school districts. In Florida, 55 counties were now able to pay back salaries to 4,461 teachers.

Delinquent Children

There were so many programs and changes that it should be no surprise that the records of FFWC fail to show that the women were aware of all that was happening in their state and nation. However, during 1933 and 1934 they kept working for change where they knew that it was needed.

Interest in the Industrial School for Girls and the one for boys at Marianna had been of major concern to FFWC. The following is quoted from the report of the Chairman of Corrections and Institutions.

> Adopting the military custom of passing over what is all right and calling attention to what is wrong, we mention the following regarding our state institutions and the work connected therewith:
>
> 1. There is no provision by the state for delinquent children under 12 years of age.
>
> 2. There are no educational facilities at the industrial schools for children who have finished the eighth grade.
>
> 3. Since 25 per cent of those admitted to the State Prison Farm last year were between the ages of 16 and 21, there should be a state reformatory for offenders of this group, especially first offenders.
>
> 4. There is no vocational training for children who are dependent but not delinquent.
>
> 5. There is no provision for the hospitalization or sterilization of adult feeble-minded and no law against their marriage.
>
> 6. There is no provision for the colored feeble-minded or for

colored delinquent girls.

7. The inadequate social work facilities in the counties increase the need of state provision.

8. There is need of mental hygiene and psychiatric and social hygiene work to prevent need of so much institutionalization at Chattahoochee.

9. There is too little attention to the provision that families who are able shall pay for care of any of their members at Gainesville or Chattahoochee.

10. There is need for more enlightened and modern methods of dealing with incorrigibles.

We must look ahead to increasing and modernizing buildings and equipment of the state institutions when economic circumstances will permit. Also, we must be alert to save what public welfare set-up we have, especially the State Board of Public Welfare.

There was a Committee on Inter-Racial Cooperation and its chairman wrote the following:

> In South Florida there is much more interest in the committee than in North Florida.
>
> In St. Petersburg there is a Jesus Worker among the colored people of the county and she makes her report to the Federation, they help her carry on.
>
> In Jacksonville the Federation has helped the colored women set up a well baby clinic — helped them carry on classes in cooking and sewing. All over the state we have distributed the left-over literature from the churches in town to the colored churches in the country.
>
> Our home demonstration agents are doing much to help the colored women with their problems, especially in the smaller counties. We find them very appreciative, and they certainly need their 'white folks' to help them.

Only by quoting these reports as they were written can the attitudes toward some of the problems with which the clubwomen dealt be understood.

The 1933-1934 Year Book reports the necessity of supporting a Pure Food and Drug Act. It also contains 10 pages of reports about the finances, plants, and management of the FFWC's Royal Palm Park, and hopes that the Everglades National Park will become a reality.

Summer Courses for Women

The University of Florida was an all male university but the

Extension Department offered short courses for women, usually during the summer when there were fewer men students on the campus. There being no system of community colleges, these intensive short courses were great learning experiences for leaders of organizations, housewives and mothers. An example is one given June 25-30, 1934.

The theme of this short course was "Essentials for the New Era". Mrs. Elizabeth Skinner Jackson and Mrs. J. W. McCollum, past presidents of FFWC, were on the advisory committee. Leaders from sixteen organizations were invited to attend the short course. The registration fee was $2.00, tickets for breakfast and lunch at the university cafeteria were 50 cents a day, rooms in the dormitories were 25 cents a night or "rooms could be had in private homes at reasonable cost". The program listed 29 lecturers, each an authority in his or her field. Women attending these short courses could not possibly attend all of the lectures, but they crammed as many as they could into their schedules.Few programs before or since those years when the Extension Department of the University of Florida was under the guidance of Dean Bert C. Riley have done so much for the hundreds of adults who took those courses and at such a small cost.

Jessie Hamm Meyer

7 – Growth, Change, War

THE 1936 annual meeting was held in Tampa with Mrs. T. V. Moore presiding. Senator Claude Pepper spoke on "What Can Florida Do to Improve Her Educational System?", a topic which would continue to generate discussion, hope, plans, committees, and attempts for consistent revenue into the twenty-first century. Support of education made some progress, but Florida remained low in ranking among other states. In 1936, Florida was still reeling from the effects of two devastating hurricanes, a land boom which left both individuals and governments uneasy about investing for economic growth, and the lingering results of the worldwide depression. Resolutions made at this meeting showed alarm concerning communistic and socialistic activities both real and imagined. Parts of two resolutions follow.

> WHEREAS: Clubwomen of America and the F.F.W.C. in convention assembled, are concerned and alarmed at the widespread Communistic and Socialistic activities in our country, as witnessed in our schools, colleges, industrial organizations, churches, civic groups, legislative bodies, newspapers, magazines and radio,
>
> AND WHEREAS: A flagrant attack upon American ideals, institutions and constitutional government of the United States was permitted and sponsored by Columbia Broadcasting System on March 5th, when it permitted Earl Browder, Secretary of the Communist Party in America, to broadcast over its network, and the advertising program 'March of Time', which promoted Browder's broadcast during the previous radio hour, thereby insuring a larger air audience, though Browder's entire address was a vicious attack upon the foundation of American Government and property rights,
>
> THEREFORE, BE IT RESOLVED, by the Florida Federation of Women's Clubs, in convention assembled, we do most vigorously disapprove and protest these widespread Communistic activities against our Government, and particularly the Columbia Broadcast-

ing System and 'March of Time' radio program for permitting this propaganda.

The members of FFWC believed that controlling immigration would be helpful in limiting communistic and socialistic influences.

"WHEREAS, known efforts to nullify our constitution, to upset our government and democratic ideals and institutions through Communistic and Socialistic propaganda and by opening our frontiers to aliens, many of whom are destructive in their attacks, therefore

BE IT RESOLVED, that the Florida Federation of Women's Clubs endorse the immigration bills of Senator Reynolds and of Representative Stormes, now pending consideration in Congress, and that the Federation disapproves of the Kerr and O'Day bills.

Mrs. O. I. Woodley, chairman of the department of citizenship, wrote in her report:

Without going further into the methods of this unscrupulous system, whose avowed purpose is the establishment of communism throughout the world and whose fighting preparation is for world revolution, I do urge that we, the representatives of the clubwomen of Florida, who are in large measure the guardians of our youth, wake up to an understanding of the menace which has already entered our fair state.

Alarm about Communism resulted in resolutions and mention in reports, but there were other events headlining the news. The Social Security Act had been passed and there were trouble spots internationally. The position of the United States was officially neutral in the Spanish Civil War although hundreds of men from both the United States and Europe joined the Communistic Loyalists fighting against the insurgents representing Fascist Italy and Germany. Japan had invaded China which was worrisome to those who thought about the significance of that invasion. However, public opinion was more concerned with Wallis Warfield Simpson's marriage to Edward VIII and his abdication of the throne of England or with the unresolved problems of Scarlett and Rhett. *Gone With the Wind* sold more copies than any previously published American novel and the search for an actress to play the part of Scarlett in the movie made news for weeks.

This convention also resolved "That the Florida Federation of Women's Clubs in convention assembled, March 17-20,

1936, declares itself as unequivocally opposed to the practice of lynching and urges its member organizations to apply such educational activities as will uphold laws prohibiting this iniquitous practice." Delegates knew that lynchings had occurred in Florida and would likely continue to occur unless a generation could be educated believing that the constitutional right of a trial by jury must not only be "on the books" but also in the minds and hearts of every citizen.

As vice-president, Mrs. Kellum had made a survey and found that 93 clubs owned clubhouses and many of them were used for libraries or nursery schools.Several clubs sponsored building community centers through federal aid projects such as the Works Progress Administration. All clubs had a few departments of the federation and some of the larger ones had nine departments. Sectional vice-presidents reported clubs engaged in welfare work, "tonsil clinics," school lunch programs and libraries. Frequent mention of WPA indicated wide use of that federal aid program.

Americanization was a topic discussed by division chairman with emphasis on club women becoming involved in school programs that would educate boys and girls to be good American citizens.

The American Home Department and its divisions made many recommendations, one of which was legislation against child marriages, Florida being only one of nine states which had no such laws.

The report of the Home Demonstration Division was lengthy. Under its sponsorship corn clubs, tomato clubs, pig clubs and canning clubs had been organized but these were being replaced by 4-H, a program which became nationwide particularly in rural areas. It emphasized balanced living, the 4-H representing Head, Heart, Health and Hands.The program planned to assure an adequate supply of food for farm families and members of 4-H clubs reported outstanding participation and production of a wide variety of foods. Improvement and beautification of homes, instruction in sewing, consumer buying, increasing family income, and healthy habits were emphasized in the 4-H programs. The population of Florida lived in mostly rural areas and the Florida Federation of Women's Clubs supported and co-operated with other organizations which were working for the betterment of individual and community life. Many of the actual programs were carried out by home demonstration agents and county agricultural agents which the Florida Federation of Women's Clubs had tried to obtain for every county. These agents were funded through joint efforts of local, state and federal governments.

School Funding

Mrs. D. R. Read, chairman of the department of education, had been discouraged at the close of the legislative session because funds were not available for more than three or four months of school. However, by the time this convention met she had found that such curtailment was not necessary; most schools would be in session for at least eight months, teacher salaries were to be increased by 10 per cent and were to be paid on time. A new tax policy adopted by the 1935 legislature had begun to generate funds for the support of rural schools and millions of dollars given to Florida through the Federal Emergency Relief Administration had enabled the schools of Florida to avoid disaster. However, no mention was made in her report of the source of the funds to keep the schools open and to pay teachers salaries. Many citizens of Florida were opposed to the New Deal of Franklin Roosevelt's administration and even those who favored it recognized that massive funds from the federal government were temporary; that local, county and state governments must respond to the needs of the people. Mrs. Read made a statement in her report that warned of repeated school crises in Florida as well as in many other states saying that friends of education must be ever vigilant.

"But our schools are in politics, or vice versa, and politics are tricky. There is no assurance that the specter of school poverty may not again stalk through our state. Friends of education must neither slumber nor sleep. Loyal vigilance and untiring interest and work for the public schools is the only hope of their success."

The legislature had passed a law in 1933 allowing the State

Board of Education to say what subjects could be taught in the schools. As a result of this law the State Board of Education had passed a regulation preventing art, music and physical education teachers from being paid from state funds. The Division of Art Chairman urged FFWC members to create such an interest in art instruction on the part of the public that the regulation would be removed.

There was a chairman on community singing and according to her report 34 clubs had participated in some activity involving community singing. Minutes of practically all state meetings of FFWC recorded assembly singing, "Suwanee River" and "America the Beautiful" being the favorites.

Edna G. Fuller, Chairman of the Department of Social Welfare, was instructive in her report since the Social Welfare Act of 1935 placed emphasis on local administration of welfare machinery. This opened the door to new fields of opportunity and service but it also required study. Mrs. Fuller was particularly interested in what this new law would do for children and the elderly. Study revealed that "Poor Laws" which dated back to 1828 authorized judges to bind out to apprenticeships orphans or children of fathers on the counties' pauper lists. The State Board of Health had been created in 1927 beginning a more modern approach of protective and supervisory responsibilities but funding had been inadequate in normal times and completely inadequate for the depression. However, it became the nucleus for the rapid development of a state social service administration which was responsible for implementing the Social Welfare Act of 1935.

Drivers' Licensing

Mrs. Meade A. Love, Chairman of the Division of Highway Safety, gave figures on the number of accidents, injuries and fatalities on the highways in 1934. She recommended that members of FFWC "endorse a Driver's License Law with fees to support a State Highway Patrol with a suspension of license penalty clause." (Generations of citizens now can't imagine a time when no one had to have a license to drive. If a child could see through the windshield and reach the brake and gas pedals, he or she could take to the road and practice — a custom which had worked well enough in small towns and on country roads before ownership of cars multiplied until existing roads became crowded. The proposed license law was not intended to test driving. It was designed only to produce funds to support the Highway Patrol.)

Chairmen of committees on roadside improvement, parks and natural scenery, playgrounds and recreation, state institutions, Indian welfare and conservation reported activity in their areas of interest.

Mrs. J. Ralston Wells, editor of the *Florida Clubwoman,* wrote that during her term of office 17 issues of the *Florida Clubwoman* had been published. Mrs. Wells said, "It is no small task to edit and publish a magazine which shall appeal to 9,000 clubwomen with a small amount of money at one's disposal, but experience shows that it can be done. The percentage of dues with a small income from advertising was found sufficient and the administration closes with money in the Publicity Fund, and all bills paid."

Royal Palm State Park

Mrs. W. S. Jennings, Chairman of Royal Palm State Park, reported that progress was being made toward getting the park accepted into the National Park system. Mrs. Jennings and Mrs. T.V. Moore had been appointed by Governor David Sholtz to the Everglades National Park Commission which had its first meeting January 16, 1936. The Royal Palm State Park had an aggregate area of 477,000 acres, but the maximum area desired was 2,000 square miles which meant that approximately 1,280,000 acres must be acquired. A gigantic task! The Works Progress Administration (WPA) and the Civilian Conservation Corps (CCC) had worked in the park building a fire tower, correcting damage done by a storm, clearing paths, and putting in a telephone line to the park. Indebtedness of the park was over $2,000 but payment of back state appropriations allowed that debt to be paid in full. Mrs. Jennings presented a list of things needed for the park such as heavy duty batteries for the Delco plant, tools, roofing, a new refrigerator, a bigger stove, new dishes and kitchen equipment and an increase in salary for the warden.

Jessie Hamm Meyer

There was a standing committee on munitions activities and its chairman, Mrs. Pearl Wamsley, gave a comprehensive and satiric report. There had been a two-year Senate investigation into the arms industry costing $132,369. Part of what she had to say about that investigation follows: "a large amount to discover that there was a World War; that billions were spent; that loans were made; that there was some bribery; huge profits; and that there was a blot on the Wilson administration in that the war president favored the British." Mrs. Wamsley expressed some hope for the future: "There is a movement now to take the manufacture of arms out of the private class, and there is a large percentage, according to the poll, favoring the idea of turning this business over to the government. This may be a solution of the question, because the profit system has been leading us to war for generations. Possibly the government system would break the cycle."

(Mrs. Wamsley expressed a vain hope. After another World War and an unequalled period of economic growth, American citizens heard President Dwight Eisenhower warn them that the military-industrial complex could become the greatest threat to the country's peace and security. That was just before he went out of office in 1960. In the last decade of the Twentieth Century, the threat appeared greater than ever before as the nation's "cold war" debt mounted while Russia and the United States engaged in an arms race which brought down the Soviet Empire and left the United States with an overwhelming debt and little to show for the money spent other than atomic bombs, intercontinental missiles and military hardware unparalleled in previous history.)

Mrs. J. G. Kellum was elected President for the following two years along with the entire slate of officers presented by the nominating committee.

In March 1937, the forty-third annual convention of the Florida Federation of Women's Clubs met at the Roosevelt Hotel, Jacksonville. Resolutions at this meeting dealt with the old problem of livestock having free range, endangering the lives of motorists and of a need for a Driver's License Law. Delegates also recommended that a portion of the gasoline tax paid by boaters be used for the improvement of waterways. The intracoastal canals on both the east and west coasts of Florida were completed and the money from this tax on gasoline used by boaters would enable the state to develop the "wonderful God-given water resources of our state."

The forty-fourth annual meeting was held in West Palm Beach. It is interesting that on March 17, 1938, Mr. M. H. Doss, Narcotics Department, State Board of Health, spoke on "Marihuana," a subject that would get little national attention until another twenty-five years had passed. There was also an address on "Some Aspects of Japanese Imperialism".

Resolutions of this convention showed concern for the preservation and restoration of wild life, a national cooperative cancer education program, a teacher retirement system, the raising of revenue to provide a uniform system of public free schools, (school districts and counties had separate systems and unequal tax bases resulting in schools which were very well supported and schools with very little support) and wider use of the radio for education and public welfare.

The American Home Chairman, Mrs. B. W. Helvensten, Jr., reported that every club in the state had at least one program on the American Home. She asked that Florida club women study a national uniform marriage and divorce law which the General Federation of Women's Clubs had endorsed.

Conservation and Beautification

Mrs. W. S. Jennings, Chairman of the Department of Conservation, reminded club members "considering the suffering caused by the dust storms in the West and the more recent fearful floods causing unprecedented erosion, forces a realization and firm conviction that life itself is absolutely dependent upon efficient and scientifically directed conservation." Among her recommendations for beautification projects was the planting of wild flowers on roadsides. The subject got nationwide publicity 25 years later when First Lady Mrs. Lyndon B. Johnson used roadside wild flower planting as her project. Mrs. Johnson's influence plus that of organizations such as garden clubs and women's clubs resulted in several states continuing to plant wildflowers on the roadsides and as a result realizing significant savings due to less frequent mowing.

Improving the Lot of "Negroes"

Under the Department of Public Welfare there were divisions of Child Welfare, Indian Welfare, Interracial Cooperation and Public Safety. All of these chairmen reported work being done. Mrs. Malcolm Smith, Chairman of the Interracial Cooperation Committee, wrote about the condition of Negroes in Florida and what several local clubs were doing. Mrs. Smith wrote:

> When one investigates the conditions now existing, one is appalled by the situation......We are a progressive state yet thousands of our school children are attending school in shacks, unsafe school houses, churches, lodges and in over-crowded double sessions. Of course they are not of the white race but of the Negro.....Hundreds of Negro schools have no blackboards or libraries...Hundreds of Negro schools have no water supply.....Hundreds of Negro schools have no toilets.

Mrs. Smith pointed out that the 1930 census showed that one in five Negroes was illiterate. Adult education for literacy and vocational education in Negro high schools would, she believed, go a long way toward bettering the life of Negroes. After education she wanted health programs instituted.

> An appalling percentage of Negroes suffer from some communicable disease. These people are in our midst, in daily contact with our children. We cannot ignore their physical well-being and expect to remain unharmed ourselves.
>
> It is a well-known fact that a large percentage of Negroes suffer from venereal disease.... Would it not be well for us to insist that our servants have a physical examination and treatment when necessary? We can do our part in fighting this scourge by sane and simple education.

Even lower middle class families employed Negro help. Clothes were often scrubbed on a washboard and boiled in a kettle in the backyard. The fabric of these clothes, sheets, table cloths, pillow cases and towels was cotton. They dried on a line, were dampened and ironed. Food was cooked "from scratch" and dishes were washed by hand. With no air-conditioning, windows were left open in the summer. In the winter houses were heated with wood, gas or oil. Houses required more frequent cleaning under these circumstances. If there was a lawn, it had to be mowed with a push lawnmower. There were homes that made no attempt to have a lawn — the sandy yard was raked and swept every day to clear it of fallen twigs or leaves and no weeds were allowed to grow — much easier to see snakes in clean sand! Even people of very modest means had at least part time help which was not expensive. Some people worked for a place to sleep and food. Day help often cost as little as three dollars a week. Many Florida children had more supervision from a kindly Negro combination maid and nurse than they had from their own parents. Most movie theaters had a balcony where Negroes were required to sit. Children growing up in the South often went to matinee movies and sat in the balcony with the maids and gardeners. White children played with servants' children and formed lasting friendships but they did not sit at a table and eat together.

Mrs. Smith wrote about thirteen clubs and the work they were doing for Negroes in their communities. Some clubs had made donations to Negro hospitals and one club had sponsored WPA training of Negro maids. Some of the attitudes and much of the work done on behalf of Negroes was patronizing or the result of long held opinions that as a class Negroes were inferior. However, many of these same women had close friendships with individual Blacks recognizing their intelligence, honesty and skills. Enlightened leaders were victims of double-think where Blacks were concerned. This writer remembers that churches and schools felt a great sense of pride when they gave outmoded worn out text books, hymn books, and library books to Negro groups. When a white school got new desks, the old ones went to a Negro school. A lack of funds for all schools during the thirties made this a better policy than giving the Negro schools nothing but how discouraging it must have been to Black children! Never a new book! Never a new desk!

The following statement in Mrs. Smith's report indicates that she was trying to raise awareness of her fellow club members to the problems of education for negroes.

> The Negro is like he is because we have neglected to teach him that there is something higher and finer in life. He will not lift himself until he is taught that there is a better way of life than that to which he is accustomed. As a more enlightened race, we have no right to withhold from him this knowledge.

Some minor changes were made in the bylaws during Mrs. Kellum's administration; the most noteworthy was a first-time registration fee to delegates attending a convention. Beginning with the 1938 Convention, delegates paid a one dollar registration fee, but delegates of the hostess club were exempted from the fee. Mrs. J. Ralston Wells was elected President, Mrs. Thurston Roberts, First Vice President and Mrs. Ralph Austin Smith, Second Vice President for 1938-1940.

Membership Growth

Mrs. Wells began her administration with a post-convention board meeting at West Palm Beach in March 1938. As was customary, she announced her appointments of department and division chairman as well as chairmen of various standing committees. She also announced a goal of 12,000 paid members for the ensuing year. The board voted to move headquarters from Tallahassee to Daytona Beach. Headquarters had no permanent home but was moved to wherever the president of FFWC lived.

There was another board meeting in June 1938 in Tallahassee. Mrs. Wells announced a budget based on 9,000 members at 50 cents each, 10 cents of which went to the General Federation of Women's Clubs. In November 1938, the board met at the Panama City Woman's Club. Delegates present at this meeting passed resolutions concerning more equitable taxation, revision of the Florida Constitution, and a request that certain land owned by the state be put in escrow as a guarantee of good faith toward doing the necessary paper work to consummate the formation of Everglades National Park.

At the forty-fifth Convention in Orlando, March 1939, Second Vice President Mrs. Ralph Smith reported that there were 175 paid clubs with a total of 9,482 members. The goal of 12,000 had not been reached but there was a gain over the 9,000 of the budget base. Among the resolutions of this convention was again one requesting that the legislature pass a driver's license law.

The convention of 1940 was held in Sarasota and Mrs. Robert T. Dewell, Chairman of the Department of Legislation, gave her report, stating that "the 1939 Legislature passed a law for State Driver's License and State Highway Patrol."

Officers made encouraging reports. Mrs. John R. Dykers, Corresponding Secretary, reported that she had started collecting photographs of club houses and up to the time of the convention she had collected 120. Each sectional vice-president gave a report of the activities of the clubs in her section. These reports showed a number of clubs reinstated in FFWC as well as new clubs formed and federated. Sectional vice presidents enthusiastically reported support of libraries, various charities and educational programs.

Department chairman and division chairman gave reports reflecting the concerns of the times. Some of the reports remind present day readers that the same problems existed in 1940 as those which cause anxiety today. Remedies were suggested. For example, Mrs. C.E. Hawkins, Chairman of the Division of Law Enforcement, wrote:

> Lawlessness is spreading and law is held in little respect on account of the ability of criminals to escape the penalty for law infraction. The most serious feature of this crime wave is the fact that the age of criminals is largely among the youth of from 16 to 22. A great deal of this crime consciousness is, I think, due to laxness of enforcement, unemployment and the overwhelming number of gangster programs on the radio and screen.... We as women voters should study the issues and support only candidates that we feel are sufficiently interested in the future of our great state to make sure that our next Legislature will repeal obsolete laws and make new ones that are practical and usable. Our great need is not for more laws but for better ones."

Chairmen of various divisions of the Department of Conservation had worked to beautify roadsides, distributed information about parks and waterways, supported the work of the Florida Audubon Society and the Florida Wildlife Federation and worked with the schools to educate the children about the value of beautifying their surroundings and protecting flowers and wildlife.

The Department of Education focused on libraries, adult education, character education, youth cooperation, and "know your schools".

Progress on Many Fronts

Janie Smith Rhyne, Chairman of the Poetry Division of the Department of Fine Arts, conducted a poetry contest in 1939-1940. The winning poems were published in the 1938-1940 Year Book. Louise Van Hood, Chairman of Bible as Literature Division, sent outlines for study to 200 general clubs and 40 junior clubs. She declared Jacksonville, club of largest membership, and Anthony, club of 10 members, honor clubs for their participation in her division. Literature and art continued to be subjects of study by club women.

The Golden Jubilee of the General Federation of Women's Clubs was being celebrated in 1940 and club members were encouraged to write poems, plays and stories in honor of this event. A program, "Fifty Years of Progress" was prepared for a special "Golden Jubilee" radio broadcast.

Twelve clubs reported sponsoring radio programs. Gladys Lyons was chairman of a standing radio committee and had persuaded specialists in their fields to prepare scripts for radio presentation on the general topic of "Thoughtful Citizens in Action." Twelve radio stations had cooperated in this effort giving a different program each month.

Ten new Junior Clubs had been formed since March of 1938 making a total of fifty Junior Clubs in the state. Junior club members could be no older than thirty, at which age they were urged to join a general club.

Mary Hollister Dewell, Chairman of the Department of Legislation, continued to urge members to support constitutional revision and a change in Florida's tax structure.

Membership had increased to 11,500. Mrs. Ralph Smith as 2nd Vice President and membership chairman had over-subscribed her goal of 25 new clubs reporting 24 new general clubs and 14 new junior clubs added to the Florida Federation during the previous two years.

There was finally $25,000 in the Endowment Fund.

The 1940 convention elected Mrs. Thurston Roberts President and Mrs. Ralph Austin Smith First Vice-President along with the slate of officers presented by the nominating committee. Mrs. Roberts presided at a post-convention meeting of the Board of Directors in Sarasota and as was customary named chairmen whom she had appointed to direct the work of the departments and the standing committees necessary to carry on the work of the federation.

Among those chairmen was Mrs. Malcolm McDonald of Coral Gables, Junior Department Chairman. Mrs. McDonald made the District Tour of the state with President Roberts in the fall of 1940. At the end of her two years Mrs. McDonald reported that 21 Junior Clubs had been organized and 17 of them federated, making a total of 51 Junior Clubs with a total membership of 1,716. In November of 1940, the Board of Directors met at the Ocala Woman's Club.

Education for Delinquent Girls

Because Florida had no institution for the care and training of delinquent negro girls, the Board of Directors recommended that the Florida Federation of Women's Clubs adopt a legislative project for the establishment and maintenance of a proper institution for the care and training of these girls who had to be left at large or placed in jail since there was no other place for them. Women of the Florida Federation had used their influence, time and energy to get an Industrial School for Delinquent Girls but in a segregated society this school was for white girls only. After years of effort, there were industrial schools for both white and negro boys. Getting the legislature to provide funds for another school was uphill work.

The forty-seventh annual convention of FFWC was held in the clubhouse of the Miami Woman's Club March 25-28, 1941. The delegates to this convention had new problems facing them. The country had passed defense legislation and Army and Navy establishments were built or were being built to take care of 81,000 enlisted men and officers. Defense programs connected with health, nutrition, housing, recreation and similar activities would need experienced and practical help. Much volunteer work would be required, but to implement the new programs, professionally trained workers would be essential. Home demonstration agents had the necessary skills and could train others in each community. Members of FFWC had supported and worked to get these agents in every county but there were still some counties that did not have this service. Delegates to the 1941 Convention asked that funds be allocated to make home demonstration agents available for help "in this emergency." They also asked that Florida's "Sugar Quota" be increased because "sugar is considered by our Army and Navy as a critical wartime material as it supplies 13 percent of man's energy."

They also resolved "to endorse the principles of the prenatal law and the law requiring the use of silver nitrate, or a recognized substitute, in newborn infants' eyes."

Dr. Walter J. Matherly, Dean of the College of Business Administration at the University of Florida, gave an address to the general assembly on "Individual Preparedness, the Basis for National Defense".

Much of the 1941 convention's time was spent in committee meetings and federation business but the delegates also enjoyed the usual banquets, luncheons, musical performances and assembly singing.

War Breaks Out

The United States had entered into lend lease agreements to help England, France and Russia in their war against Nazi Germany and its ally, Italy. Clubs had been busy preparing "Bundles for Britain" and were encouraged to keep up this work because Britain was fighting for its existence as German war planes bombed British cities almost every night.

On December 7, 1941, the Japanese attacked the United States at Pearl Harbor and the next day President Franklin D. Roosevelt announced that Congress had declared war not only against Japan but also against Germany and its allies.

In April of 1942, the Florida Federation of Women's Clubs met in Jacksonville for its 48th Convention. This was no ordinary convention. The nation was at war and the women assembled in Jacksonville knew that their lives had changed and might never be the same again. None knew what sacrifices lay ahead.

Claude Pepper, Junior Senator from Florida, spoke on "A Democracy Mobilized," Senator Pepper emphasized that "There must be a nucleus of purposeful people after the war to plan for a new world so that our generation shall have kept our rendezvous with destiny and been true to God and man." The minutes of that Wednesday evening session record: "Mrs. Roberts pledged to Senator Pepper that the Federation would do all it could to plan for a better new world."

As was customary, a memorial service was held for members who had died during the previous year. This service was personal with each district director reading the names of deceased members from her district and as each name was read the first vice-president and the second vice-president placed a white gladiola in an urn. The 1940-1942 year book records the 134 names which were read. This custom continued to be followed for many years.

On Thursday evening, Governor Spessard Holland spoke on "Florida's Contribution to Victory" with "a heads up, sure we can win" attitude. However, many in his audience had to "screw their courage to the sticking point" because every house was required to have blackout curtains, especially along Florida's coasts. Coast Guardsmen patrolled the shores and any window that was not blacked out would get its owner a warning and a stern reminder. People understood that non-compliance gave the patrol the right to shoot out the light. Restrictions of various kinds affected the every day life of each person. Governor Holland said that Florida had more than her share of sons in the service and that 125,000 persons were active in civilian defense.

This convention repeated its resolution of 1941 that the legislature provide funds to build and maintain a proper place for delinquent negro girls.

Endorsing the WACS

Mrs. Robert T. Dewell, Chairman of the Department of Legislation, presented three resolutions to the delegates all of which were approved. One of these was endorsement of a resolution of GFWC concerning the support of legislation to establish a Women's Auxiliary Army Corps by voluntary enrollment for service in the Army of the United States. Another resolution asked for the curtailment of non defense activities by the government and her third resolution asked for endorsement of a resolution by GFWC opposing the enactment by Congress of a law requiring filing of a joint income tax by husbands and wives.

Infantile paralysis was a dreaded crippling disease which had become epidemic particularly among children. A method of treating victims of this disease was developed by Elizabeth Kenny and was widely accepted as being the best treatment available. However, trained practitioners were in short supply. The delegates to this convention "earnestly implored and urged the State Board of Health to act promptly in providing for the training of physicians, nurses and teachers in the Kenny method of treatment of infantile paralysis, and to spare no effort to see that the treatment be available to any future victim of that disease in any section of the state."

Clubhouse USO's

Vice-presidents of sections reported clubs having defense programs, allowing their club houses to be used for Red Cross work or for recreational purposes by the United Service Organization (USO). There were fund-raising campaigns for Red Cross and sewing for both Red Cross and Bundles for Britain. Clubs encouraged their members to buy war bonds and stamps. They cooperated with County Defense Councils, contributed nearly 100,000 books to be used by service men, sent truck-loads of magazines to Camp Blanding, conducted first aid classes, served as airplane spotters, had their blood tested in order to be ready in case of an emergency, registered citizens for Civilian Defense Work, sponsored aluminum drives, conducted nutrition classes, encouraged "victory gardens", collected old paper, jars, clothing and tin foil, and some clubs collected sacks for sand bags to be used in case of air attacks. With German U-Boats prowling off the coast of Florida and Britain under constant attack, it is understandable that the women of the Florida Federation of Women's Clubs pitched in to do everything possible to help the government in its efforts. The remarkable fact is that most of the clubs carried on their regular programs in addition to their war work.

The five-year plan for each member to pay fifty-cents toward the endowment fund had fallen far short of the $150,000 goal. In fact the endowment fund chairman, Mrs. Thomas Shackleford, reported that the fund had only $26,467.88. Twenty clubs had paid up in full, a few clubs had used the war as a reason not to pay but most clubs had directed their energy and priorities toward more pressing demands. Mrs. Shackleford regretted that the next chairman would have to struggle as she had to get the clubs to contribute toward this much-needed fund.

War Bonds, War Stamps, Warsages

Delegates to the 1942 Convention elected Mrs. Ralph Austin Smith president and Mrs. Joseph L. Gray first vice president. Mrs. Smith and her board began an all out campaign to inspire club women to do their utmost to help our country in its war against Germany and Japan. The war impinged on every facet of life. No detail of speech or action was too small either to help or hinder the country's war effort. Posters warned that the enemy might be listening. Everyone was urged to buy defense stamps (10 cents each) and war bonds ($25 or more). During her term of office Mrs. Smith discouraged the use of corsages. (For several years custom had demanded that women be presented corsages for every function in which they had part in the direction of the meeting whether social, charitable, educational, political, religious or civic.) Instead of flowers, Mrs. Smith led the women in the use of WARSAGES which were made of defense stamps and colored cellophane. She gave every club a book with one stamp in it and encouraged the club to fill the book. A book would purchase a twenty-five dollar war bond. More than $3,000,000 was raised by Florida Federation clubwomen toward a "Buy A Bomber" war bond drive making Florida among the most successful state federations in the nation in the campaign to finance the war against Germany, Japan and their allies.

The Fall Board of Directors met in Sanford, October 20-22, 1942. Delegates adopted resolutions reflecting problems more noticeable because of the war. One of these resolutions was against an existing discriminatory tax on oleomargarine which on the surface might not seem at all related to the war but was keenly felt by women who were stretching their budgets in every way to meet household needs.

> "WHEREAS, margarine is conceded by chemists and food experts to be a wholesome and nutritious food, and one that is vitally needed by millions of low-income families, and
>
> WHEREAS, the Congress of the United States and about twenty northern and mid-western legislatures have passed laws which tax and otherwise unfairly discriminate against margarine and therefore against the products from which it is made, and
>
> WHEREAS, domestic vegetable oils, chiefly cottonseed oil, are used in the production of margarine, and
>
> WHEREAS, these southern vegetable oils are important farm products and are as much entitled to free market outlets in interstate commerce as are northern butter-fats, and
>
> WHEREAS, it is unfair and un-American to tax or otherwise discriminate against wholesome products of one group of American farmers for the alleged benefit of another group of American farmers presenting a threat to national unity, it is economically unsound public policy to maintain state trade barriers which are unfair and injurious to public health to deprive millions of low income families of the only table spread within their reach, which situation is made doubly paradoxical by the existence of an annual shortage of table spread (butter and margarine) indicated by the U. S. Department of Agriculture to be over two billion pounds annually, now therfore
>
> BE IT RESOLVED, that the Board of Directors of the Florida Federation of Women's Clubs in convention assembled urge the Congress of the United States and the several northern and mid-western states to repeal all discriminatory restrictions that hinder free and unmolested sale and use of margarine in the United States.

At the time the delegates approved the above resolution, margarine could be sold only in its white, unattractive form. Each pound came with a little capsule filled with yellow color which could be worked into margarine when softened.

Because selective service examinations had revealed a high percentage of physical defects among the young men of the country, the delegates assembled at this Fall Board meeting resolved "as a contribution to the war effort of STATE and NATION, the Florida Federation of Women's Clubs does agree to sponsor a 'Health for Victory' educational program". This program encompassed "personal fitness, nutrition, sanitary eating and drinking establishments, safe food and water supplies, adequate housing facilities, immunization and vaccination, rodent control, adequate sewage disposal, venereal disease control, repression of prostitution and other allied problems."

No problem was too small or too large to get the attention of club women invigorated by patriotism and determination to do their best to help both in the war effort and to make the home front function in the best possible way. Their resolutions often over-reached their ability to implement them but they raised public awareness to existing problems.

The 49th Convention of FFWC was held in New Smyrna Beach, March 23-25, 1943, with President Mrs. Ralph Austin Smith presiding. Fearing that an isolationist policy might prevail in the country when the war was over, this convention went on record supporting a policy of International Co-operation.

Golden Jubilee

The meeting held in Tampa, April 1944, was known as the Golden Jubilee Convention. In spite of the fact that the energies of the women's clubs had been chiefly directed toward the war and the problems it caused in every day life, the 50th anniversary of the Florida Federation of Women's Clubs could not pass without proper celebration. At a pre-convention banquet, past presidents who were deceased or not present were honored. Nine of the eleven living past presidents attended the Jubilee Convention and were asked to give highlights of their terms of office. Miss Bessie Williams, a charter member of the Crescent City V.I.A., gave a piano selection. A group from the Winter Park Woman's Club gave a pantomine depicting the early days of the federation and the five charter member clubs: Green Cove Springs Village Improvement Association, Fairfield Village Improvement Association (Jacksonville), Crescent City Village Improvement Association, Orange City Village Improvement Association and the Village Improvement Association of Tarpon Springs. The women of today were depicted in uniforms of the various departments of the

Jessie Hamm Meyer

Red Cross, WACS (Women's Army Corp), SPARS (members of the women's reserve of the coast guard), the WAVES (members of the women's reserve of the U.S. Navy), the woman legislator and the modern housewife.

Speakers at the convention were business, government, education, health and religious leaders. Mrs. John Whitehurst, President of the General Federation of Women's Clubs, spoke at this convention as well as at the 1943 convention. Gubernatorial candidates had been invited to speak at the convention and six of them accepted.

The 1942-1944 administration began four months after the Japanese attack on Pearl Harbor and ended with the fiftieth convention. The two years had been war years. More men and women were in training for war service per square mile in Florida than in any other state in the nation. Clubwomen entertained these service people with picnics, Sunday dinners, dances and songfests. Clubs were organized for wives of service men. Women's federated clubs conducted active campaigns to enlist women of the state in the WACS, WAVES and SPARS It was a time of gasoline rationing; tires were almost impossible to replace; many foods were rationed; shortages of both luxuries and necessities caused belt tightening never before envisioned and yet the officers and club members made war service an integral part of their work. Many clubs discontinued meeting during the war years having turned their clubhouses over to the USO or the Red Cross surgical dressing units.

Mrs. Ralph Austin Smith recalled those war years to this writer in 1992 saying, "I used the gasoline ration stamps of three cars and I still did not have enough gasoline to drive my car to all the districts and meetings that I should visit and attend. Train connections from north to south in Florida could be made to most clubs and districts (not to Key West) but there were few east-west connections so there was nothing to do but ride the buses. Buses were always crowded. Many times I stood on those hot un-airconditioned buses getting to meetings in distant parts of the state but I never missed a meeting."

Mrs. Smith had named Mrs. Thurston Roberts, War Service Chairman and in September of 1942, Mrs. Smith and Mrs.

Roberts were called to Washington along with other state presidents to be briefed on how to conduct campaigns to raise money through Liberty Bonds sales. Mrs. Roberts as war service chairman reported that the Florida Federation participated in the "Buy-A-Bomber" campaign and "from August 16 through September 30, 1943, the club women sold war bonds to the value of $3,894,197." The reported cost of a bomber at that time was $300,000. Mrs. Roberts praised Florida Federation club women for their help in drives for aluminum, tin, rubber, paper and fats.

"In one drive the women of Florida led the nation in the salvaging of house-hold fats."

Royal Palm State Park, managed by FFWC, contributed to the war effort by allowing thirty radio experts from the American Telephone and Telegraph Company to stay in the park and study the effect of dense vegetation on radio transmission and reception.

Combatting Black Markets

A number of clubs gave assistance to the Office of Price Administration in determining food values (The OPA controlled prices and prevented inflation although black-markets of scarce goods were a problem.) The clubs of the state cooperated in stamping out black markets. Club women worked regularly on rationing boards and a number of clubs held classes in point rationing. Clubs had a part in the program of housing. One club reported placing eight hundred families. Thousands of families of servicemen flocked to Florida and records show that clubs helped establish fair rents in individual communities.

In spite of all the war work, departments and divisions made reports at the 1944 convention which showed that most of the clubs continued to carry on their regular programs.

Mrs. Joseph L. Gray was elected President and Mrs. L. J. McCaffrey First Vice-President for 1944-1946. Mrs. Gray held a post convention board meeting at which she named department chairmen and chairmen of divisions. The Board of Directors met October 23-25, 1944, at Lake City. Department chairmen reported and business of the federation was conducted by the 82 club women registered. Five new clubs were admitted to the federation.

There was no convention held in the spring of 1945. The war had finally caused a disruption in the agenda of the Florida Federation of Women's Clubs. However, the war in Europe ended with Germany's unconditional surrender May 8th, 1945, and the war against Japan ended with the dropping of atomic bombs on Hiroshima and Nagasaki on August 6 and August 8. With the unconditional surrender of Japan on August 15, 1945, many soldiers could resume civilian life and the United States could begin to convert to a peace time economy. The women of FFWC could once again turn their full attention to improving their communities, their state and the quality of their own lives.

The Board of Directors met at Fort Lauderdale in October 1945. Dropping of the atom bomb had ended the war, but the weapon's potential for destruction was so great that the world was in awe and fear of its consequences. Discussions and programs at this convention centered on international relations and ways to achieve a lasting peace.

Clubhouse Photos

The following illustrations were selected from 120 pictures of clubhouses collected by Mrs. John R. Dykers during the late 1930s and others collected by Miss Maude Knight in the early 1940s. In 1950 President Helen MacKay reported that "of the 185 clubs in Florida, 138 owned their own clubhouses, which of course were shared by juniors."

Selections were made in an attempt to show a wide range of architectural styles and Florida locations, as well as houses representing clubs with small, medium and large memberships.

Fig. 11. (Top) Fort Lauderdale Woman's Club, built 1917. Fig. 12. (Center) Coco Plum Woman's Club, South Miami, built 1915. Fig. 13. (Bottom) St. Petersburg Woman's Club, built 1929.

Fig. 14. (Top) Sorosis Club of Lakeland, built 1922. Fig. 15. (Lower) Lakeland Woman's Club, built 1927. These two clubs merged to form the United Women's Club of Lakeland. In 1993, they were building a new clubhouse.

Leading the Way: A Century of Service

Fig. 16. (Top) The Woman's Club of Jacksonville, built 1927.
Fig. 17. (Lower) Sorosis of Orlando.

Jessie Hamm Meyer

Fig. 18. (Top) Palmetto Club of Daytona Beach, as built in 1905.
Fig. 19 (Lower) Palmetto Club of Daytona Beach as remodeled in 1925.

Fig. 20. (Top) Miami Woman's Club, built in 1913 on land given by Henry Flagler — sold to advantage in 1923 for $345,000. Present club was financed by the sale. Fig. 21. (Lower) Julia Tuttle House, a pioneer home (of one of Miami's founders) used temporarily by the Woman's Club for 18 months in 1923-1924.

Jessie Hamm Meyer

Fig. 22 (Top) Woman's Club of Delray Beach; original club and multi-use building. Fig. 23. (Lower) The Woman's Club of West Palm Beach, built 1915, remodeled 1937.

Fig. 24. (Top) The Woman's Club of Tallahassee, built 1926.
Fig. 25. (Lower) The Woman's Club of Sarasota, built 1940.

Fig. 26. (Top) The Monticello Women's Club, built 1920.
Fig. 27. (Lower) The Wauchula Women's Club, built 1925.

Leading the Way: A Century of Service

Fig. 28 (Top) The Madison Women's Club, built 1939.
Fig. 29. (Lower) The Key West Women's Club, built 1902.

Jessie Hamm Meyer

Fig. 30. (Top) The Colahatchee Woman's Club, Oakland Park, built 1939. Fig. 31 (Lower) The Vero Beach Woman's Club, built 1917; the original timber was delivered by ox team. Remodeled more than once.

8 – Beginning Another Fifty Years

The fifty-first annual convention was held in Lakeland, April, 1946. Mrs. LaFell Dickinson, President of the General Federation of Women's Clubs, gave the opening address. She spoke for equal rights for women, urged women to take more responsibility in electing the right men for office, emphasized that women support the National Health Bill and reminded those present of the importance of youth conservation. There were also speeches made by a school principal pointing out the crisis in education and one by a professor from Southern College who spoke on "Education at the Cross Roads". Lewis G. Scoggin, Director of Park Service, gave a talk on "What Shall Our Memorials Be?" in which he stated, "Every city and village should have a park, every city should have a playground and every county should have a park or a forest. State Parks should be developed within fifty miles of every individual. Jook joints and unsightly signs should be eliminated from our waterfronts."

Leland Hiatt, Welfare Commissioner, spoke on the "Stepping Stones to Security". He stated that 50,000 individuals are being assisted in Florida through the welfare program. Mr. Hiatt named the following as the five stepping stones that are essential to security:

1. Opportunity for academic training
2. Vocational training
3. Recreational opportunities
4. Social development and development of personality
5. Spiritual training

This 1946 convention directed members to set goals for a

peacetime society.

Among the resolutions approved was one that had been made several times before concerning the need for an industrial school for Negro girls. The Florida Legislature had at last made some funds available for building the school. Delegates to the 1946 convention specified that it should be staffed by trained and capable Negroes.

They also went on record as favoring "Living Memorials" (parks or forests) to those who served during World War II and they insisted that the State Board of Education extend and expand music and art courses in the public school system.

Because of increased speed and traffic on the highways, the delegates went back to a problem addressed by the Florida Federation of Women's Clubs at its first meeting in Green Cove Springs. Once again they petitioned the Governor and the Legislature to pass a fence law so that an owner of livestock could not allow his animals to roam on open range. The destruction of landscape planting and the creation of a mess of manure in the streets were no longer principal reasons for such a law. The safety of those using the roads and highways was at stake. The delegates did not think "it right that Florida entice tourists to come to the state where their cars could be demolished or their lives lost because of wandering cattle and hogs on the highways."

An Office for the Federation?

The 1945 Board of Directors had authorized setting up a business office with a full time paid secretary. President Gray reported to the 1946 convention that the Seminole Hotel in Jacksonville had offered a room free of charge for this office and an experienced woman had been secured. "Such an office would insure continuous methodical records, a proper filing of the organization papers in one place, a home for various materials now scattered over Florida in many homes of past presidents and chairmen, and above all would release the president from routine office duties so that she could give her time and effort to leadership of the ever growing organization in this very large state of ours."

This office was not set up and it was left to the incoming

executive committee to make a decision. There was some opposition to the location of a headquarters office in Jacksonville since it would not be as centrally located as somewhere toward the center of the state.

Mrs. L. J. McCaffrey was elected President and Mrs. A. T. MacKay First Vice-President.

The 52nd Convention was held in West Palm Beach, April 1947. At the opening session, Dr. Kathryn A. Hanna, a noted Florida historian and lecturer, spoke on "Education for the Atomic Age." She urged the delegates to further their education. She said, "We are attempting to solve present crises with knowledge that is thirty or forty years old. As adults, we must grow ourselves if we are to live in the world of 1947. We cannot live by labels and slogans. If you do you will kill your brother and allies. We cannot survive as a country if the 'grown-ups' don't continue to grow."

The problem of livestock on the highways still existed causing the delegates again to resolve to ask the legislature to pass a law allowing for a referendum vote on a State Stock Law at the next general election. They also asked that necessary legislation be enacted establishing a State Tax Commission which would have as its prime function the equalization of assessments throughout the state of Florida.

It was at the 1947 convention that the decision was made to give Royal Palm State Park with its 477,000 acres and the three story brown shingle lodge to the Federal Government as the nucleus for Everglades National Park.

A Pan American Convention

During the post-war years a tremendous growth in membership of the General Federation of Women's Clubs showed that of the 10,743,121 members almost half of them lived in countries other than the United States of America. Programs of GFWC had focused on building a more peaceful world. Efforts on behalf of the United Nations, the European Recovery Program, assistance to those in need abroad, an educational rehabilitation project, scholarships for foreign students, and an international good will program to promote friendly contacts among women of the world resulted in the growth of membership in women's clubs in other countries. Florida club women had contributed their part in these post-war efforts toward a more peaceful world.

President McCaffrey stressed the International Relations Department during her tenure. Isolationism as a political ideology was no longer a factor in the thinking of most citizens. Optimism prevailed.

The fifty-third annual convention of FFWC known as the ASSEMBLY OF WOMEN OF THE AMERICAS met in St. Petersburg, April, 1948. Women from the Dominican Republic, Cuba, Brazil, Ecuador and Canada participated in a panel on "Citizenship" led by Margaret Carter from the U.S. Dept. of State. However, records show no other programs during this convention were directed toward hemispheric interests.

The United States had put its tremendous energy into winning the war; its people had done without scarce commodities and had sacrificed lives and lived in fear of the forces of Fascism. The late 40s began a period of catching up on home building, car buying, domestic spending and young families producing a "baby boom generation." The Florida Federation of Women's Clubs reflected this peace time enthusiasm in 5,251 new members and 36 new clubs brought into the federation between 1946 and 1948 bringing the total membership to 21,200.

Three resolutions adopted by the 1948 convention put FFWC on record against certain types of radio programs during the evening hours when children would be listening, against current literature that approved and encouraged profanity, intemperance and low moral standards, and against moving pictures showing the use of alcoholic beverages as an acceptable custom.

Rejecting Federal Aid to Education

The fifty-third convention passed resolutions approving a universal military program and disapproving federal aid to education, a subject which had generated much public discussion. Fear was constantly expressed in newspaper articles and magazines that once the federal government gave money to schools it could control the curriculum. There was also apprehension that the federal government would dictate exactly how the money would be spent. Apparently no one remembered or knew that federal money had enabled Florida to pay its teachers and keep schools open more than three or four months during the thirties when bank failures and economic depression had caused Florida to have to pay its debts with IOU's euphemisticaly referred to as State Warrants. There was fear and much discussion of required desegregation. On the other hand there was a recognized need for more equitable funding of schools throughout the country, some areas of the country being either too poor or in some cases unwilling to provide state or local taxes sufficient to give children an education equal to that provided in other sections of the country. The Florida Legislature passed an advanced school law in 1947 which provided limited equalization of opportunity by dividing the state into school districts by counties. However, this law was not funded until 1957.

The delegates recommended that "legislative action be taken to require all paroles and pardons be endorsed by the committing judge or the prosecuting attorney in the court concerned, and that notice of such intention be filed in the daily papers of the community where the crime was committed, at least thirty days before action taken by such board."

Some by-laws concerning Junior Clubs were redefined: The Chairman of the Junior Club Women (a junior club woman who had been president of a junior club) would be appointed by the president with the approval of the executive board. The Junior Chairman would be an exofficio member of the executive board. There were to be two classes of junior clubs: (a) Sub-Juniors, girls under eighteen years of age; (b) Junior clubs, young women from eighteen to thirty years of age.

Apparently, nothing was done about establishing an office with a secretary because the treasurer's report for 1947 shows only $11.50 disbursed for typing and clerical help and in 1948 "clerical salaries—$10.00." Jacksonville which had been proposed as a headquarters was not centrally located and was not a favored area.

Jessie Hamm Meyer

Everglades National Park

Royal Palm State Park had been deeded to Everglades National Park and was dedicated December 6, 1947 with President Harry Truman and other dignitaries attending. Mrs. Paul Sears, Chairman of Royal Palm State Park, reported that the plaque ordered by the 1947 convention to commemorate the Florida Federation of Women's Club's gift to Everglades National Park was beautiful and had been set in native coral rock and placed at the entrance to the park on Paradise Key near Florida City. The funds of the park, always reported in a separate account, were transferred to the Endowment Fund. Mrs. Sears as the last Park Chairman closed her report with this statement:

"We, the members of the Florida Federation of Women's Clubs, are proud to have had a part in preserving the only area of its kind in the world for the perpetual pleasure and enjoyment of the people."

For several years, Mrs. Frank Stranahan had been chairman for Indian Welfare Work and she felt that great progress had been made in getting the Indian children into public schools. McKinley Osceola had sat on the platform with President Truman during the dedication of Everglades National Park and showed unquestioned evidence of his tribe's good will. Mrs. Stranahan had talked with Osceola and his friends and found that they were very happy to have had a part in the dedication of the park with a large attendance of Indians present all day. The government school at the Brighton Reservation was well attended; the Indians were working on a road building program; the government nurse served a vast area in spite of a cut in funds; however, various churches and local organizations had been generous with contributions for medical supplies. Several FFWC clubs contributed financially to the Indian welfare program.

Florida was experiencing unprecedented population growth. Thousands of young men and women had been stationed in the state during their training periods for World War II; after the war was over, these veterans returned to Florida to make their homes, to start new lives or to further

Fig. 32. Dedication of plaque to commemorate the Florida Federation of Women's Clubs' gift to Everglades National Park, placed at the entrance to the park on Paradise Key near Florida City.

Fig. 33. Park Lodge built and maintained by FFWC principally for naturalists and scientists visiting and studying the flora and fauna of Royal Palm State Park.

their education through allowances from the "GI Bill". Colleges and universities were overrun with these mature men and women seeking a basic college education or higher degrees. Many of these veterans had children who soon crowded classrooms. New schools had to be built and teachers had to be trained. Teachers were recruited from other states which were not experiencing Florida's population growth. All of the social, educational and health services of Florida were challenged and while the clubwomen of Florida had risen with remarkable strength to the problems of the war years, they found that new problems came with peace and growth.

Delegates to the 1948 convention elected Mrs. A. T. MacKay, President; Mrs. Raeburn C. Horne, First Vice-President and Mrs. Wiliam W. Armstrong, Second Vice President.

Fall Board was held in Ocala, October 5-6, 1948. Two resolutions were passed concerning the health and welfare of children. Delegates said that it was a known fact that babies were being sold in Florida and they urged the "Florida Legislature of 1949 to pass child placement legislation which will correct the evil of selling children." The other resolution urged the establishment of full time health services in every Florida County.

A National Convention

The General Federation of Women's Clubs had accepted the Florida Federation's invitation to hold its convention in Florida in 1949. Such a convention presented both a challenge and an opportunity to Mrs. McKay and her officers. Mrs. L. J. McCaffrey was named general chairman to coordinate plans for the convention. Each club of FFWC was asked to contribute 35 cents per capita to pay the costs of this international convention and the response was almost 100%. The Housekeeper's Club of Coconut Grove made 100 Seminole capes for Florida workers to wear during the convention. Souvenirs were donated by the thousands. Tropical flowers were featured at each event; especially impressive were the thousands of orchids at one of the evening banquets. The Convention was held at the Hollywood Beach Hotel in Hollywood, Florida, and was attended by more than 1600 delegates and a total of 2100 registrants. Senators George Smathers and Claude Pepper were there to welcome guests. Mrs. Eleanor Roosevelt spoke on "Human Rights" at the principal banquet. The entire Hollywood Beach Hotel was closed to the public while Mrs. Roosevelt was there. Publicity for the GFWC Convention was handled by Mrs. Mildred White, a member of the Palmetto Club of Daytona Beach and editor of the *GFWC Clubwoman*. This international convention of club women was declared one of the "most glamorous and beautiful" of GFWC conventions and was a credit to Mrs. McKay and her administration.

Opposing "Socialized Medicine"

The Florida Federation of Women's Clubs streamlined its convention meeting in Hollywood, April 24-25, 1949 for just a day and a half before the GFWC Convention thus giving Florida club women a chance to attend both meetings. Hosting the national organization did not divert the attention of the delegates from their own agenda. They passed a strongly worded resolution disapproving "a proposed Compulsory Insurance Bill or Bills, or any form of government medicine, known as socialized medicine." They ordered copies of the resolution sent to the entire delegation in Washington. This action reflected widespread propaganda on the part of special interest groups against any form of socialized medicine. England and the Scandinavian countries had instituted programs guaranteeing universal health care for their citizens. There was much debate; newspapers in the United States published articles on both sides. Members of the American Medical Association worked diligently to discourage the adoption of any government plan to guarantee health care to all citizens. FFWC delegates to the 1949 convention voted the conservative opinion held by those people who could afford medical care or who believed that local, county and state governments could more adequately furnish care to those unable to afford it than could the national government.

Because "Insanitary conditions exist in the many rest rooms throughout the state of Florida", the FFWC delegates voted to request the Railroad Commission to make "a ruling that bus terminals be required to employ attendants eight hours a day at the carrier's expense, whose duty it shall be to keep the premise in a clean and sanitary condition." It is interesting to note that it was the Railroad Commission that would be held responsible for the condition of restrooms in bus stations. They recommended that the legislature increase its appropriation to the State Library Board. Many communities continued to be without library services and the amount that had been appropriated was far below that appropriated for library services in neighboring states.

The Fall Board held in Orlando, October, 1949, amended Article XV, Section 2 of the constitution to read, "The minimum annual dues for each federated club shall be 75c per capita; 25c for direct membership in the General Federation; the balance to be distributed in such manner as the Board of Directors shall determine." Dues had been only fifty cents per capita for years. Clubs were asked to pay 60¢ per capita for

1950 and 75¢ would be the amount for FFWC and GFWC beginning in 1951.

In the summer of 1949 Mrs. Armstrong resigned and Mrs. Walter Jones was appointed to fill the unexpired term of 2nd Vice President.

Banishing the "Sacred Cow" At Last

The matter of cattle on the highways had finally been settled. Fuller Warren in his campaign for the governorship of Florida had promised that if elected, he would get the cattle off the roads and highways of Florida. The Chamber of Commerce had also taken up the cause and people in general were upset by the many accidents caused by cars being wrecked and people injured or killed when cars hit cattle or hogs. It was particularly dangerous to drive at night because cattle found the roads an ideal place to rest. It was not uncommon in certain areas for a passenger to get out of the car, walk in front of it to get the sleeping cows to wake up and move on. A night time trip could take many hours. Fuller Warren was elected and under his leadership the 1949 legislature barred cattle from all of state roads beginning July 1, 1950. Two years later the state took over maintenance of county roads and cattle were barred from these roads also. FFWC clubwomen had worked for fifty-five years to get the animals off the roads but it was the increasing number of accidents which turned opinion around. In 1947 and 1948, 933 accidents were reported which injured 257 people and killed 24, all caused by cattle or hogs on the highways. The days of free ranging cattle came to an end as cattlemen complied with the new law which required fences to be built around grazing land.

The convention in April 1950, at Tampa brought Mrs. MacKay's administration to a close. A highlight of her term was the GFWC convention held in Hollywood, Florida. The number of clubs as well as the number of individual members had increased during her tenure as president. Mrs. MacKay's theme of "Women alert" had borne fruit in many women being elected to school boards; both junior and general clubs had won awards from GFWC for their outstanding work.

Reports of district directors told of club activities. Many

clubs were building, remodeling or repairing club houses. Most of them had a library project. The Coco Plum Woman's Club of Coral Gables started a bookmobile service in 1948 as an extension of the library started by this club in 1913. This was Florida's first bookmobile. Clubs made gifts and donations for veteran's hospitals and were particularly interested that there be hospital rooms suitable for WACS and WAVES. Hookworm eradication was an objective of some clubs with education programs and elimination of unsanitary privies as part of that on-going effort. They sponsored health clinics, Brownie and Girl Scout troops, collected clothes for the poor, gave books to Negro schools, and generally involved themselves in community projects.

Some clubs added "to the social graces of teenagers by organizing cotillion clubs."

Mrs. MacKay reported: "Of the 185 senior clubs in Florida 138 owned their own club houses, which, of course, are shared by juniors. The number of club houses in Florida is most unusual and this ownership of buildings is a great help in carrying on work in various communities."

Because the ever increasing multiplication of signs along highways was defeating the roadside beautification efforts of the women of FFWC, delegates to the 1950 convention made a strong recommendation that roadsides be zoned. Zoning should prevent private land owners from leasing rights for billboards. Passing laws to get signs off highway rights-of-way were not sufficient to prevent this blight on highway beautification. (In the 1990s it appears that getting signs off the highways and adjoining land may take longer than it did to remove cattle from the roads. The billboard lobbies have consistently had a stronger voice than women who want the roadsides free of billboard blight.)

During Mrs. MacKay's administration 78 students were awarded $21,417.17 by the federation and individual clubs; in addition, three scholarships amounting to $15,000 were given to foreign students.

The new officers elected and installed while the delegates met in Tampa were Mrs. Raeburn C. Horne, President; Mrs.

Leading the Way: A Century of Service

Walter E. Jones, First Vice-President; Mrs. E. D. Pearce Second Vice President, Mrs. F. B. Orr, Recording Secretary; and Mrs. Wm. W. Armstrong, Treasurer. Mrs. L. J. McCaffrey became Recording Secretary for GFWC.

Jessie Hamm Meyer

9 – The Fifties

Mrs. Raeburn Horne chose "Service" as her theme when she assumed the presidency in 1950. The welfare department added a division of mental health which worked with the legislative department to get added facilities for the mental and feeble-minded of the state; as a result three new wards were erected for the feeble minded at Gainesville, two for whites and one for negroes.

A review of resolutions passed and topics studied by women members of the Florida Federation of Women's Clubs in the 1950s shows continuing involvement in national, state and local issues.

Mrs. Horne conducted the Fall Board meeting in Tallahassee in November of 1951, where delegates passed a resolution against building dams on the Colorado River that would destroy the scenic beauty of valleys and canyons in Dinosaur National Park. In their resolution they asked that Congress not allow the building of dams in national parks for commercial or any other purposes.

The 56th Annual Convention of the Florida Federation of Women's Clubs was held at Daytona Beach, April 1951. Resolutions adopted at this convention addressed the problem of inflation and consumer protection.

> WHEREAS: Inflation is second only to war itself as a menace to the National economy and to individual welfare, and
>
> WHEREAS: The United States now faces grave dangers of uncontrolled inflation and
>
> WHEREAS: Temporizing with the situation undermines our whole economic structure as a nation and brings disastrous and unjustifiable hardship to our people
>
> THEREFORE BE IT RESOLVED, that the Florida Federation of Women's Clubs in convention assembled April 5, 1951, urges the

Leading the Way: A Century of Service

> Government of the United States to act with promptness and firmness for the period of the emergency by adopting and enforcing control measures without regard to partisan or political considerations of the interests of special groups, and
>
> FURTHER BE IT RESOLVED, that the Florida Federation of Women's Clubs declares its conviction, despite difficulties involved, that food prices should be rolled back to those prevailing about June 1, 1950, and other consumer items to levels relatively in balance with food prices of that date.

(A reader might well question how or why a group of well intentioned, intelligent women would vote against a system guaranteeing health care to its citizens and against the Federal Government giving financial aid to schools and then pass a resolution which would give the Federal Government the power to control prices of food and consumer items thus inserting the Federal Government into practically every private business in the country. All too often women in convention failed to study resolutions. They attended workshops on how to get and keep members, how to raise funds for their various projects, and they received information on a wide variety of topics but when it came time to vote on resolutions there was usually little meaningful debate. Often the resolution was so general that there could be no specific results; for example, delegates endorsed a resolution recommending that "a permanent joint committee of the House and Senate be formed for the purpose of inquiring into all matters affecting health, welfare and protection of the consumer.")

Cops and Kids

One of the chief concerns of members of FFWC was the welfare of children. At the meeting in Tallahassee, delegates "whole heartedly" endorsed the Proposed Juvenile Court Amendment to the Florida Constitution, which was intended to establish a statewide uniform system of juvenile courts.

In previous years FFWC had repeatedly asked the Florida Legislature to establish a highway patrol. They were happy when this was accomplished and praised the Department of Public Safety and Division of the Florida Highway Patrol for its work. The delegates at the 1951 convention recommended to the Florida Legislature that the duties of the Highway Patrol be continued and that it be adequately financed by paying a "living wage commensurate with their twelve hour a day working schedule and present-day cost of living".

An industrial school for delinquent negro girls had been built in Ocala but it had not been funded for maintenance, operation and staffing. The delegates passed a resolution urging the legislature to appropriate funds for this project.

Pines and Paintings

At the Fall Board meeting held at Gulf Beach, St. Petersburg, in October a "Pennies for Pines" program was begun. Pine seedlings could be secured at nominal expense and the state would supervise the planting. The plan was to plant a pine forest known as a Florida Federation of Women's Clubs Forest, with the first one to be specifically in honor of the President, Mrs. Raeburn C. Horne. They recommended that this program be continued during each successive administration.

Various funds existed within the federation such as the "Penny Art Fund" the intended use being to buy copies of paintings of great artists. These pictures were to be passed from school to school for the purpose of teaching art appreciation among Florida's children. There was also a War Veterans' Birthday Fund, a Florida Veterans' Fund, and an Indian Work Fund. Some funds were often gifts given by members or friends with specifications as to how they could be used.

Jacksonville Woman's Club hosted the 57th annual convention in April 1952. To establish better understanding and solidarity with Central and South America the delegates at this convention resolved to urge the Florida Legislature to stress the teaching of conversational Spanish in all the schools and they also urged individual clubs to organize study groups in conversational Spanish.

There was also a resolution that Congress "restore the balance of power between the three branches of government as our forefathers created and intended" and "that taxes be lowered by the practices of such sensible economies in government as we would practice in our homes or our clubs or as a reasonable business man would use in the conduct of his own business."

Leading the Way: A Century of Service

A resolution to ask for an amendment to Florida's Constitution which would provide for the state and county superintendents of public instruction to be appointed rather than elected was voted down by the delegates to the 1952 Convention.

Fourteen new clubs were voted into the federation during Mrs. Horne's administration bringing the total to 190 senior clubs, 70 junior clubs and 18 county federations with a total membership of 25,519. The Endowment Fund had been increased by over $2000 giving it a total of $43,796.00. Eight girls were attending colleges on loans from FFWC. The amount of the loan fund was $5,000.00 so none of the loans were for huge amounts but they were helpful to the girls using them and they paid the loans back according to agreements governing the fund. In addition to the aid given to students by FFWC, 33 individual clubs and 3 county federations had given a total of $40,000 to students in Florida to further their education beyond high school.

Adult education programs got help from the University of Florida through short courses held by the Extension Division. Edith McBride Cameron was head of the Department of Auditory Instruction and Women's Activities and Bert C. Riley was Dean of the Extension Division. They were often mentioned by various chairman and officers of FFWC as being helpful and available whenever needed for any continuing education endeavor. Mrs. Bert C. Riley was a loyal worker for FFWC, holding many chairmanships.

Crowding in Mental Hospitals

Clubs were concerned about the overcrowding of seven thousand mental health patients in the one antiquated hospital and a single branch. Three hundred patients were waiting for admittance, some of them in jails. Individual clubs sent hundreds of Christmas presents to these "forgotten people" and they also sent records, playing cards, games, money and materials to be used in an occupational therapy department. More mental hospitals were needed and delegates discussed the obvious need for them to be built in places accessible to population centers. Two days travel were required to admit patients or to visit them from the southernmost part of Florida to the hospital located in Chattahoochee.

A listing of the departments and divisions of FFWC at mid-century shows the principal interests and concerns of clubwomen at that time.

> DEPARTMENT OF THE AMERICAN HOME, Home Beautification and Gardens, Consumer Information and Family Finances, Urban-Rural Cooperation, Bible Study.
> DEPARTMENT OF CITIZENSHIP
> DEPARTMENT OF CONSERVATION, Protection of Animals, Birds and Wild Life, Forestry and Waterways, Parks and Roadside Beauty.
> DEPARTMENT OF EDUCATION, Adult Education, Library Service, Public Instruction.
> FINE ARTS, Art, Drama, Music, Literature and Poetry.
> DEPARTMENT OF INTERNATIONAL RELATIONS, Pan-American Relations
> DEPARTMENT OF JUNIOR CLUBWOMEN
> DEPARTMENT OF LEGISLATION
> DEPARTMENT OF PRESS AND PUBLICITY
> DEPARTMENT OF PUBLIC WELFARE, Corrective Institutions, Playgrounds and Child Welfare, Inter-Racial Cooperation, Indian Welfare, Public Health, Mental Hygiene.

Mrs. Walter S. Jones was installed President; Mrs. E. D. Pearce, First Vice President; Mrs. C. M. Washburn, Second Vice President; Mrs. Neil Bitting, Recording Secretary; Mrs. Art S. Witmer, Treasurer for 1952-1954. For several years the Florida Federation of Women's Clubs had shown evidence of maturity by electing leaders who had served the organization through many years of responsible chairmanships and elected offices. Previous responsibilites trained women to be dependable and loyal administrators of a growing federation of clubs whose influence often affected change not only in their communities but also in the state and nation.

Mrs. Jones held her Fall Board Meeting in DeLand in early October 1952. The 58th annual convention was held in Miami in April 1953. This convention endorsed several bills, most of which had to do with institutions: "Appropriations for additional Buildings at State Mental Hospital, Enlargement of Facilities at Florida Farm Colony, Enlargement of Facilities at

Boys Industrial and Girls Industrial Schools." They also endorsed legislation for a Home Nursing Bill and a Library Bill.

During the administration of Mrs. Jones, 22 new clubs and one new county federation were added to the Florida Federation of Women's Clubs bringing the total membership to 27,767, a result of incentive awards for districts presenting the most new clubs and also for the district presenting the most new members for federation.

State Headquarters

Mrs. Jones had established the building of a State Headquarters as her principal goal and the 58th annual convention appointed a committee to study the project and report at the next Fall Board meeting. The Board of Directors was given the power to act on recommendations of the Committees' investigation of the Headquarters project. Among those on the committee were: Mrs. W. A. Gillian, Miss Mary Ruth Rivers, Mrs. Henry Shaw, Mrs Joseph Gray, Mrs. Robert Marshall, Mrs. Guy Mills White, Miss Odessa Morris, Mrs. T. M. Shackleford, Mrs. A. T. McKay, Mrs. Ralph Smith, Mrs. John Kellum, Mrs. O. P. Herdon, Mrs. Lawton Swan and Mrs. Marietto Benevento. Mrs. Jones had met with the location committee in Orlando, Lakeland, and Jacksonville to study offered building sites, before the Lakeland decision was made.

The Fall Board meeting at the Shamrock Village in Fort Pierce, October 5, 1953, adopted the recommendation of the Headquarters Committee that the new Headquarters be located in Lakeland. (Interesting addenda — an advertisement for the Fall Board meeting appeared in the *Florida Clubwoman*: "Three days, seven meals — including banquets — tax and tips — $25.00.")

A called meeting of the Executive Board, January 6, 1954, authorized the President and the Corresponding Secretary to execute a lease with the City of Lakeland for a lot to be used for a Headquarters Building. The Headquarters Committee was dissolved and a continuing Special Building Committee was formed. The Executive Board authorized all surplus monies in the Publicity Fund and the General Fund transferred to a Building Fund.

The 59th annual convention was held in Tallahassee in April 1954. An amount of $28,100 cash and pledges was reported to be in the Building Fund and the names of clubs and individuals contributing to the fund occupied one and a half pages in the reports for 1952-1954. Revision of Article VI, Section 3 was adopted. This article had read, "At a meeting of the Board of Directors immediately following the biennial election of officers of the Federation, the Board shall designate the official headquarters of the corporation at the place of residence of the President." The revision deleted the words "at the place of residence of the President". The Florida Federation of Women's Clubs at last would have a home with all of its records in one place instead of being stored in the homes of its presidents.

By the time Mrs. Jones administration came to an end, she could report that there was $30,000 in the Building Fund. The City of Lakeland had donated a lot in the heart of the city, a 99 year lease, and $1000.00 toward the Building Fund. Plans to employ an architect were underway and it was hoped that building could be started at an early date.

Clubs had shown interest in corrective institutions, volunteered countless hours and money for the control of disease, dental and well-baby clinics, school lunches, audiometer testing in schools, rodent control, and proper disposal of sewage and garbage.

Club women had worked to get people to vote, quoting Plato, "The penalty that good men pay for indifference to public affairs is to be ruled by evil men."

Mrs. Jones had served as chief counsel to the Juvenile Court of Duval County and sponsored a movement to remove children from jails and house them in children's shelters.

Vice and Comic Books

Two resolutions passed at the 1954 Convention addressed the problem of child molestation and juvenile delinquency. The first asked that child molesters over Juvenile Court age who were mentally competent be given mandatory life imprisonment. If the offender was not mentally competent the molester was to be given treatment until cured, or, if incurable, custodial care in a mental institution for life. The other resolution stated:

> WHEREAS, It is the contention of the Florida Federation of Women's Clubs that a large majority of the 'so-called' comic books available through news stands and similar agencies are degrading to the morals of American youth and are direct contributors to juvenile delinquency through pictorial and written suggestions,
>
> RESOLVED, that the Florida Federation of Women's Clubs recognize this threat to youth and establish a program which will abolish such publication for all time.

Just how these women planned to implement such a program is not recorded.

The Florida Federation was granted an Epsilon Sigma Omicron charter—Sigma Chapter—in 1953 making it the eighteenth state federation to receive a charter. Epsilon Sigma Omicron was founded by Mrs. Quincy A. Myers in 1928, assisted by Indiana University and organized as a project of the Adult Education Division of the Indiana Federation of Clubs to promote adult education among its members. The first national convention of ESO was held in 1932 at the same time as the GFWC Convention. ESO affiliated with GFWC in 1934 and in 1950 became a division of the GFWC's Education Department. ESO provides planned reading programs and membership is earned by completing any four home reading courses, a course being five books. A wide variety of subjects are offered as courses with published lists of books in each course.

Mrs. E. D. Pearce, President; Mrs. C. M. Washburn, First Vice President and Mrs. C. L. Menser, Second Vice President, Mrs. R. D. Gray, Jr, Recording Secretary, Mrs. Henry Shaw, Corresponding Secretary, and Mrs. S. B. Taylor, Treasurer were installed at the Tallahassee convention to serve for the 1954-1956 administration.

Mrs. Pearce had been president of the Miami Woman's Club in 1939 and her record of volunteer work in various other organizations was impressive. She had taken a full time job during the World War II years and it was then that she decided that she had neglected her own self-improvement while rearing her family. She had finished two years of college before she married. After her war work, she enrolled in the Adult Education Department of the University of Miami taking a course one night a week, determined to continue until she got her degree and after six years she reached her goal without having slackened her volunteer work. She was an outstanding leader among Florida women and in 1966 became President of the General Federation of Women's Clubs.

Celebrating Sixty

At the Fall Board Meeting in Gainesville, authorization was given that a "60th Anniversary Year, Federation History be written giving 60 years of achievement." A Federation Forest near Ocala was also approved and a resolution was passed that the Florida Federation of Women's Clubs working through their twelve districts make a survey of the entire state to determine the number of mentally retarded children living in the state in need of institutional care. The results of the survey were to be given to the Florida Association for Mental Health by March 1, 1955.

The 60th Convention was held in Tampa, April 19th-20th, 1955. Ground breaking for the new Headquarters Building was scheduled for April 22nd at 11:00 A.M. It was a busy convention. New awareness of Florida's ties to Latin America influenced the delegates to pass a resolution urging that conversational Spanish be taught in Florida's elementary schools; the delegates pressed all concerned to strengthen the Public School System: they recommended that state legislation be enacted banning objectionable comic books and urged strict enforcement of "present state laws against the selling and distribution of obscene, lewd, immoral and licentious material in any form." The delegates also urged the 1955 Legislature to set up a Legislative Commission with "the sole duty to write a new Constitution for the State of Florida." (Florida's Constitution was written in 1885 for a sparsely settled state and had been amended more than 100 times.) The women who were assembled in Tampa wanted funds appropriated for a new nursery for the Forest Service in order that more pine seedlings could be produced for replanting Florida's forests.

Leading the Way: A Century of Service

CAROLYN PEARCE (Mrs. E. D.).
President of FFWC, 1954-1956; President of GFWC, 1966-1968.

Fig. 35. Entrance to FFWC Headquarters, 106 East Orange Street, Lakeland, Florida. Dedicated April 23, 1956. Bought by City of Lakeland, 1988.

The Chairman of Credentials, Mrs. Lee Skipwith, reported that the total attendance at the convention was 915 with 661 paid registrations at $1.00 each.

Dedication of the new $35,000 Headquarters Building at 106 East Orange Street, Lakeland, was held April 23rd, 1956, just before the beginning of the 61st Convention which was also held in Lakeland.

Championing Education

Mrs. Pearce had an informed and intelligent mind particularly concerning steps Florida should take to better educate its children. Governor Leroy Collins appointed her to be a member of the Continuing Education Council and to attend the White House Conference on Education.

At the Lakeland Convention Dr. John L. Buford, President of the National Education Association, gave the principal address. The state slogan was "Better Schools Make Better Communities" and under the leadership of Mrs. Pearce, club members resolved to study, understand and work closely with the schools in their communities. Emphasizing that education is the most important function of government for citizens to live in a democracy, club members recognized the important position of teachers and insisted that a minimum average salary be adopted. "To strengthen the position of the teacher in the community is to strengthen the whole school system." Delegates adopted a resolution exhorting members of clubs in their local communities to assist in securing and maintaining equitable salary schedules for teachers and to participate in a state and nationwide recruitment program with the objective to get a sufficient number of qualified and prepared teachers for the schools of the United States. They also recommended that courses in United States history be provided and required in all high schools and colleges in the United States.

Among the projects of the Juniors in the 1954-1956 administration was the printing and distribution of 100,000 "grace cards" to public restaurants. Printed on these cards were "table blessings" considered appropriate for those of Protestant, Catholic or Jewish faiths. .

Mrs. Pearce announced at the Tampa Convention that a

house for Billy Osceola, a recipient of federation help while attending a seminary, and a hut for Indian Cub Scouts had been built on the Brighton Reservation. "Pennies for Pines" had paid for planting 30,000 pine seedlings for a 35 acre Federation Forest located in the Ocala National Forest.

FFWC club members showed interest in the projects and work of the General Federation of Women's Clubs by an unusual number of delegates attending the national and international conventions in 1954 and 1955: 63 going to Denver, 77 to Philadelphia, 25 to Geneva, Switzerland, and 2 to an Inter-American Conference in San Jose, Costa Rica.

Florida was recognized with first place awards from GFWC for its Indian Affairs work and also for having the most subscribers to *GFWC Clubwoman*.

The Treasurer, Mrs. S. B. Taylor, reported that $38,758.30 had been disbursed for the headquarters building between May 1, 1954 and April 30, 1956. (This figure included some furniture for the building.) There was $48,844.00 in the Endowment and Scholarship Funds which were invested in U.S. Bonds. The two years had seen 12 new senior and 15 new junior clubs added to the Florida Federation with 2,094 new members bringing the total membership up to 29,861.

The Department of Welfare added a Division of Gerontology and the Department of Public Affairs added a Division of Status of Women. The Department of Youth Conservation's Chairman, Mrs. W.L. Maxwell reported that 160 clubs had Youth Conservation Departments which worked with local organizations to provide youth centers with recreational facilities.

Vigilantes Against Crime Comics

Some club women maintained "constant vigil of newsstands and worked closely with law enforcement officers to prevent sale of objectionable crime, sex, and horror comic books." The Florida Legislature had not enacted legislation against the sale and distribution of objectionable comic books but there had been several local ordinances passed. Mrs. Garland E. Bell, Chairman of the Division of Juvenile Protection, reported that 100 clubs had studied the crime comic book situation in their communities and had those which dealt with adultery and cannibalism removed from the newsstands. Two clubs found that a large number of juvenile delinquency cases also proved to be remedial reading problems and one club was paying for remedial reading instruction for children who needed it.

Responding to the resolution passed by the 1954 Fall Board meeting authorizing a survey of mentally retarded children, Mrs. F. F. Ravlin, chairman of the Department of Welfare, reported that 26,000 women had carried out the survey over the entire state of Florida, compiled the data concerning the mentally retarded children in need of institutional or hospital care and had sent the data to the state legislators in the hope that it would enable them to determine the extent of new facilities needed for a new Southwestern Mental Hospital.

Mrs. Pearce was appointed Chairman of the Western Hemisphere Division of International Relations by GFWC.

Mrs. C. M. Washburn was elected President; Mrs. C. L. Menser, First Vice President; Mrs. Art S. Witmer, Second Vice President; Mrs. L. M. Lewis Hall, Recording Secretary; and Mrs. Charles H. MacDowell, Treasurer for the 1956-1958 years. Mrs. A. M. C. Jobson became Recording Secretary, and Mrs. Charles Campbell, Director of Juniors. The post-convention board meeting elected Mrs. S. B. Taylor to the Headquarters Maintenance Committee. At the Fall Board Meeting Mrs. Avery Thomas was employed as Headquarters secretary.

The 62nd Convention met at Palm Beach in April 1957, and took care of the usual business of the organization. Officers and delegates felt that much progress had been made when they were told that books containing minutes of all past administrations had been filed in locked cabinets at FFWC Headquarters.

Resolutions passed at the 1957 convention asked that figures and facts govern the location of a new training institution for the mentally retarded. An appropriation of $5 million was pending for building this new institution and the governor and cabinet had approved the advisory committee report which stated "Site should be located within one hour's driving time of major trading areas to take advantage of labor pool, medical centers, universities, accessability of housing for staff, close proximity to civic clubs and parents' groups.

Because of rapid growth of school population, the delegates to this convention declared that the "present provisions of the Minimum Foundation Program are no longer adequate" and they urged that the next session of the legislature support those proposals which would meet the needs of the state's children. They also recommended that a beginning salary of $4200 be provided for each teacher unit filled by a teacher with a B.S. degree.

Comics Vs. The Bible

The Coral Gables Woman's Club asked the FFWC to endorse the legislative program of the Decent Literature Council of Dade County, which proposed a state statute designed to prohibit the sale to minors of objectionable and obscene literature. The program was endorsed and immediately transmitted by wire to the Speaker of the House and the President of the Senate.

In 1939, the Florida Legislature had passed a law requiring that members of the instructional staff of the public schools "have once every school day, reading in the presence of the pupils, from the Holy Bible, without sectarian comment." There were a significant number of citizens opposed to this law, but the delegates to the 1957 convention deemed it "inadvisable and detrimental to our youth to discontinue the requirement of daily Bible reading."

They urged study about and protection of the water resources of the state and also endorsed a resolution of the Tropical Audubon Society which was aimed at conservation of Key Deer.

Because the industrial schools for girls and boys had been of particular interest to members of FFWC and were considered to be primarily institutions for education, the delegates strongly opposed these institutions being placed under the Director of Prisons—"an act that would stigmatize these pupils." The Governor, the Cabinet and the Legislature were informed of these objections.

Fears of Nuclear Destruction

The 63rd Convention met in St. Petersburg in April 1958. Alarm over nuclear destruction was not mentioned in the reports of that meeting but a resolution passed by the delegates reflects some of the fear that had become a part of the lives of people everywhere.

> WHEREAS, it has been brought to the attention of the Florida Federation of Women's Clubs by the Miami Woman's Club of the necessity in time of invasion, aerial raid or disaster to provide for orderly continuation and functioning of our local, state and national government and that it be
>
> RESOLVED, that the Florida Federation of Women's Clubs, join the Miami Woman's Club in requesting the Governor of Florida to include in his message recommendations to the next Legislature for the creation of a Legislative Committee to explore and fully study the problem that such an emergency would present and that pursuant to such study there be enacted proper legislation for the
>
> CHAIN OF GOVERNMENTAL COMMAND AND AUTHORITY in the state of Florida and for the several local governments, including cities and counties, should the emergency arise where our various duly qualified and elected governmental officials are killed or so wounded as to render them ineffectual and unable to fulfill the obligations of their respective duties and offices.

It was their wish also that similar action be taken by the nation's Congress but without doing anything that would lead to the suspension of our Constitution or Bill of Rights. There is little in the records to indicate the real fear and constant concern about atomic destruction. Children in schools practiced getting under their desks or gathering against an inside wall. Individuals built air raid shelters. Movies and novels about radiation sickness and the total destruction of civilization added to both the fear and fascination of talk about nuclear holocaust.

An article had appeared in *The Miami Herald* which estimated that there were some 400 additives in use in food only 100 of which had been tested because under existing law, food processors and manufacturers were not required to test such additives prior to use. The delegates wanted Congress to enact a law that would require pretesting when the additives were not a natural content of such food.

With 27 new clubs, Florida had the greatest net increase in clubs and in membership of any state in the General Federation of Women's Clubs during the 1956-1958 reporting period. A new district was organized bringing the total to 13 districts; the Endowment Fund passed the $50,000 mark; a $2000 medical loan fund was established at the J. Hillis Miller Medical Center, University of Florida, Gainesville; the first Florida Federation Tour was promoted with 19 members enjoying four days in Cuba; $3000 was given for Indian scholarship and welfare and a 40 acre Federation Forest was established near Tallahassee.

The treasurer's report reflects expenses of having a headquarters building with maintenance, insurance, utilities, salary for the secretary, yard upkeep, furnishings and tax reserve listed under disbursements.

An outstanding event for the Juniors was the adoption of a new bylaw which gave them a voice in the selection of the Junior Director and put her on the Executive Committee with full voting rights.

There was strong emphasis on getting all club members to register to vote. Some clubs amended their bylaws requiring a prospective member to be registered either in her Florida precinct or at her northern home in order to become a club member. There were 88 clubs reporting 100% voter registration by their members.

The 1958 Convention installed Mrs. C. L. Menser, President; Mrs. Art S. Witmer, First Vice-President; Mrs. M. Lewis Hall, Second Vice President; Mrs. J. Porter Tyner, Recording Secretary; Mrs. S. B. Taylor, Corresponding Secretary; Mrs. Olin B. Hamilton, Treasurer and Mrs. Joseph C. Clark Director of Juniors.

Mrs. Menser chose "Progress Through Understanding" as the theme for her administration. Mrs. Menser is listed under Past Presidents as Irene Schweitzer (Mrs. Leslie).

At the Pre-Convention Board Meeting April 14, 1959, in Jacksonville, a citation of "First Vice-President Emeritus" was given to Mrs. Art S. Witmer who had resigned due to illness.

Mrs. M. Lewis Hall was appointed First Vice President and Mrs. A.P. Drummond, Second Vice President. The Executive Committee gave its report which was mostly concerned with scholarship funds and allocation of other funds. Mrs. E. D. Pearce was unnanimously endorsed for the office of Recording Secretary of the General Federation of Women's Clubs.

The delegates to the 64th convention in 1959 voted to sponsor a Library Service Bill which would provide that state monies be appropriated for use in establishing or enlarging facilities of counties for free libraries or library services.

Driver Education

Resolutions recommending that the Citizens Committee on Highway Safety be enacted into law contained provisions which the committee hoped would decrease the number of highway traffic deaths and accidents.

Legislation was recommended requiring that every person under eighteen should have successfully passed a driver education course before being issued a license; that every new Florida resident be required to pass a driver's license examination before being issued a license; that the number of on-the-road highway patrol be increased; that a chemical test with "implied consent" DUI laws be adopted and that the fee for a driver's license be increased to $1.75 with seventy-five cents of the amount designated specifically for driver education.

There were resolutions dealing with "Sobriety Law Enforcement," glamorization of social drinking through liquor advertisements, air pollution control, and the repeal of the Excise Tax Bill (federal) which was a tax on luxuries passed during World War II and still being collected. The Conservation Department recommended that both state and federal governments halt the widespread use of heptachlor and dieldrin for the eradication of fire ants until "adequate research studies can determine its effect upon wildlife resources and human health."

Because of the "Berlin Crisis" and the ability of the Soviet Union to wage intercontinental nuclear war the delegates passed an "Emergency Resolution" requesting the Florida Members of Congress to urge the House and Senate Appropriation Committees to act favorably on the President's request for $87 million for the Office of Civil and Defense Mobilization.

Another emergency resolution showed FFWC's continued interest in providing care for the mentally retarded. A new school was almost finished at Fort Myers but the waiting list for the Sunland Training School in Gainesville alone would fill the new school. Instead of building overly large institutions more were needed and could be smaller. "One was needed in the Central Panhandle, one in Southeastern Florida and another on the axis between Orange and Pinellas counties."

The Fall Board Meeting was held in Pensacola, September 24-26, 1959. The Executive Committee reported that air-conditioning equipment had been placed in the office space at headquarters; the address plates for the *CLUBWOMAN* had been moved from Jacksonville to headquarters and the printing of the magazine had been changed to the Rose Printing Company, Tallahassee. The Fall Board approved extending an invitation to GFWC to hold their Convention in Florida in 1961.

Polio Vaccine

The Junior clubwomen of the Florida Federation of Women's Clubs had adopted and supported polio immunization as a state project for 1958-1960 and they asked that FFWC delegates request the next session of the legislature to pass a bill requiring that any child between the ages of two months and six years be given an "immunizing dose of prophylactic agent against poliomyelitis."

The 65th Annual Convention was held April 26-29, 1960, in Miami Beach with the Coco Plum Woman's Club as the hostess club. The Miami Beach Woman's Club presented a resolution urging clubs and individual members to use constructive criticism, voluntary agreements, laws, boycotts, visits and letters to uphold the moral code of the Ten Commandments. They saw the nation in moral decay because of moral laxity, divorce, juvenile delinquency, theft, murder and rape. The Northeast Miami Junior Woman's Club presented a resolution asking the Motion Picture Industry of America to take whatever action necessary to bring about a betterment of motion pictures.

Support for the Arts

The Fine Arts Department had six divisions. The Art Division sponsored art shows, stimulated creative art in schools and colleges, gave cash awards, conducted art classes for handicapped children and encouraged members to support art museums. The Crafts Division conducted sewing contests and craft exhibits. The Drama Division stimulated interest in writing, producing and sponsoring drama as well as supporting Little Theater movements. Awards were offered for the best skits written by club members. The Division of Music encouraged the participation of club members in choral groups and offered scholarships and grants to music students. Mrs. J. Riley Staats, Chairman of the Poetry Division and herself a poet of some distinction, encouraged club members to write poetry. Women responded with an increasing number of award winning entries. The Literature Division encouraged club women to give books to family and friends and they reported approximately 6000 books given. They supported libraries and kept up a "drive to eradicate salacious literature."

The Education Department reported that $9,210.00 was contributed to Guidance Clinics as well as several thousand service hours. Clubs had contributed $9,101.00 and 2,755 books to libraries. Forty-four clubs had given 62 scholarships. Interest in recruiting and developing excellent teachers resulted in GFWC setting up a plan to give "Oscars" to teachers. This was begun in Florida in 1956 and became known better as "Teacher of the Year" award. (However, there was some controversy over this award. Mrs. J. P. Ashmore, Chairman of the Adult Education Division, received 20 letters asking that the "Teacher of the Year" program be discontinued.) Judging teacher effectiveness has proven to be a most difficult task because teaching methods which work well with some children fail completely with others.

The International Affairs Department sent medical supplies, food and agricultural implements to Mexico through CARE. They sent educational materials to Ecuador. One hundred and fourteen clubs held International relations programs.

Club Histories

The Florida Federation of Women's Clubs was 65 years old in 1960 and could boast of 228 Senior clubs, 109 Junior clubs, 17 County Federations, and an overall membership of 32,151.

Mrs. Fred Heath, Historian for FFWC, had promoted the writing of club histories by giving awards in two classifications: (1) the best dramatic presentation of a club history either in the form of a play or as a pageant. (2) the best narrative form history. Mrs. Heath emphasized the importance of keeping a record or history of individual clubs and she placed the histories that she received in the archives at headquarters. The treasurer's report for April 1960, listed $746.88 in the Archives Fund—a long step toward maturity from the time when the records of the organization were moved in paper cartons from one FFWC President's residence to another. The history of FFWC that was to have been written when the organization was sixty years old had not been written until Mrs. Mabel Meadows Staats who had served as Poetry chairman wrote *History of the Florida Federation of Women's Clubs 1895-1960*. No history of FFWC had been written since the one written by Lucy Worthington Blackman in 1939. Mrs. Staats' history was typed and copied. Its 12 single spaced pages were sold by Headquarters to those interested in learning about the history of their organization.

Mrs. Menser reported that 34 new clubs had been added to the Florida Federation during her two year term. She had held state meetings in the extreme corners of the state, St. Petersburg, Pensacola, Jacksonville, Orlando and Miami. Florida had the largest delegation to travel to GFWC Convention in Manila in the Philippines and the largest delegation to travel with the GFWC "Around the World."

Two delegates from Florida had traveled with the GFWC team to Alaska to present the Flag of Florida in the official ceremonies for admitting Alaska to the Union.

Leading the Way: A Century of Service

10 – The Sixties

OFFICERS elected for 1960-1962 were: Mrs. M. Lewis Hall, President; Mrs. A. P. Drummond, First Vice President; Mrs. Edward J. Clark, Second Vice President; Mrs. Albert Huth, Recording Secretary; Mrs. Frank C. Martin, Corresponding Secretary; Mrs. Mark Emmel, Treasurer; Mrs. John G. Mahon, State Director of Juniors. A post-convention board meeting in the Napoleon Room of the Deauville Hotel in Miami Beach ratified appointments of department chairmen. Departments were reduced from nine to seven and Mrs. J. Porter Tyner was elected Member-at-Large.

At the fall board meeting in Lakeland five new general clubs were accepted into membership and one new junior club. Plans for the 1961 GFWC convention at Miami Beach were discussed and to defray expenses of the convention the delegates asked for a voluntary contribution of twenty-five cents per capita of FFWC members.

The 1940-1942 president of FFWC, Mrs. Thurston Roberts, died May 25, 1960, and the delegates at the 1960 Fall Board expressed their deep sympathy to her family.

The board also recommended the endorsement of Mrs. E. D. Pearce as a candidate for third vice-president of GFWC.

At the pre-convention board meeting in Miami, June 2, 1961, the appointment of Mrs. J. R. Glover as Second Vice President was approved. Mrs. E. J. Clark had resigned. There were thirteen other appointments approved indicating many previously appointed chairmen of departments and heads of standing committees had resigned since the manual for 1960-1962 was printed.

Anti-Communist Panic

The 66th convention was held at the Barcelona and Eden Roc Hotels, Miami Beach, June 2nd and 3rd. 1961, with a total registration of 868. Resignations from four junior clubs were accepted, two general clubs resigned and one general club was dropped. Two new clubs were accepted for membership. The delegates to the 1961 and 1962 meetings were facing national and international changes and problems hardly known before in peace time.

The Soviet Union had put a rocket-powered earth satellite into orbit, October 4, 1957, a feat that shocked the entire educational system of the United States which since World War II had known without a doubt that "its science and industry were the best in the world." Because of Russia's Sputnik, curriculums were overhauled with more emphasis on mathematics and science. Programs were planned and funded to enable the United States to again become first in science, particularly in the exploration of space.

Meanwhile, an extreme right wing group known as the John Birch Society had been founded in 1958, and by 1961 had spread widely, causing great uneasiness. This society said that the United States was in more danger from Communists within than from without the country, prompting "witch hunts" throughout the nation for anyone with possible connections to any organization which might have at any time spoken in favor of a communist idea.

Russia and East Germany began to build the Berlin Wall. The United States fired its first intercontinental ballistic missile. Congress approved a $3,500,000,000 increase in defense funds and authorized President Kennedy to call up 250,000 reservists to active duty for up to one year and to extend the length of duty for regular forces. Over-riding all other fears was that of nuclear annihilation.

In March of 1961, President John F. Kennedy established the Peace Corps for service abroad by American volunteers, who were to aid general education, technical instruction and social development in underdeveloped countries and Congress in September allotted $30 million to implement the program.

Fear of communism resulted in the following resolution:

WHEREAS, The openly avowed Communist objective of world domination is a clear and present danger to the free world and

WHEREAS, Communist institutions planning subversion, and training skilled and dedicated workers to carry out subversion throughout the world, have no counterpart in the free world, and

WHEREAS, The Congress of the United States has before it proposals to found a FREEDOM ACADEMY to plan counteraction and train skilled and dedicated workers to counteract Communist subversion

THEREFORE BE IT RESOLVED: That the Florida Federation of Women's Clubs does hereby endorse the proposed FREEDOM ACADEMY and urge the Congress of the United States to enact necessary legislation without delay.

Because the Supreme Court had ruled that the Secretary of State had no authority to deny passports to people who were Communists, the delegates to this 1961 convention "urged Congress to promptly pass a law making it illegal to issue passports to members of any organization dedicated to the overthrow of our Constitutional Republic by force or violence".

Recognizing that many young women of the armed forces were stationed in Florida, a resolution recommended that clubs which had young women of the armed forces stationed near them "begin a Pal Day honoring the young women of the Armed Services such as had been observed by the Woman's Club of Jacksonville as an annual event."

Some by-laws were amended or changed. The definition and object of Junior Women's Clubs stated that "membership should be entirely of women ages 18 to 35 and that such clubs must undertake one or more projects of civic, social or cultural interest and shall hold active membership in the Federation and participate in its programs."

Because of her work and dedication from 1949 through 1960 to increase interest and knowledge of writing poetry, fourteen past presidents of the Florida Federation of Women's Clubs presented Mrs. J. Riley Staats a certificate of appreciation which designated her as the "true Poet Laureate of the Fine Arts Department."

Jessie Hamm Meyer

The Fall Board meeting was held in early October 1961 at the Galt Ocean Mile Hotel of Fort Lauderdale. An archives committee was appointed. Sale of "Reflections of Life and Installations" written and published by Mrs. L. J. McCaffrey, past president of FFWC, was approved. Price was $1.00 and profits were to go to the Endowment Fund. The "Fosett Fund for Retarded Children" was created from $1200 given by Mr. Fosett. (No initials or first name recorded.)

The pre-convention board meeting held April 24, 1962, at the Tampa Terrace Hotel ratified action taken by the Executive Committee called meeting October 20, 1961. Mrs. A. P. Drummond had resigned as First Vice President, Mrs. J. R. Glover was elected First Vice President; Mrs. Mark Emmel, Second Vice President; Mrs. J. Porter Tyner, Treasurer and Mrs. Allen H. Dawson, Member-at-Large. The appointment of Mrs. J. B. Davis, Director of District 3 to replace Mrs. S. C. Edwards was ratified.

The 67th Convention was held in Tampa, April 24-27, 1962. Three new junior clubs were accepted for membership and five general clubs. However, three general clubs resigned and four were dropped. Often clubs that were dropped became reinstated. Club treasurers sometimes missed deadlines for reporting their clubs membership and payment of FFWC dues. Membership totaled almost 33,000.

America First

The delegates to the 1962 Convention passed two AMERICANISM RESOLUTIONS, one of which emphasized preparedness with special recollection of Pearl Harbor, and the other implored recognition in every way possible of "What's Right with America" and observance of "Know America Week."

Another resolution gave the support of FFWC to the After-Care Bill sponsored by the Florida Council of Juvenile Court Judges. The delegates also resolved to use all their resources to prevent any change in the Narcotics Control Act of 1956.

In her administration report Mrs. Hall wrote:

> We have accomplished many new 'firsts' in this administration. Under GFWC Public Affairs program, clubs have responded to Civil Defense and Home Preparedness programs. Florida's most vital

concern continues to be providing for 90,000 Cuban refugees, who have infiltered into our state since October.

The Freedom Academy's program and study course based on J. Edgar Hoover's "Masters of Deceit" has afforded knowledge and means to combat Communism. Florida law, requiring teaching of "Americanism versus Communism" in our public schools has been an education of our youth on this problem. J. Edgar Hoover has referred to the FFWC program as a model one.

Radio Free Europe, CARE, libraries, "Good Will Ambassador Scholarships" and help to the Sunland Centers were part of FFWC's program during these years.

The FFWC Manual for 1960-1962 states:

The dues of the Federation are now one dollar per capita member. This pays for General Federation dues, Florida Federation expenses, printing of the Florida Federation Clubwoman Magazine, and maintenance of State Headquarters in Lakeland. The Florida Federation has an Endowment Fund invested in government bonds. Only the interest from these bonds is used for expenses of the officers and chairmen and to promote the work of the Federation. Contributions to this fund are always acceptable. Special funds are set up for specific projects by voluntary contributions: such as, Penny Art Fund, Pennies for Pines, Indian welfare, scholarships etc.

There had been a drop in membership of the Juniors but they had accomplished much between 1960 and 1962. They had worked for the Sunland Training Centers located in Gainesville, Orlando and Lee County as their special project. Legislation passed in 1957 allowed mentally retarded and epileptics to be admitted at any age. Some of the residents of these centers could be rehabilitated while others left the center only at death. Juniors gave gifts valued at $17,661 to these centers.

Juvenile courts claimed the attention of 230 clubs which participated in the "Day in Court" program aimed at better understanding and improvement of the treatment of juveniles who had been accused of being delinquent.

In 1961, the Florida Federation had hosted the General Federation's Convention in Miami and had endorsed past president of FFWC, Carolyn Pearce as Second Vice President of GFWC. During Mrs. Hall's administration almost $128,000 had been given for various scholarships and over $4,000 had been given to CARE. There was $56,613.12 left in the treasury for the next administration

A total of 1360 women registered for the 1962 convention. Mrs. J.R. Glover was elected President, Mrs. Mark W. Emmel First Vice President, Mrs. Albert Huth Second Vice President, Mrs. James G. Matheny Recording Secretary, Mrs. Thomas Harrison Treasurer, and Mrs. Herbert R. Savage State Junior Director for 1962-1964. Mrs. J. Porter Tyner was appointed Corresponding Secretary.

The fall Board meeting was held October 1-3, 1962, at the Daytona Plaza Hotel in Daytona Beach. The appointment of Mrs. Walter Schroeder Corresponding Secretary to fill the vacancy caused by the resignation of Mrs. J. Porter Tyner was ratified. A resolution dealing with Comprehensive Long-Range Studies of Florida's Water Resources was passed. This resolution recognized that the growing population of Florida would make demands on the water resources of some sections of the state in excess of the available supplies and urged the Legislature of Florida to approve and support with adequate appropriations the comprehensive long-range studies program of Florida's water resources initiated by the State Board of Conservation, Division of Water Resources and Conservation.

Another resolution passed by the Fall Board of 1962 asked that the Florida Legislature create a Senior Citizens' Commission with a paid staff of workers to give special attention to the needs and welfare of the growing number of Florida citizens over the age of 65.

Cuban Missile Crisis

Delegates to the Fall Board meeting left for their homes not knowing that in two weeks the nation and Florida particularly would face a threat of nuclear attack. On October 14th surveillance flights over Cuba took photographs furnishing incontrovertible evidence that Russia had installed medium range missiles and that sites for more advanced missiles were under construction. The purpose of these missile sites had to be to provide nuclear strike capability against the Western Hemisphere. On October 20th, the United States began a naval blockade of Cuba and on October 22nd, President Kennedy explained the situation to the American people. It was a frightening time in Florida and the nation. Some citizens had built bomb shelters, stored food and water out of fear of nuclear attack. Schools had drilled children — having them duck under their desks or hunker against inside walls of their schoolrooms. With missiles as close as Cuba all that preparation appeared to be useless. Many school children were told by their parents, "If it happens, try to get home so that we can all die together."

The two great nuclear powers were "eyeball to eyeball". An awesome gathering of military forces in Florida added to the breath-holding tension of Florida citizens as they went about their daily tasks. On October 28, 1962, Russia agreed to dismantle the missile sites in Cuba. The people of Florida and the nation breathed a collective sigh of relief and hoped that they could get on with their lives and work.

The 68th Annual Convention was held April 16-19, 1963, at the Palm Beach Biltmore, Palm Beach, with total registrations of 1,015.

The Florida Legislature was in session and was considering a bill to appropriate money for a Sunland Training School in Dade County. Surveys had long since shown the need for this facility and the delegates to the convention approved an emergency resolution supporting the bill and urging that it be passed.

A resolution allowing that the age range for Juniors be extended from 35 to 40 lost by a vote of 174 to 300.

A resolution *against* the registration of firearms passed.

A resolution asking that the Florida Legislature of 1963 separate the School for the Blind at St. Augustine from the School for the Deaf was approved.

The delegates asked that the legislature pass and enforce a law which would keep children 16 and under from attending "Adults Only" movies. Another resolution asked that adequate facilities be set up for the treatment of psychotic children under the age of 12.

A "Teacher of the Year Award" continued to be given but

there continued to be several members who were against such an award.

The Fall Board of 1963 met September 30, October 1 and 2 at Panama City with 340 paid registrations. Clubs in Putnam County were transferred from District 6 to District 4.

The 69th Annual Convention met at the George Washington and Robert Meyer Hotels in Jacksonville April 12-16, 1964.

A Switch on Gun Control

The delegates to this convention amended the resolution about registration of firearms. This new resolution expressed belief that there was a need for limited restrictions in the purchase of firearms through mail order to counteract irresponsible and anonymous purchase of weapons. This resolution urged "all member clubs to study thoroughly ALL proposed congressional legislation on the subject of mail order purchase of weapons, with the purpose of approving appropriate legislation to members of Congress to prevent irresponsible purchase of weapons by mail order." Minutes are supposed to record only the actions taken at a meeting but a history needs to explain why such actions were taken. The reason for the amendment of a resolution passed only a few months previously was the assassination of President Kennedy on November 22, 1963. On November 24th, his alleged killer while in the custody of the police was shot by Jack Ruby.

Millions of Americans still in shock over the assassination of the President saw Lee Harvey Oswald killed as they were watching a news broadcast on TV. The gun that was used by Oswald was said to have been purchased by mail order. Previous to that time there had not been much thought given to the fact that anyone could get a gun simply by ordering it from a gun catalog.

The delegates went on record as favoring the "Becker Amendment" to the Constitution, This amendment had been proposed as an answer to the Supreme Court decision that barred reading of the Bible and prayer in the public schools. The Becker amendment contended that the Supreme Court's decision was in violation of the second part of the 1st Amendment which says that Congress can pass no law which prohibits the free exercise of religion. Those in favor of the Becker Amendment believed that listening to the Bible being read or to prayer in schools was completely voluntary while others contended that public schools were supported by taxes and to read the Bible or have prayer was unconstitutional because it supported an established religion.

Scholarships

Mrs. Glover's theme during her administration had been "Growth Through Education" and she was particularly pleased with the response of the clubs in making loans or scholarships available in the amount of over $150,000.00. A Good Will Ambassador scholarship of $1000.00 was given by the Federation to a girl from Latin America.

Along with the high school students throughout Florida, club women also studied programs on "Americanism versus Communism". Gifts went to Radio Free Europe, Indian Welfare, Salk Institute, the Arthritis Foundation, "Dimes for Liberty" and to a program set up by the General Federation to be used to furnish a room at the base of the Statue of Liberty to depict American life.

Executive officers made two tours of the districts logging 5,000 miles of travel. Membership increases were emphasized and 126 clubs reported increased membership. During the year, 17 new clubs were accepted into membership but 14 clubs dropped out. Membership at the end of the administration was 26,233 generals and 4,909 juniors.

Installed for the 1964-1966 administration were Mrs. Mark Emmel, President; Mrs. Albert Huth, First Vice President; Mrs. Thomas Harrison, Second Vice President; Mrs. J. C. Pratt, Recording Secretary; Mrs. Charles Outen, Corresponding Secretary; Mrs. A. M. Romer, Treasurer; and Mrs. J. Frank Johnson, Director of Junior Clubs.

Mrs. Emmel chose "Time for Believing, Learning and Doing" as the theme for her administration.

The Post Convention Board meeting accomplished some reorganization to conform to GFWC, reducing departments from eight to six.

The Fall Board met at Cocoa Beach, September 24-26, 1964. The appointments of departments and committee chairmen were ratified and changes in International Affairs Department making the department comparable to the GFWC department were ratified. This change resulted in four Divisions: America, Europe, Middle East and Far East. Six clubs were accepted into the federation.

The 70th Annual Convention was held at Hollywood-by-the-Sea, April 19-23, 1965. The 1216 delegates unanimously endorsed Mrs. E. D. Pearce (Carolyn) for the office of the President of GFWC. Mrs. Pearce would be the first club worker from Florida to lead the General Federation of Women's Clubs. Because of her work not only in FFWC and GFWC but also on state educational committees and boards, Mrs. Pearce was loved and respected by those who had worked with her. Florida Federation women were especially proud that Mrs. Pearce would have an opportunity to serve as the leader of the General Federation of Women's Clubs.

Because of increased enrollment in the Florida schools and a decreasing supply of teachers, equipment and space, the Florida Education Association was making an extensive study of the problems. The delegates to the 1965 meeting adopted a resolution to study and support the recommendations of the FEA.

The FFWC had caused to be prepared a bill defining obscene literature. A resolution urging the passage of this bill was adopted. The delegates also adopted a resolution urging the passage of legislation which would establish a moral code of decency to cover showing and advertising of movies.

Other subjects considered by the delegates were: raising the age of drivers' learner permits from 14 to 16, mandatory testing of infants for metabolic disorders, abolishing special registration for women being called for jury duty, separating Mental Health from Mental Retardation by establishing a Division of Mental Health and a Division of Mental Retardation, providing for exemption from civil liability of persons rendering emergency care in case of traffic accidents, and prohibiting

Leading the Way: A Century of Service

cigarette vending machines from being put in public places unless supervised by an adult. (Surveys had shown that the law regarding sale of cigarettes to minors was not being enforced because of children's access to vending machines.)

Not all of the subjects resulted in resolutions or actions, but the fact that clubs all over the state decided to study and try to affect laws showed interest in a wide range of problems.

Lakeland was the site of the 1965 Fall Board Meeting held September 23-26. There had been discussion and a committee formed to investigate the use of the Lakeland Headquarters for more state meetings. The final result was a recommendation that meetings should be held in different areas of the state.

The military action in Vietnam had escalated and there was disenchantment among many young people. Objections to the war had resulted in young men of draft age questioning whether it was their patriotic duty to allow themselves to be drafted. Rebellion against the established society showed in alternative dress and hair styles, dropping out, drugs, communes, and peace marches. Concern over the development of a serious "generation gap" was existent but not overt in established organizations. Generally the women of FFWC went about studying and acting on projects where they felt that they could effect change. Reports of chairmen and district directors give evidence that Mrs. Emmel and her board persevered in all Departments and Divisions of their federation. Membership had increased from 30,900 to 32,050 with a net gain of 22 new clubs giving the Florida Federation a first place award for "Percentage Net Gain in New Clubs" at the GFWC Convention. Sixteen county federations were lost. Contributions to scholarship funds amounted to $371,000.00. The chairman of the Youth Guidance Division reported over $240,000 in contributions and 228,467 hours of work.

Defending the Everglades National Park

Everglades National Park had been a chief concern of the Florida Federation of Women's Clubs until it was turned over to the National Park Service in 1947. The Conservation of Natural Resources Department of FFWC continued to be concerned and presented an emergency resolution to the Fall

Jessie Hamm Meyer

Board:
> WHEREAS, The Florida Federation of Women's Clubs was instrumental in securing the Everglades National Park for the citizens of Florida, for our visitors and for posterity; and
>
> WHEREAS, in 1948 the United States Congress approved a project of the U. S. Corps of Engineers to control future flood waters in Florida, with the assurance that the project would not damage or interfere with this great National Park, there being abundant water to supply the Everglades National Park if properly used; and
>
> WHEREAS, the park is actually being destroyed by lack of sufficient water because of the Central and Southern Florida Flood Control Project; and
>
> WHEREAS. The State of Florida has turned the management of the area over to a five man governing board, which so far apparently represents only real estate and financial interests, although 80% of the cost of the project comes out of the pockets of the nation's taxpayers; now therefore be it
>
> RESOLVED, that the Florida Federation of Women's Clubs urge the Congress of the United States and the Florida Legislature to approve and support the guaranteeing of an adequate amount of water for the Everglades National Park, and be it further
>
> RESOLVED, that a copy of this resolution be sent to the Florida State Board of Conservation, with copies to the President of the U.S.A., the Senators from Florida, the Governor of Florida, the President of the Florida Senate and the Speaker of the Florida House of Representatives.

The 71st Annual Convention was held at the Jack Tar Hotel in Clearwater, April 12-15, 1966. Amendments to the Bylaws having to do with resolutions and elections were adopted and the fiscal year was defined as beginning July 1 and ending June 30. Resolutions concerned with the dumping of raw sewage from toilets of railroad passenger trains, the licensing of child care facilities and allowing Bible reading and prayer in the public schools were submitted to the delegates of the 71st convention

Juniors had been supportive of the five Sunland Training Centers both in time and money. They had also given contributions to the Hospital Ship Hope and to CARE. Most of the Junior clubs had participated in "Operation Healthy Babies".

The Distinguished Awards Jury of the Freedom Foundation presented FFWC the George Washington Honor Medal for the

"Know Your America" program in 1965 and the honor medal plus a check for $100.00 in the "Community Program Award Category" in 1966 for "outstanding accomplishments in helping to achieve a better understanding of the American Way of Life". Three more Federation Forests were planted in cooperation with the U. S. Forest Service and the "Lois Emmel Conservation of Natural Resources Scholarship Fund" was established.

The Florida Federation of Women's Clubs hosted the reception following Mrs. E. D. Pearce's installation as President of the General Federation of Women's Clubs. Mrs. Emmel reported: "The brilliant reception in the Grand Ballroom of the Conrad Hilton Hotel in Chicago in honor of President Pearce was a Florida wonderland and tropical paradise and truly a night to remember, not only for the large Florida delegation of more than 200 members all dressed in green or gold with orange corsages who were hostesses, but the approximately 1400 who attended to enjoy the missiles, fountains of orange juice, orange trees and a little bit of Florida hospitality."

An Unpopular War

When Mrs. Pearce assumed the General Federation presidency, she said:

> We yearn today for peace. Many of us have lived through the ravages and the holocaust of two world wars, of the Korean War, and now Vietnam ...
>
> Whatever else we may do during the two years of this administration, one objective will be paramount: we will work for peace...There only is one way that we will ever acquire a peaceful world— and keep it so— and this is by instilling in our young people a love of peace that will permeate their thinking and guide their deeds.... And so our General Federation theme for this administration will be 'Build our Youth for a Better World'.

Mrs. Pearce spoke of the modern woman pioneering in the Space Age:

> We have no forbidding mountains or scorching plains to conquer, but we do have the perplexing and dangerous problems concomitant with a thriving advanced civilization....illiteracy, school dropouts, water and air pollution, illnesses to eradicate, salacious magazines, crime on inadequately lit streets, increasing traffic

accidents and the needs of the underprivileged at home and abroad.

She asked that clubs "walk hand in hand with youth for community betterment through community service." She encouraged the formation of a new category of membership known as the Juniorettes, teenagers between 14 and 18 years old. Many clubs had sponsored groups of teen age girls, affording them a chance to learn social skills, but Mrs. Pearce was looking at the Juniorettes as a training time to learn how to volunteer. From this group, she envisioned the leaders of the federated women's clubs of the future.

Mrs. Pearce and 114 other members of GFWC attended a conference of the Federation of Asian Women's Associations in Manila. This conference did not dwell upon international problems or politics but there was a "constant consciousness of the proximity of the Vietnam War". She visited Clark Air Force Base in the Phillipines where wounded were being brought from the conflict in Vietnam only two hours away.

Like other presidents of GFWC, Mrs. Pearce traveled widely visiting countries of the Orient, the Pacific Basin, Australia, New Zealand and Europe. Her visits with women of other countries and cultures caused her to "marvel not about their differences but about their similarities of interests."

During the administration of Mrs. Pearce, GFWC delegates reaffirmed the Equal Rights Amendment.

Florida Federation Officers elected for 1966-1968 were Mrs. Albert Huth, President; Mrs. Thomas Harrison, First Vice President; Mrs. J. C. Pratt, Second Vice President; Mrs. Stanley Buss, Recording Secretary; Mrs. Paul B. Wallis, Corresponding Secretary; Mrs. Joseph I. Mathis, Treasurer and Mrs. Charles E. Hunt, Director of Juniors.

Mrs. Huth presided at the Fall Board September 26-28, 1966, at the Galt Ocean Mile Hotel, Fort Lauderdale. and at the Convention April 17-20, 1967, at the Daytona Plaza Hotel in Daytona Beach. However, on April 29, 1967, Mrs. Huth married Henry H. Carleton and is listed among the FFWC past presidents as Edythe Carleton (Mrs. Henry H.).

The 1968-1970 manual did not include reports of departments and divisions for the previous administration as yearbooks previously had done. However, minutes from fall boards, conventions, reports of officers and resolutions endorsed were printed in soft back book form and this pattern for manuals was followed for the next several years. Mrs. Carleton reported that her administration's main project, law enforcement training, resulted in the co- sponsoring of four courses ($6,000) at the Florida Institute for Law Enforcement, giving 160 police officers reduced tuition. Individual clubs paid tuition and expenses for 50 more police officers to get additional training. The 356 federated clubs and their 31,291 members contributed an estimated $88,000.00 to scholarships,"Pennies for Pines", Sunland Training Centers, CARE, SHIP HOPE, Radio Free Europe and to the upkeep of the FFWC headquarters building.

The 1967 Convention at Daytona Beach honored Mrs. E. D. Pearce, GFWC President, who also gave the keynote speech for the convention.

Delegates adopted resolutions:

1. Suggesting legislation on driver education, uniform state regulations, inspections, importance of wearing helmets and other safety measures for motorcyclists.

2. Enforcement of existing laws regarding child molesters.

3. A requirement that all school children in Florida show proof of small pox vaccination.

4. Establishment of a statewide program of licensing away-from-home child care facilities.

5. Legislation to provide adequate safety at highway- railroad grade crossings.

During Mrs. Carleton's administration, more than ninety thousand copies of a booklet entitled "Who Me?" (Florida Law for Teenagers) were printed and distributed to 8th and 9th grade social studies classes. The booklet was prepared by Judge Bowden Hunt and paid for through a separate account set up by FFWC. Some money formerly designated for Indian scholarships was transferred to that account.

Delegates to the Fall Board in Gainesville, September 6-8, 1967, urged that legislators charged with drafting a new Constitution for Florida retain the statute which exempted FFWC clubhouses from ad valorem taxes. They argued that a tax on club houses would work such a hardship on some clubs that they could not do the charitable work for which they were organized.

At the 73rd Convention held in Jacksonville, April 28-May 2, 1968, the Miami Woman's Club, alarmed at the increase in violent crimes in Dade County, asked and got the adoption of a resolution which urged total dedicated commitment of all public officials toward all-out support and implementation of an effective action program against crime in Dade County.

A Wave of Protests

Statistics showed that Dade County was not alone in the increase of violent crime. There were protests, riots and "non-violent" disturbances all over the country which added to the general air of social unrest. Delegates at this convention took note of the preponderance of young people participating in these demonstrations and generally blamed what they considered unpatriotic acts on a lack of knowledge of Americanism. A resolution "seeking to instill in our youth the meaning and the privilege of being an American" was adopted. Women who had been a part of the great patriotic effort to save the world from fascism were frustrated and puzzled by young people refusing to answer their country's call for a war which was supposed to stop the spread of communism.

There were many causes for the demonstrations, the seeming lack of patriotism and the widening gap between generations. The war in Vietnam was shown on TV screens of homes everyday and became known as America's first "Living Room War." Civil rights and school integration had supportive laws but there was not enough will among the people to peaceably enforce the laws. The use of drugs was a greater problem than ever before.

Martin Luther King, Jr., the leading black proponent of non-violent protest against injustice, was shot to death in Memphis, Tennessee, on April 4, 1968, and Robert F. Kennedy, Democratic nominee for President, was killed in Los Angeles, June 5, 1968. Student demonstrations were disrupting college campuses and many young men of draft age went to Canada.

President Lyndon Johnson refused to run for the Presidency again when he could neither win the war in Vietnam nor admit defeat. The Republican Nixon-Agnew ticket promising to win the war won in one of the closest elections in the history of the country, but the conflict did not end until 1975.

Women of the Florida Federation addressed issues and implemented long range plans to make lives better at the local level. They took their stand on national problems from the standpoint of their historical and cultural experience.

Mrs. Charles Hunt, State Junior Director, reported that the 4,574 Florida Juniors gave $628,500.00 to philanthropies and sponsored 14,300 projects. Sunland Training Centers continued to be the Juniors' principal project but they also supported all Federation projects. The treasurer's report showed a total membership of 31,287, counting both generals and juniors.

Officers elected to serve the Florida Federation of Women's Clubs for 1968-1970 were Mrs. Thomas Harrison, President; Mrs. J. C. Pratt, First Vice President; Mrs. Karl F. King, Second Vice President; Mrs. Arthur Zimmet, Recording Secretary; Mrs. O. E. Slotterbeck, Treasurer; and Mrs. Wm. H. Winsemann, Director of Junior Clubs.

Mrs. Harrison chose "Cherish the Past — Challenge the Future" as the theme for her administration and her project was "Operation Crime Stop." The 1968 Fall Board meeting was held at the Robert Meyer Motor Inn in Orlando, September 16-18, and delegates to the Convention of 1969 met in Miami, April 21-24 at the Carillon Hotel.

A strong resolution deploring obscenity, nudity and immorality in the motion picture industry and its influence on the young people of the nation was adopted. The same resolution solicited the support of individuals, churches, government officials, clubs and other organizations and asked assistance in a letter-writing campaign to the Motion Picture Association of America and the American Guild of Variety Artists. Delegates to the 1969 Convention also adopted a resolution asking legislative bodies to strengthen the laws against pornography.

Ecologists were warning that alligators were becoming an endangered species and pointing out their role in swamp ecology. Delegates supported legislative bills concerning endangered species and discouraged the purchase of articles made from alligator hides.

Demonstrations against the Vietnam War and the success of the Tet offensive in 1968 had put the country through a traumatic time, but on July 20th, 1969, Neil Armstrong, Commander of the Apollo ll mission, walked on the moon. People all over the world watched their TV screens or listened to their radios in absolute awe and the general feeling throughout the United States became optimistic. "If we can put a man on the moon and bring him back to earth, we can do anything."

It was in an atmosphere of hope that FFWC's Fall Board met at the Beach Club Hotel at Naples, September 15-17, 1969. Dr. Henry Stanford, President of the University of Miami; Frederick F. Fox, Assistant Special Agent in charge of the Federal Bureau of Investigation and Donald R. McClure, Director of Department of Child Services spoke to the delegates. No workshops were mentioned in the report of this Fall Board meeting other than one on procedure and another on public speaking but plans traditionally were made for officers and chairmen to hold working sessions for new club presidents, treasurers and department chairmen.

Divided Sympathies

Protests against the war in Vietnam continued with the march of 250,000 protestors on Washington November 15, 1969. College campuses were scenes of sit-ins and protests of various kinds testing both the patience and the skill of those who had to deal with students who were being asked to fight in a war which had never been declared. The older generation, remembering their patriotic response to World War II had little understanding of these draft card burning, rioting young people. No mention of these troubles appears in the records of the meetings of those days. Some delegates had sons who had volunteered or been drafted into the military, others had sons who had fled to Canada to escape the draft and others had managed to get their sons exempted from the draft for one reason or another. Perhaps they considered it best to limit their activities to the business at hand as they met at their 75th Convention April 20-23, 1970, at the Sarasota Motor Motel in Sarasota.

Amendments to the by-laws fixed annual dues to FFWC at "$1.25 per capita, but not to exceed $1.50 per capita for active, associate and life members. Dues include membership in the General Federation of Women's Clubs. At least ten cents per capita of the Junior Clubs' dues shall be allocated to a Junior Fund to promote work of the Juniors. The publication *Florida Clubwoman* is furnished to participating members as part of their annual dues." The by-laws also defined eligibility for district directors and junior district directors.

Bills had been introduced in both the U. S. Senate and House of Representatives prohibiting the dissemination of materials harmful to persons under the age of eighteen and exhibition of movies or other presentations harmful to such persons. Delegates to the 75th convention urged the enactment of these bills into law. Another resolution urged FFWC members to request the legislature to increase funds for child welfare and youth services. Under community improvement, the Coral Gables Woman's Club presented a resolution asking that the Florida Power Service Commission adopt tariffs, rules and regulations which would require placing all overhead utility lines, except major electric distribution lines, underground. This resolution was adopted as well as one against artificial school districts which required busing children out of their natural school districts. No mention was made of the cause for these artificial school districts which was that the courts were attempting to integrate the schools, resulting in black children being bused to formerly all white schools and vice-versa.

An emergency resolution asked the Florida Legislature to enact a law requiring that all food markets have a state inspected scale accessible to patrons to give consumers protection against dishonest or negligent dealers.

11 – The Seventies

FFWC officers for 1970-1972 were: Mrs. J.C. Pratt, President; Mrs. Karl F. King, First Vice President; Mrs. E. Ross Harris, Second Vice President; Mrs. Harold Wayne, Recording Secretary; Corresponding Secretary; Mrs. C. Hubbard Davis, Treasurer and Mrs. Richard Conibear, Director of Junior Clubs.

A New Focus

While the 75th Convention was meeting April 22nd, millions of Americans participated in anti-pollution demonstrations which marked the celebration of the first EARTH DAY. Both GFWC and FFWC began a concentrated effort to encourage members and communities to observe responsible consumption and awareness of the necessity to take care of the planet. Many organizations such as the Sierra Club, Nature Conservancy, National Wildlife Federation and Audubon Society were researching and publishing their findings which warned of the diminishing quality of air and water and the extinction of species. Air over some cities had become so polluted that citizens with breathing disorders were admonished to stay inside on certain days when the quality of the air was particularly bad.

The theme of Mrs. Pratt's administration was "Build for a Better Future." Mrs. Earl A. Brown, President of the General Federation of Women's Clubs had declared that the issue of the 70s was a "Better Environment" and she had urged the six departments of the General Federation to attempt to accomplish projects within their spheres of influence which would contribute to cleaning up and salvaging litter from their own back yards, crusading for clean air and clean water and pressing for laws to "insure your survival".

Green Stamps for the Homeless

It was during Mrs. Pratt's administration that Hacienda Girls' Ranch became a project of the Florida Federation. The idea of a home for "homeless" girls originated with concerned citizens in Brevard County. Much credit is due to Rollin W. Zimmerman, a lieutenant in the Brevard County Sheriff's department. In the early 60s there was no provision for girls who through no fault of their own needed a safe place to live. It was because of "Zim's" concern that the idea of Hacienda Girls' Ranch was born. Their first home was a temporary one — an old house in Cocoa which housed eight girls. Members of women's clubs in Cocoa and Melbourne helped to make the old house habitable for the girls. These club women alerted the members of the Florida Federation to the need for a home for girls who were not delinquent but for various reasons either had no home or had to be removed from the homes where they were. Under Mrs. Pratt's leadership FFWC adopted Hacienda as its state project and began a state-wide fund raising effort to build the first cottage. The 1971 spring issue of *The Clubwoman* asked for a green stamp book (value $2.00) from each club member to help Hacienda. (During the 70s many retail stores gave green stamps with each $1.00 purchase and these could be pasted into books and taken to a "green stamp store" where one could purchase household merchandise in exchange for books of stamps.) Various money raising projects for Hacienda were enthusiastically begun. Clubs as well as individual club members responded to FFWC's fund raising efforts so well that the treasurer's report ending March 15, 1972, showed receipts of $46,814.08 in the Hacienda Fund. "Pratt Cottage" at Hacienda Ranch for Girls opened its doors to ten girls in June of 1972.

In 1972 the Junior Sorosis Club of Orlando won first place and an award of $10,000 in the GFWC Community Improvement Program (CIP). This program, sponsored by Sears Roebuck, had 100 per cent participation by FFWC clubs and it was the second time the Junior Sorosis Club of Orlando had won first place.

Mrs. Pratt reported that FFWC held the first state wide conservation conference and led workshops on local problems of water and air pollution. Many clubs became interested in the legislative process and wrote letters to their legislators concerning the vital problems of conservation. Cooperating with the U. S. Forestry Service, FFWC began the Trout Pond Park project which was the only recreational area in the United States for the handicapped. Ninety-seven per cent of the Florida Federation's clubs contributed to the outstanding success of this project and money remaining in the "Pennies for Pines" fund was transferred to the park fund. At the dedication of Trout Pond Park located in the Appalachicola National Forest near Tallahassee, David and Julie Eisenhower shared the speaker's stand with Governor Claude Kirk.

In the Home Life Department, the primary emphasis was on the welfare of children and senior citizens, and the education of the public about the need for early diagnosis and treatment of epi lepsy. Geriatrics and Gerontolgy were subjects for study and discussions as Florida increasingly became a haven for retired and aging people.

Just after the FFWC 75th Convention, May 4, 1970, four students were killed at Kent State University in Ohio by National Guardsmen called out to quell student protests against the war in Vietnam. There was general disagreement among the citizenry about the event. Many people felt that force was the only way to control the protesting students but many others were against the use of deadly force and deeply regretted the Kent State tragedy. Those seeking easy and simple answers blamed all the protests on Communistic influences. Certainly the generational gap grew increasingly wider and there was much hand-wringing, but it solved no problems.

The 76th Convention was held in April, 1971, in Jacksonville. In addition to the usual business of FFWC, delegates responded to the general concern of citizens all over the country with the unknown fate of more than 1500 American citizens who were missing in action or were prisoners of war in Southeast Asia. A resolution was adopted demanding that the government of Vietnam adhere to the clearly stipulated terms of the Geneva Convention which accorded basic humanitarian protection to prisoners of war.

The Fall Board meeting was held in September, 1971, in Fort Lauderdale and the 77th Convention was held in April, 1972, at the Fort Harrison Hotel in Clearwater where delegates reacted to the problems of the country reaffirming a resolution of GFWC concerning the preservation of our free institutions which read in part:

> WHEREAS, Subversive methods being used to undermine the free institutions of the Government of the United States are: organized rioting, crime in the streets, trafficking in narcotics, smut, pornography, obscenity and perversion, promotion of disrespect for authority and disrespect for the flag of the United States of America, breakdown of law and order, destruction of the family and attack on our educational and religious institutions, and
>
> WHEREAS, The Congress and others in authority have been apathetic about enacting and enforcing laws needed to combat the forces in our country bent on destruction of our free way of life, therefore, the Florida Federation of Women's Clubs urges its members to join a mobilzation of woman power through Leadership Foundation and other organized women's groups, for the restoration of a moral climate and perpetuation of our free institutions.

This convention also adopted a resolution against the forced busing of children away from their neighborhood schools.

Smut on the Tube

A strongly worded resolution was directed to the Columbia Broadcasting System and those of other networks asking that the decision to broadcast X-rated movies after 11:30 at night be reversed. They declared that "The invasion of American homes with profanity, vulgarity, adultery, incest, homosexuality, child molestation, nudity and sadism represents a moral challenge of major proportions and dirty movies making their debut at 11:30 p.m. will soon move into prime time, and the urgent need to dam this flood of smut and filth that threatens to invade our homes and give false impressions to our children demands courageous action on the part of those who care."

Officers elected for the years 1972-1974 were: Mrs. Karl F. King, President; Mrs. E. Ross Harris, First Vice President; Mrs.

Elmer Norton, Second Vice President; Mrs. John O'Steen, Recording Secretary; Mrs. Edward L.Mockler, Treasurer and Mrs. Raymond Faubion, Director of Junior Clubs.

FFWC projects under Lucille King's administration were: Hacienda Girls' Ranch, restoration of FFWC Headquarters and promotion of the Endowment Fund. Her theme was "Restore: Honesty, Integrity, Morals and Truth."

In September of 1972, Fall Board met in St. Petersburg and in April of 1973 the 78th Convention was held at the Carillon Hotel in Miami Beach.. An emergency resolution "BIG CYPRESS SWAMP ACQUISITION BY THE FEDERAL GOVERNMENT" was sent back to committee for further consideration. An emergency resolution endorsed House Bill #1 which provided for construction of bicycle trails and footpaths along state roads.

More than $27,900.00 was raised for the restoration of the headquarters building which was more than enough to replace the roof, air-condition the building, buy some new furniture, paint inside and out, refurbish the landscaping and buy a new copy machine.

Contributions to Hacienda amounted to $50,079.92 thus assuring that a second cottage would be built. The Endowment Fund was increased by $7,000.00. FFWC sponsored overseas tours and made more than $12,000.00 for the organization. Donations to Trout Pond amounted to almost $7,000.00.

The Environmental Responsibility Division promoted projects for the recycling of aluminum cans, glass and paper, controlling litter and managing solid waste.

Registration at Fall Boards and Conventions broke all previous attendance records during Mrs. King's administration with 1,194 registering for the convention of 1974. Jeannine Faubion, Director of Junior Clubs, and Lucille King worked together with remarkable success. The Juniors contributed generously to all FFWC projects as well as raising $4,700.00 for their own project at the Sunland Training Centers. They also participated in two GFWC projects giving $1,900.00 to the National Kidney Foundation and more than $1,200.00 to the National Association for Retarded Citizens. Under Mrs.

Leading the Way: A Century of Service

Faubion's leadership 138 Junior clubs reported on "youth" projects and 164 clubs incorporated leadership development training in their programs.

Integration in the Bylaws

In April of 1973 a revised addition of the CHARTER and BYLAWS of FFWC was completed. An important change was made under membership — previously, eligibility had stated that the federation members should be white women. The revised eligibilty stated only that members should not be members of any subversive group or organization. The matter of race had caused a problem in the early days of General Federation. Previous to 1902, club women of Montana did not wish to join GFWC for two reasons: one being the distance they would have to travel, the other was that they did not want to get involved in the discussion of the color question. Georgia had a plan that left no doubt that only clubs of white women could belong to the General Federation. The Massachusetts plan would have the General Federation made up of state federations with each state controlling its own membership. In 1902, Missouri offered a compromise which was accepted based on states' rights. If a club was a member of a state federation regardless of its rules about color, it could also be eligible for membership in the General Federation. The color question was considered settled in 1904 and 25 clubs from Montana joined the General Federation.

With transportation, restaurants, schools and other public facilities being integrated, the word "white" was taken from the eligibility requirements of FFWC in 1973. This did not mean that local clubs immediately recruited black members. Clubs for the most part remained white and there were few black delegates at FFWC Conventions until the 90's except for occasional international visitors who were warmly welcomed.

Dues were raised in the 1973 by-laws from $1.50 to $2.00.

A Troubled Time

While the published annual reports of the Florida Federation of Women's Clubs recount many accomplishments of departments and clubs during the 1972-1974 administration,

Jessie Hamm Meyer

newspapers, radio and television reminded the citizens of the country that problems world wide and at home grew. The U.S. resumed bombing of Hanoi in retaliation for the North Vietnamese attack across the demilitarized zone; the cold war went on in spite of a strategic arms pact with Russia; Alabama Governor George Wallace was shot and severely wounded while campaigning for the presidency; trials for the "Watergate burglars" kept the attention of the country riveted on the alleged conspiracy of the White House to cover up and obstruct justice.

In spite of disturbing events, the women of the Florida Federation showed amazing strength and perseverance in their aims to make a difference where they were. When Mrs. King and Mrs. Faubion decided on the theme, "Restore Honesty, Integrity, Morals and Truth" at the beginning of their administration they could have had no idea how the entire country would long for those qualities in its government and in the actions of its elected officials only two years later.

The Fall Board met in St. Petersburg in September 1973. Mrs. E. Ross Harris, First Vice President, became President-Elect in January of election year according to the By-laws which had been completely revised in 1973. The 79th Convention was held at the Robert Meyer Hotel in Jacksonville. Elected for the 1974-1976 administration were: Mrs. Elmer M. Norton, First Vice President; Mrs. Raymond Faubion, Second Vice President; Mrs. Wyatt O. Crane, Recording Secretary, Mrs. E. Sinclair Eaton, Treasurer and Mrs. Kenneth Perkins, State Director of Juniors.

Patriotism Sparks Action and Reaction

Mrs. Harris had a comprehensive theme for her administration: "Women United - To Rededicate Ourselves - Our Efforts, Our Influence, Our Personal Example - To a Rekindling of the Fires of Patriotism, A Renewed Respect for Law and Order, A Return to Basic Values of Life and the Fulfillment of the American Dream of Peace for All Nations." The Bicentennial Celebration theme was a part of almost every activity of the years 1974-1976. The clubs sold over 1,000 Bicentennial commemorative plates and presented others to various foreign representatives.

Meanwhile, the King-Harris Cottage was completed at Hacienda Girls' Ranch and dedicated April 10, 1976. The total cost including carpeting (except where vinyl was indicated), draperies, kitchen equipment and landscaping was $59,902.14. TOT LOT, a playground for handicapped and retarded children was created at Trout Pond at a cost of $13,497.71.

Seventeen new clubs were added to the federation making Florida one of the few states honored by GFWC at the 1975 convention for a gain in membership. Mrs. Faubion as chairman of district directors worked closely with the directors to achieve the organization of the new clubs. She also updated and reprinted the District Director's Manual and brought the FFWC history up to date.

As Director of the Junior Clubs, Lois Perkins emphasized at all membership levels the development of leadership giving continuous opportunities to members for self-improvement and self- confidence. Mrs. Perkins worked particularly toward making Juniors feel a part of the Florida Federation and they responded with $861,303.32 worth of support through 16,851 projects in federation projects as well as $150,442.11 (in monies and goods) in support of the State Junior Project — Mental Retardation.

President Richard Nixon resigned on August 4, 1974, and Vice- President Gerald Ford became President. On September 8, 1974, Gerald Ford issued a full pardon to ex-President Nixon for any and all federal crimes which he "committed or may have committed." The action of President Gerald Ford stopped any trials, just as Nixon's resignation had stopped impeachment proceedings. The country could now to some extent put the headlines of the Watergate cover-up, abuse of power, and obstruction of justice, behind them and press forward on the problems at hand.

Opposition to Equal Rights

The Fall Board meeting was held at the Hilton Hotel in Gainesville, September 22nd-25th, 1974, and the 80th Convention was at the Diplomat Hotel in Hollywood.

Delegates to this convention adopted resolutions:

1. Opposing a petition to the Federal Communications Commission to ban all Christian broadcasting.

2. Opposing confinement of mentally ill patients with hardened criminals.

3. Urging Congress to repeal the earnings limitation on Social Security

4. Opposing the plan to destroy the old State Capitol Building.

5. Opposing the Equal Rights Amendment to the U.S. Constitution. Delegates also voted to file a minority report opposing the Equal Rights Amendment with GFWC.

The Equal Rights Amendment was introduced in Congress in 1923 and after much study the General Federation of Women's Clubs endorsed it in 1944. In 1967, during Carolyn Pearce's presidency, GFWC reaffirmed its support for ERA. In 1971 GFWC again reaffirmed its support for ERA and published articles in the General Federation *CLUBWOMAN* magazine. One article written by Mrs.A.Paul Hartz, chairman of the GFWC Legislative Committee, stated:

> For over a quarter of a century, the General Federation of Women's Clubs has been on record for the passage of the Equal Rights Amendment to the Constitution of the United States, believing that only through such an amendment can women be guaranteed the full protection of the law.

A pamphlet was written, printed and distributed in the hope that it would be helpful to women in their efforts to obtain passage of the amendment. The pamphlet was in the form of questions and answers, the first of which was: "Why an Equal Rights Amendment?" The answer was:

> An Equal Rights Amendment is essential to assure equality under the law for men and women. At the time the U.S. Constitution was adopted, women acquired no rights as citizens. Those who drafted the Constitution never considered changing the status of women from what they 'enjoyed' under the English Common Law; married women could not own personal property, make contracts, sue in court, or serve as legal guardians for their own children. In fact, a woman was not a legal entity but a chattel. She had no absolute right to employment or education. There are still many laws which restrict women's ownership and control of their property rights, or their enjoyment of full equality of civil and political rights.

There were twenty-three other questions and answers included in the pamphlet.

Arguments against the amendment presented in the press in the early 70s included such ideas as: "the amendment would do away with separate rest rooms for men and women; it would undo much legislation that had been passed particularly to protect women." Certainly, delegates to the 1974 convention in Hollywood had a difference of opinion with GFWC.

Delegates who voted their opposition to the amendment probably never had to confront an employer who frankly said, "For this work we pay men $115 but for women doing this same job we pay $85." Even school boards often had dual pay scales for men and women teachers. Their rationale was "Women teach for pin money, men must support families."

By 1974, dual pay scales were not as prevalent as they had been, but in many areas, it was very difficult for women to rise to higher paying jobs. Women professors in universities were often held in the lower paying assistant professor jobs while men rose through the ranks to full professorships. With no Equal Rights Amendment, change had to come through proof of discrimination rather than through an amendment to the Constitution giving women equal rights.

In the case of the ERA Amendment there were many differences of opinion among women all over the country. The Florida Federation of Women's Clubs opposed the ERA Amendment and by June of 1982, the deadline for ratification showed 35 states had ratified, three short of the 38 required for ratification. As late as 1993, statistics showed that women workers from laborers to PhDs still earned only 69 cents to the dollar of their male counterparts and at many state universities women made up only 13 per cent of the tenured faculty.

Defending the CIA, the Canal, School Prayer

The Fall Board of 1975 was held September 28-October 1 at the Americana Hotel in Miami Beach. Delegates to this meeting voted to "urge Congress to act in such a way as not to impair the effectiveness of the Central Intelligence Agency." A reader of the minutes of that meeting must question why such an action was taken. It was undoubtedly prompted by the June 10th report of a "blue ribbon" panel headed by Vice President

Nelson Rockefeller which described illegal CIA operations, including records on 300,000 persons and groups and infiltration of agents into anti-war, political and black movements. Delegates recognized that these illegal activities had taken place and were in favor of an "oversight committee" to prevent such illegal activities in the future but they felt that the U.S. Government's ability to deal with international intelligence should not be diminished.

Another resolution of the Fall Board supported "Undiluted United States Sovereignty over the Panama Canal Zone". (According to historians the United States never had sovereignty over the Panama Canal Zone — one proof of this being that babies born at Gorgas Hospital in the Canal Zone of Panamanian parents did not become United States citizens. Babies born of any foreign parents while in the United States are automatically United States citizens since they were born on the sovereign territory of the United States.) The text of the resolution was long and delineated the history of treaties and the United States' undisputed ownership of the Canal. (The debate may have confused ownership and sovereignty but it was heated and continued among citizens long after a treaty was signed that gave up the United States' role in operation of the Canal by 1999.)

Delegates also voted to endorse Senate Bill 283 and House Bill 2414 "limiting the jurisdiction of the Supreme Court of the United States and the district courts to enter any judgement, decree, or order, denying or restricting, as unconstitutional, voluntary prayer in any public school."

Opposing Day-Care Centers, Blessing the B-1

The 81st Convention met at the Plaza Hotel, Daytona Beach, in late April of 1976. Delegates to this convention voted two emergency resolutions. One opposed the Child and Family Services Act which would create a network of day-care centers funded by the federal government. Fear that the "bill would commit the vast moral authority of the national government to the communal approach to child rearing" prompted their opposition. The second emergency resolution favored a strong defense and the building of the B-1 bomber. Fear of an attack of "missile aggressiveness" from Russia was the reason given for this resolution.

Mrs. Elmer Norton, President-Elect, automatically became President. Elected for the 1976-1978 administration were: Mrs. Raymond Faubion, First Vice President; Mrs. Wyatt O. Crane, Second Vice President; Mrs. George A. Gant, Recording Secretary; Mrs. Richard H. Conibear, Treasurer and Mrs. William Blount, Director of Juniors. Mrs. John Mace was Member-at-Large; Mrs. Ralph N. Wood. Sr., was appointed Corresponding Secretary; Mrs. James Matheny, Finance Chairman and Mrs. Paul Bearrs, Parliamentarian.

Mrs. Norton chose "Unity through Unselfish Understanding" as the theme for her administration and introduced an ambitious FFWC 5 star program:

Point 1 — 2,800 new quality members per year

Point 2 — 28 new quality clubs per year

Point 3 — $25,000 per year to the Endowment Fund

Point 4 — $25,000 per year to the President's Project, Special Olympics

Point 5 — $25,000 per year for Pennies for People - a conservation program to preserve lands, beauty and energy for us, the people.

"The money programs are an appeal to the individual club member," she said, "not the club treasury, to give two cents (2¢) per week to each. If this is done, the monies can be raised without placing an undue burden on your club. This is our aim."

The 82nd Fall Board Meeting was held at Hilton-on-the Bay at St. Petersburg, September 16-19, 1976. The Board of Directors accepted the resignation of Mrs. Wyatt O. Crane with regret and elected Mrs. John Mace, FFWC Second Vice-President and Mrs. Kenneth Perkins, Member at Large. The Florida Indian Scholarship Fund was renamed the Florida Indian Fund.

Anti-Gay, Anti-Abortion, Anti-ERA

The 82nd Convention was held April 20-24, 1977, at the Sheraton Towers in Orlando. Four emergency resolutions were adopted:

1. Endorsed the Kissimmee River Restoration Act of 1976

2. Opposed H.R. 2998 to amend the Civil Rights Act of 1964. (H.R. 2998 was intended to prevent discrimination against homosexuals)

3. Opposed the drafting of women into military service

4. Urged legislation to lower automobile insurance rates.

Delegates also voted to go on record as opposing any plan for additional gasoline taxation as a means of reducing energy consumption; or any additional taxation on automobiles because of gasoline consumption.

September 21-25, 1977, the 83rd Fall Board met again at the Sheraton Towers in Orlando where delegates took their stand in the form of resolutions in which:

1. Opposition to relinquishing sovereignty over the Panama Canal was reaffirmed and messages of this action were sent to Senators Lawton Chiles and Richard Stone, Florida members of the House of Representatives and to the State Department.

2. An investigation of the tax-funded I.W.Y. (International Women's Year) Convention in Houston was demanded since "most of the resolutions adopted do not represent the views of this organization."

3. Retention of the Florida Cabinet system was urged.

4. An earnest appeal was sent to Congress to adopt the Hyde Amendment to the 1977-78 Labor-HEW appropriations bill prohibiting Medicaid funding for abortions except where the life of the mother was at stake if the fetus were carried to term.

5. Endorsement of the GFWC resolution opposing the establishment of a national consumer protection agency was made, and GFWC and all Florida Congressmen notified.

FFWC's 83rd Convention was held April 11-15, 1978, at Sarasota Hyatt House. President Eve Norton's aims for her administration were partially realized when FFWC presented a check for $25,007.35 to Special Olympics' Director, Bill Crutchfield, and another for $13,685.97 for "Pennies for People" to the Supervisor of the Florida Division of Forestry. The Endowment Fund showed a marked increase but the number of new clubs and new members while considerable did not reach the goals set by Mrs. Norton. Much effort was put into membership drives and there was some net gain, although clubs all over the country were finding their members decreasing as more and more women joined the work

Leading the Way: A Century of Service

force and had less time and energy to devote to club work.
Resolutions at the 83rd convention:
> 1. Reaffirmed opposition to the Panama Canal Treaty and supported Undiluted U.S. Sovereignty Over the Panama Canal.
> 2. Opposed the ERA Extension Time Bill.
> 3. Adopted an emergency resolution in behalf of oil production in America.

(Heavy dependence on imported oil was brought to the attention of U.S. citizens in 1973 when Arab oil-producing states declared a total embargo on all exported oil to the United States. The embargo was lifted within a few months but the price of oil increased greatly and resulted in higher prices of all oil related products.)

Officers for the 1978-1980 administration installed were: Mrs. Raymond Faubion, President; Mrs. John W. Mace, First Vice President; Mrs. Kenneth Perkins, Second Vice President; Mrs. Glen Mathews, Recording Secretary; Mrs. J.M. Parker, Corresponding Secretary; Mrs. John D. Simmons Treasurer; Mrs. Louis E. Lutz, Director Of Junior Clubs, Mrs. Donald Weber, Finance Chairman and Mrs. Donald J. Taylor, Member-at-Large.

Accomplishments reported by Jeannine Faubian during her presidency were as she said "both amazing and gratifying." A new "Energy American Style" energy education program was co-sponsored by the Florida Petroleum Council and FFWC. Speakers were made available on all energy resources and clubs were encouraged to hostess NEED (Nuclear Energy Education Day) programs. Nuclear plants had become a topic of much discussion since an accident occurred March 28, 1979, at the Three Mile Island Nuclear Plant in Pennsylvania.

In September of 1979, the Florida Federation received a special recognition plaque from the president of the International Special Olympics Committee for the most outstanding contributions made by a volunteer organization.

The Home Life Department took the lead with 96 per cent of the clubs participating in a statewide immunization program called "Protect Every Child." The Public Affairs Department reported work on "Get Out the Vote" campaigns, workshops designed to help stop the crime of shop lifting and work with the Bureau of Highway Safety.

The Arts Department participated in all sorts of creative arts projects with art contests, festivals and creative writing classes. Some members trained as docents in museums and others hosted concerts. One of the Arts Department projects searched for and encouraged nonprofessional artists by giving them opportunities to display their work. In some cases clubs gave scholarships so artists might continue to study.

Mrs. Louis E. Lutz received reports from junior clubs which indicated that the "Florida Juniors had a total of 18,421 programs and projects, 437,785 hours of service and a grand total of $1,984,449.50 donated or disbursed through club, private or public channels." Juniors worked both at membership extension and retention using the theme "Let It Begin With Me." Membership in FFWC totaled 26,554 in 225 general Clubs and 108 junior clubs.

Interest rates during the late 70s were higher than they had been previously thus bringing a greater return on FFWC's Endowment Fund. Among other budgeted items, this allowed elected officers and chairman a more reasonable amount to cover desk expenses and necessary travel. (The ever present concern of any volunteer organization has been and perhaps always will be that talented and capable people may not be able to afford the expenses that serving in an office requires. When an organization can allow desk and travel expenses for its officers and chairmen on the local level as well as the state level, the pool of available talent is greatly enhanced.)

The Treasurer's report for 1979 showed that the headquarters' secretary salary was $7,261.00 and $6,817.00 had been paid for extra help.

The Fall Board meeting of September 1978 was at the Lakeland Civic Center and the 84th Annual Convention was held at the Americana Hotel at Bal Harbour. Some amendments to articles and bylaws were adopted and a resolution "Opposing any additional increases of the Federal Government's role in providing health care for the nation" was adopted. The Fall Board meeting September 23-26, 1979, was held at the Hilton Inn Gateway at Kissimmee. Some restoration funds were allocated to enclose a porch at the headquarters building and to purchase a reverse cycle wall air conditioning unit.

Also approved was sending of the following mailgram to each U. S. Senator and to President Jimmy Carter: "The Florida Federation of Women's Clubs has long been opposed to second-rate military power of the United States of America. Therefore, the Board of Directors of FFWC strongly urges the unequivocal defeat of the Salt II Treaty. Your NO vote is extremely important in view of the upcoming election year." (Mailgrams included the number of members in FFWC; the cost of sending the mailgrams was underwritten by the Palm Springs Woman's Club, District 11.)

The 85th Convention was held April 19-23, 1980, at the Dutch Inn, Lake Buena Vista, with a total of 1,376 women attending. A resolution "requesting the Florida Legislature to petition the United States Congress to begin an amendment to the Federal Constitution permitting voluntary non-sectarian prayers in Public Schools and religious symbols or music," was adopted.

Jessie Hamm Meyer

12 – The Eighties

OFFICERS for 1980-1982 were Mrs. John W. Mace, President; Mrs. Kenneth Perkins, First Vice President; Mrs. Louis E.Lutz, Second Vice President; Mrs. H. Lake Hamrick, Recording Secretary; Mrs. Lee A. Thornburg, Jr.,Treasurer; Mrs. William N. Babcock, Director of Junior Clubs.

Mrs. Mace chose to use the stated goal of GFWC as part of her theme: UNITY IN DIVERSITY - LIGHT THE WAY. Her special emphasis areas were:

Crime Reduction/Anti-Shoplifting

Energy American Style

Hacienda Girls' Ranch

Special Olympics

Legislation

FREE (A program of GFWC to "make members and communities knowledgeable about the benefits of our American Free Enterprise System."

Fall Board delegates met at Sheraton Twin Towers, Orlando, September 21-24, 1980. Approximately 27 workshops were held for departments and divisions.

The effect of OPEC's oil embargo by Arab member states in 1973-74, although lasting only from October until March, had shaken the economy. Alternate sources of energy were uppermost in the minds of many citizens. The price of gasoline and all products using oil had sky-rocketed, although gasoline was still cheaper in the United States than it was anywhere else in the industrialized world. The delegates to the Fall Board adopted a resolution favoring a bill that granted coal pipelines full, eminent domain over non-federal lands yet preserved state water rights.

Crime and Energy

The 86th convention met at Lakeland, April 26-30, 1981. Violent crime was reported up 27% in 1980 and burglary was up by 25%. Delegates adopted a resolution urging Congress to pass legislation introduced by Florida Senator Lawton Childs directed at strengthening the ability of law enforcement officials to deal with organized crime and to clarify the existing law in order to allow expanded cooperation by the military in drug law enforcement.

Crime reduction and anti-shoplifting programs continued during the administration of Mrs. Mace. Both General and Junior clubs were involved in educational programs and Court Watching Seminars around the state as FFWC volunteers gave 62,161 hours to 1,380 projects and spent $80,753.07 trying to educate people on crime prevention and anti-shoplifting programs. The Florida Federation gave $8,568.49 for educational material on crime prevention to the State Library of Florida in Tallahassee and this material was available to all the people of Florida through their local libraries. A pamphlet entitled *Crime Prevention*, a bibliography of books and films on the topic of crime prevention, was printed in cooperation with the Department of State, the State Library of Florida and FFWC. This project was praised by judges and law enforcement officers because it served as a link between the private sector, volunteers, government, educational institutions and law enforcement. Being a part of the President's Task force on Private Sector Initiatives, FFWC was able to add to the national effort on education for crime prevention.

Realizing the powerful influence of television on the American family and believing that both public and commercial television could be a force for family unification, delegates to the 1981 Convention resolved that "the Florida Federation of Women's Clubs work with and through the Parent Participation TV Workshop and with individual broadcasters to advance the use of commercial television as a vehicle through which family communication can be improved, school skills increased, and critical viewing habits enhanced."

Fall Board September 18-23, 1981, was held at the Dutch

Inn Resort Hotel, Lake Buena Vista. A motion was approved that "the Board of Directors of FFWC go on record supporting President Reagan's stand upholding the laws which prohibit striking by Federal employees in the case of the recent air controllers' strike."

The 87th Convention met April 30-May 5, 1982 at the Diplomat Resort and Country Club, Hollywood. There were reports of accomplishments during the 1980-82 administration. "Energy American Style" continued as an educational program for both club members and the public with classes and seminars on meter reading, ways to save energy, and the advantages and disadvantages of the use of particular kinds of energy. These programs totalled 1,639 with 31,345 volunteer hours and $60,713.90 spent. Sponsors of the energy program were: Gulf Oil, Tenneco Oil, Chevron U.S.A., Exxon,U.S.A., Florida Rural Electrification and Florida Petroleum. The aim of the "Energy American Style" program was "to prevent OPEC (Organization of Petroleum Exporting Countries) from dictating the future of America."

Hacienda Girls' Ranch received $62,818.60 plus many gifts of clothing, books, household equipment and special occasion gifts and for the first time each club appointed a Hacienda Chairman.

A Special Olympics project to "Sponsor an Athlete" at $34.50 each provided more than $12,000.00 for approximately 350 handicapped or impaired athletes. The Hugh O'Brien Youth Seminar for Youth Leaderhip (HOBY) received financial support from FFWC and local clubs.

The "I Did It" buttons, originated by Mrs. Mace, were intended to be an incentive to club members to get new members into their clubs and at the end of her administration she reported that there had been a significant increase in the membership of the Florida Federation.

Mrs. E.D. Pearce installed the following officers to serve during 1982-1984: Mrs. Kenneth Perkins, President; Mrs. Louis E. Lutz, First Vice President; Mrs. Lee Thornburg, Jr., Second Vice President; Mrs. W. L. Wood, Jr., Recording Secretary; Mrs. Donald Weber, Treasurer and Mrs. Michael G. Foerster, Director of Junior Clubs. Appointments were Mrs. Edward Boyack, Corresponding Secretary; Mrs Eugene Smith, Finance Chairman and Mrs. Paul Bearss, Parliamentarian. Mrs. William Babcock was elected Member-at-Large.

Leadership Programs

Lois Perkins (Mrs. Kenneth) chose "Leadership — Building Pathways to a Successful Tomorrow" as the theme for her administration. Mrs. Perkins used the President's Project Fund toward the training of Juniorettes. Trained leadership was a goal of her administration and she initiated Leadership Incentive Awards which were co-sponsored by Chevron, U.S.A. Recognizing that the nation's future depends upon its youth, her emphasis area of youth crossed all departments and special project areas. Development of our youth as future federation members and community service leaders became a reality as the 1983 Convention body accepted the Juniorette category into the FFWC structure. Eight Juniorette Clubs with 496 members were admitted at the Fall Board of 1983 and one more at the convention in 1984. While Carolyn Pearce was President of GFWC (1966-1968), a new category of membership was organized known as the Juniorettes. Mrs. Pearce had said,"I can think of no better means of assuring continuity of federation work and the influence for community good that we represent than by encouraging the formation of GFWC clubs for Juniorettes."

Mrs. Perkins, her officers, committee chairmen and members of FFWC had the privilege and the task of hosting the General Federation of Women's Clubs International Convention in 1983. Mrs. Perkins appointed Carole McLeod, Chairman for the GFWC Convention.

Fall Board of Directors met in September 1982 and the principal speaker was Juanita Bryant, GFWC International President. Workshops emphasized recruiting new members, orientation programs, membership retention, and federation interaction.

The 88th Convention met in Kissimmee, April 1983. A skit written and co-ordinated by Julie Babcock was presented to the delegates. It was the FFWC skit used at the 1982 Convention inviting GFWC to hold its 1983 Convention at Twin Towers in Orlando. Carole McLeod reported progress on plans for the GFWC Convention and announced chairmen who were working on various functions relating to the Convention. President Perkins thanked the hundreds of members who had been working for months and the clubs that had contributed to the finances of successfully hostessing the 92nd GFWC International Convention. She urged all Florida clubwomen to take advantage of their unique opportunity to attend the International Convention to be held in Orlando.

In the Fall issue of the *The Florida Clubwoman* Martha Jane Ramsay, Editor, reported:

> The theme of the GFWC Convention was "Volunteers in Action." The Florida Executive Committee were clad in identical Federation Green linen suits and white blouses with a small print — the logo of Mrs. Perkin's administration, yellow roses.
>
> Howard K. Smith, journalist and newscaster, Hugh O'Brian, HOBY Founder and George Bush, Vice-President of the United States, were among the speakers.
>
> Florida clubwomen ran the gamut, embellished tables at every meal function, 'Florida' was everywhere .....citrus, driftwood, pelicans and fish ... to name a few. This meeting was highlighted by ladies in lovely native costumes from around the world and visited by illustrious dignitaries ... Shamu and Al E. Gator.
>
> Plaudits for Carole McLeod, the Convention Chairman. Of course, there was a great deal of help and cooperation but Carole was responsible for putting committees together.

The 92nd GFWC Convention unanimously approved the GFWC Women's History and Resource Center as a permanent part of the General Federation of Women's Clubs.

During Lois Perkin's administration the merits of the Hugh O'Brien Student Leadership Program were recognized by increased financial support for students to attend the seminars. A total of $15,202.00 was contributed and enthusiastic student ambassadors from the HOBY program inspired delegates at FFWC Conventions.

There was strong emphasis on volunteerism from both GFWC and FFWC during the 80s and President Perkins' officers and chairmen reported that a total of 318,619 hours were given toward 1576 projects during her administration.

Energy Awareness Award

"Energy American Style" renewed its goals in the areas of education, legislation, consumerism and youth. FFWC received recognition as the outstanding organization in the nation for its work in energy awareness.

Membership showed an increase of five hundred and twenty-one. Members with fifty years of service were honored at the Fall Board of 1983. Thirty-six were there to receive their certificates and one hundred forty-six requested them. At that same Fall Board, Special Olympics presented FFWC with a special recognition plaque as being the largest single contributor in support of the Special Olympics program.

Hacienda Girls' Ranch was adopted officially as an on-going project by Mrs. Perkins' administration. A building fund was established and $100,000 collected to construct a building that would serve multiple purposes such as medical, library, crafts, storage and office space. A ground-breaking ceremony for the Rainbow Building-Perkins Hall was held on April 14, 1984.

The Public Affairs Department in the Crime Prevention Division introduced a new program, OPERATION CON GAME, which aimed at education in the prevention of con games, bunco and fraud and was endorsed by Florida's Attorney General.

Elected to serve for 1984-1986 were Mrs. Louis F. Lutz, (Judy)President; Mrs. Lee A. Thornburg (Vi), First Vice-President; Mrs.Eugene Smith (Jimmie), Second Vice President; Mrs. W. L. Wood(Phyllis), Treasurer and Mrs. Braxton Bright (Marcia) Director of Juniors.

At the Post-Convention Board of Directors' meeting, Tam Duggan was elected Member-at-Large. Appointments were Carole McLeod, Corresponding Secretary; Julie Babcock, Finance Chairman and Mary Bearss, Parliamentarian.

Mrs. Lutz chose "The Future Belongs to Those Who Shape It with Friendship, Humility and Service" as her theme for 1984-1986. Her special Project was "Good Health-Catch it" and the special emphasis projects were:

Hacienda Girls' Ranch
Disabled-Special Olympics

Leadership Development
HOBY
FFWC Energy in the 80's

The Fall Board Meeting September 28-October 1, 1984, was held at the Grenelefe Resort, Grenelefe, Florida. Delegates kept busy trying to attend as many workshops as possible. Routine financial business involved putting funds to work in CDs that would bring the best rate of interest to the organization.

No Smoking, Please!

The 90th Convention was held at the Orlando Marriott, April 19-23, 1985. This Convention adopted a motion requesting the executive committee to consider as a standing rule NO SMOKING at business sessions, meals and workshops at Fall Board and Convention. This brought about a major change in the atmosphere of meetings and meals where meeting and banquet rooms had been so smoke-filled that many club women could not attend state meetings because the smoke made them ill. Virginia Weber was Chairman of President Lutz' project "Good Health-Catch It". Incentive awards of $50.00 to one club in each district and $200.00 to an overall winning club determined by the percentage of members who quit smoking and total number of pounds lost by members during 1985.

Delegates to the 1985 Convention changed the bylaws to create a new office — that of a third vice president whose duty would be to serve as membership chairman.

Resolutions adopted at the 90th Annual Convention:

1. Pledged support and assistance of FFWC toward accomplishing the assigned tasks and goals of the Florida Rivers Study Commission, whose aim was to devise further means of protecting, preserving and restoring Florida's river systems and wetlands.

2. Urged that funds be appropriated for the enlargement of the Immigration and Naturalization Service to enable it to control illegal immigration effectively,(large numbers of illegal aliens were crowding schools, prisons, health and welfare facilities of the state) and also asked that severe penalties be imposed on those hiring illegal aliens.

3. Pledged support and assistance to the preservation, protection

Leading the Way: A Century of Service

and wise use of Florida's water resources and requested that the Florida Legislature continue to fund and support those agencies dedicated to protecting and preserving Florida's water resources.

The 1985 Fall Board met at the Sheraton St. Johns, Jacksonville, September 20-23. The Executive Committee recommended that a continuing and permanent fund known as the "officers and chairmen's fund" be adopted thus assuring that at least part of the traveling and desk expenses of officers and chairmen of FFWC would be reimbursed.

The 91st Convention met April 25-29, 1986, at the American Dutch Inn, Buena Vista. Again there were amendments to various articles and by-laws. It has been said that nothing delights members of women's organizations more than "tinkering with their by-laws." (This history would be much too long if all changes were noted.)

Resolutions adopted by the delegates to the 91st Convention were:

> 1. Support of increased offshore development of oil and natural gas on submerged federal lands; opposition to "offshore leasing moratoriums as both unnecessary and extremely harmful to the nation's energy and economic future."
>
> 2. Encouraged "the Department of Education and every local school board to recognize the need for change in our schools by upgrading the current school curriculum, evaluating the grading and promotion requirements so that illiterate students are not allowed to graduate; upgrade standards for teacher certification and education; review teacher evaluation processes and salaries and review textbooks at the elementary school level for their emphasis on the phonetic approach to reading.
>
> 3. Urged clubs to educate members and communities about learning disabilities and to encourage discussion of the need for preschool screening programs to determine which children need help and encourage member participation on a volunteer basis to enter into support programs to teach children with learning disability problems in the local community.

President Lutz reported that during 1984-1986 the equivalent value of $9,359,759.67 was disbursed by FFWC clubs and 11,572,700 hours of volunteer service recorded. In May of 1985, the FFWC Rainbow Building was dedicated at Hacienda Girls' Ranch. Contributions from 232 clubs amounted to $255,000 for building and operational funds.

Support of HOBY during 1984-1986 resulted in a total of $32,580.

"Health breaks" were included in many club events and medication education, immunization and health fair activities were promoted and endorsed by FFWC ACTION VOLUNTEERS during these two years.

Incentives were offered individuals as well as local clubs for adding new members and retaining old members. Workshops and "market place" targeted specific ideas to help volunteers cooperate with other organizations. Membership skits, booklets of "Installation Services" and "How to Organize a New Club with Helpful Membership Ideas", a three page pamphlet on "What Is the Florida Federation of Women's Clubs" and a "Guide Line for Treasurers" were prepared and distributed to all districts.

Marcia Bright, Director of Juniors, reported that more than 500 new members had been added to the Juniors' ranks and that 86% of the junior members were employed outside their homes. An astounding $2,299,467 was generated through 19,283 projects and programs along with 680,165 hours of volunteer service.

The Age Structure Committee presented a by-law change that was adopted by the 1986 Convention which allowed juniors to remain in their clubs beyond age 40 if they had joined their club before age 40.

A Note on Names

Officers installed to serve for the 1986-1988 term were Mrs. Lee A. Thornburg (Vi), President; Mrs. Eugene Smith (Jimmie), First Vice President; Mrs. Michael Kevorkian (Virginia), Second Vice President; Mrs. Malcolm Duggan (Tam), Third Vice President; Mrs. Ralph Walby (Sandy), Recording Secretary; Mrs. Gordon Zellers (Diana), Treasurer and Mrs. Dennis Donohue (Karen-Lee), Director of Juniors. Mrs. Alan McLeod (Carole) was elected Member-at-Large. Mrs. W.L. Wood (Phyllis) served as Finance Chairman, Mrs. Braxton Bright (Marcia) as Corresponding Secretary and Mrs. Paul Bearss (Mary) as Parliamentarian. Serving GFWC from the Florida Federation were: Jeannine Faubion - GFWC Recording Secretary; Lois Perkins -

Free Enterprise Chairman; Judy Lutz - Fundraising Chairman; Marcia Bright - Junior Public Relations Chairman.

During the decades of the 70s and 80s growing informality in social, business and organizational situations was reflected in the minutes and all records. Where previously women were referred to only as Mrs. (husband's name), the next step acknowledged that women had names of their own by adding her given name in parentheses and finally records listed officers and chairmen simply by their first names or nicknames and their last names. This was not only a growing informality of customs but also recognition of women for their own achievements and not just as wives.

President Vi Thornburg chose "Volunteers: The Keys to Caring and Sharing" as the theme for her administration and her President's Project was "Endangered Species - SOS (Save Our Species)." Special projects of President Thornburg's administration were:

"A Gift a Life" — Donor Program

"Hands Helping Hacienda" Cookbook

"K.E.E.P. IT - FLORIDA" (Key, Energy, Environmental, Population, Issues To Florida)

Fall Board met at the Sheraton Sand Key Resort, Clearwater, October 3-6, 1986, with a total registration of 1089.

President Thornburg's project "Save Our Species" was given special emphasis at the 1986 Fall Board by the presence of "Tracker," a Florida panther and his caretaker, Jim McMullen, author of *Cry of the Panther*.

Delegates to the Fall Board of Directors' meeting endorsed Jeannine Faubion for 2nd Vice President of GFWC. Treasurer, Dianne Zellers' resignation was accepted with regret and Phyllis Wood was appointed Treasurer for the remainder of the 1986-1988 administration. Other projects of "Save Our Species" was the Bald Eagle rehabilitation program, Audubon's "Adopt a Bird" program, and "Save Our Manatee." Florida club women gave $8,821.22 to these programs and another $4,000 to other organizations working with endangered species. One club invested $5,000 in printing pamphlets about panthers so that all fourth graders in

Florida's public schools could learn more about this endangered species. Each district director helped distribute the pamphlets.

Hope Lodge, a Winn Dixie Corporation project in Gainesville, was designed as a place for cancer patients and a family member to stay while the patient was under-going treatment. Volunteer organizations contributed both services and funds to make Hope Lodge a home away from home for cancer patients. The Florida Federation of Women's Clubs reached its goal of $10,000 to be used to furnish a suite in the lodge.

Energy Education

K.E.E.P. IT FLORIDA was designed as an awareness and educational program to focus on the fast growing population of Florida and to meet the demands on energy and environmental issues. Twelve district workshops, two regional seminars and three energy roundtables were co-hosted with Westinghouse Electric Corporation. Regional Seminars were also co-hosted with AWARE (Alerting Women about Resources and Energy). This far reaching program resulted in an OFFALOT ENERGY EDUCATION PROGRAM. A grant of $208,000.00 was obtained through the Governor's Energy Office from an oil overage fund enabling the FFWC to work with the Governor's Energy Office, the Department of Education's Business Partnership Coordinators and five electric utilities to furnish 6,000 kindergarten classes with the complete OFFALOT COURSE — badges, puppets, workbooks and teacher guides. More than 180,000 kindergarten children participated in the program. Teaching children while very young to save energy was the aim of the program. It was successful in a multitude of ways. In fact, teachers had to warn their pupils that not every switch should be turned "off a lot" after an enterprising and dedicated kindergartner turned off the switch on his grandmother's freezer.

Florida was growing at the rate of 1000 new permanent residents per day overburdening schools, social services, utilities, streets and highways. Added to the already large Hispanic population of South Florida that emigrated from Cuba when Castro's Communists came to power, were

Nicaraguans leaving their country because of the Sandinista-Contra conflict. Florida had become a multi-cultural society with children entering the schools speaking as many as thirty-five different languages.

Although Florida was among the top states in wealth, it continued to be among the lowest in percentage of money actually allocated to education. To Florida's credit, its aim to establish a junior college within driving distance of every student had been largely realized. These junior colleges served three major purposes: first, two years of college preparatory to entering a four year institution; second, two years of specialized vocational training and third, adult education for special skills regardless of previous schooling. The program of establishing junior colleges put Florida at the forefront of most other states in that area. Because there remained much to be done particularly for pre-kindergarten children through their high school years, the FFWC Education Department continuously urged its members to volunteer help at their local schools with tutoring, reading to young children who never had anyone read to them at home, doing clerical duties or working in any way possible to enrich the schools' curriculum.

During the 80s ecology, conservation, the environment, health (dire predictions about the spread of AIDS, a disease for which no cure had been found were being widely publicized), and international tensions affected programs and workshops of club women. Training sessions for new club presidents, vice presidents, treasurers and other officers were held at state meetings during every administration. One of the aims of every president of FFWC was increased membership.

A Threat to Headquarters

Having a headquarters building had been a source of pride as well as a place which enabled the executive committees of each administration to meet and work. An employed secretary kept records readily available and clubs could call the secretary for needed information. The executive committee and chairmen could have planning sessions and workshops at a headquarters that had become "home" to all members of the Florida

Federation. Dismay and shock followed a letter of information that the City of Lakeland intended to buy the remaining 66 years on FFWC's land lease where their building stood. The city planned to build a new City Hall, Electric and Water Administration complex and would exercise the right of eminent domain offering $175,000. The executive committee hired an attorney who got an extension of time from April 30, 1988 until July 1, 1988 for FFWC to vacate their headquarters. The work of the attorney and an appraisal resulted in FFWC receiving $208,000 for its building and the remainder of the lease with $8,000 going to the attorney.

Although occasional drives helped raise money for the on-going expenses of Hacienda, Hands Helping Hacienda committee members thought that an FFWC Cookbook would answer the need for a constant income. (Many clubs publish cookbooks that bring in publication costs at first and then continue for years to produce more funds as orders come in. Churches, Junior Leagues, medical associations, regions, states, countries and individuals write and sell cookbooks.) Members were asked to submit their favorite recipes in various categories and work was begun. It was a monumental task to read, screen, and arrange recipes, get art work, and publish the 350 page *The Florida Cooking Adventure* by cookbook chairmen Betty Taylor and Gloria Kasouf, and their committee, Virginia Weber, Joan Young and Tamara Taylor. Clubs and individuals donated time, recipes and money to help with the development of the cookbook. It was completed, and 10,000 copies were printed in 1987. President Thornburg's theme, "The Keys To Caring And Sharing, was reflected throughout the book with the use of KEYS as a border, and the SHARING of treasured recipes by CARING people."

The 92nd Convention was held at the Peabody, Orlando, April 24- 28, 1987. Delegates adopted a resolution declaring Mabel Meadows Staats "Poet Laureate of FFWC". Another resolution was adopted requiring the elimination of the use of firearms and dogs within the Fakahatchee Strand State Preserve in order to protect the few remaining endangered Florida panthers.

Leading the Way: A Century of Service

Frances Weaver, author and humorist, entertained the 1,290 registrants at the 1987 Convention. Phyllis Wood entertained and instructed delegates with her talk "Let Me Tell You About My Club," a hilarious description of women in a club without parliamentery discipline or guidance. At Fall Board, September 1987, Phyllis Wood (by popular demand) gave a special presentation of Part 2, "Let Me Tell You About My Club".

The 93rd Convention, April 22-26, 1988, met at the Orlando Airport Marriott. Increasing awareness of the environment was reflected in resolutions adopted at this convention.

Because the wetlands of the Everglades area were being degraded by contaminates pumped from the Everglades watershed, the Florida Federation of Women's Clubs "urged that the Governor and Cabinet take all necessary steps to insure that state agencies involved develop and implement a comprehensive plan for achieving compliance with all state and federal regulations at each location where contaminates enter the Everglades wetlands."

Another resolution adopted by the delegates to the 93rd convention urged the "Legislature of the State of Florida to include in its Solid Waste Legislation of 1988 a continuing program of Hazardous Waste Amnesty Days for the health and well being of the people of Florida." They also requested that the solid waste legislation include a beverage container deposit law.

There being no physical examination required of food handlers in Florida, the delegates adopted a resolution stating that the Florida Federation of Women's Clubs take the initiative in introducing a law requiring such examination for food handlers and processors of food consumed by the public and that they support the enactment of such a law.

Jimmie Smith as President Elect became President and elected to serve with her for the 1988-1990 administration were Tammerson Duggan, First Vice President; Marcia Bright, Second Vice President; Bert Alberti, Third Vice President; Judy Martin, Recording Secretary; Elizabeth Tesdorpf, Treasurer; and Pat Warbritton, Director of Junior Clubs. Phyllis Wood, Corresponding Secretary; Mary Bearss, Parliamentarian; and

Jane Parker, Finance Chairman were appointed. Ilo Cox was elected Member-at-Large at the post-convention board meeting. A major job of any incoming president was appointing chairmen for departments and divisions. The 1973 change in the bylaws requiring the First Vice President to become President Elect in the year of elections had proved to be a great improvement because it allowed the incoming president to find members willing to serve as chairmen or in appointive positions before the election and installation of officers at spring convention. The later bylaw change allowing the First Vice President to become President Elect in November of the interim year gave her a longer time to plan her administration.

Mrs. Eugene Smith (Jimmie) chose as her theme "Changing Times — A Quest for the Best". Her projects were Winn-Dixie Hope Lodge, "A Gift - A Life" Donor Progam, and OFFALOT/K.E.E.P. It Florida. FFWC would continue to emphasize Hacienda Girls' Ranch, Membership, Leadership/HOBY, the "Hands Helping Hacienda" Cookbook, and Special Olympics.

The Fall Board met at the Hyatt Regency Westshore, Tampa, September 30 — October 3, 1988. Delegates represented a total membership of 23,142.

The executive committee recommended that scholarship loans remaining on the books all of which had been uncollectable for seven or more years be written off. (There was some doubt as to whether those persons receiving the loans understood that the money was a loan rather than a scholarship.)

Delegates endorsed Jeannine Faubian for GFWC First Vice President. Mrs.Faubion had worked as a board member of FFWC for twenty years, had served as its President (1972-1974) and for twelve years she had been a member of the GFWC Board of Directors. Her education, business experience, training and service would fit her for the presidency of the General Federation. Not since Carolyn Pearce ((1966-1968) had been President of GFWC had Florida had a candidate to lead the world's largest volunteer organization. The Executive Committee recommended that an "I'm For Jeannine" fund be established for the GFWC 1994 Convention. The installation of Mrs. Faubion as President at the GFWC Convention in Atlanta in

Leading the Way: A Century of Service

1994 would require generous funding for a reception and various functions that would showcase the Florida Federation of Women's Clubs not only nationally but internationally.

Florida Federation of Women's Clubs joined all those belonging to the General Federation of Women's Clubs in a celebration of the Centennial of GFWC. The history of the woman's club movement was studied, costumes of 1890 were made and worn, skits were performed and appreciation for early club women deepened during the 1990 Centennial celebration.

The 1989 Convention adopted the concept of establishing a National Children's Day to be observed the first Sunday in October.

Both Pratt and King-Harris cottage at Hacienda Girls' Ranch needed new roofs which were provided through the generosity of the Florida Roofing Association.

One of the major jobs of Jimmie Smith's administration was addressing the problem of a new headquarters. The executive committee was empowered to decide by a two thirds vote on a location and or relocation of FFWC Headquarters within budgetary means. Phyllis Wood, Tam Duggan, Marcia Bright and Joan Young were named to the relocation committee of the new permanent headquarters office.

FFWC Headquarters remained in Lakeland but was moved into temporary quarters twice between 1988 and 1990. Archives, books, and records of all kinds were stored in paper cartons and stacked in storage rooms next to the temporary headquarters office.

The Relocation Committee considered several options including various buildings which could be renovated and used by FFWC but decided to buy a lot in Lakeland and build a headquarters specifically designed to meet the needs of the Florida Federation. A Building Committee was appointed composed of:

Tammerson Duggan, Chairman

Bert Alberti	Jane Parker
Mary Bearss	Jimmie Smith
Marcia Bright	Elizabeth Tesdorpf

Jessie Hamm Meyer

Ilo Cox   Pat Warbritton
Judy Martin   Phyllis Wood

This committee hired Architect Warren H. Smith and Contractor Robin Young, both of Lakeland. The new headquarters building was dedicated May 6, 1990, and declared debt free. Busloads of delegates traveled from the 95th Convention held at the Hyatt Regency in Tampa to tour the new building and to participate in its dedication. Clubs and individuals donated furniture and furnishings. Office and work space provided ample room for storage of supplies, computers and copiers. Two sofas could be converted to queen sized beds for authorized persons wishing to work in the archives or on records for more than one day. A well equipped kitchen was another convenience for volunteers working at headquarters. A large combination archives and board room assured that records could be stored in orderly fashion and were accessible when needed and that the executive committee or any officers or chairmen had a convenient place to work.

A $500,000 grant from the Governor's Energy Office insured further funding for the OFFALOT program and made possible a follow-up program for first graders entitled BRIGHTLAND. The OFFALOT/BRIGHTLAND program reached over 750,000 pupils in the kindergarten and first grades of the 67 school districts of Florida. The project provided material for the parents to understand the program. It was estimated that each pupil shared the program with at least two adults thus reaching at least 1,500,000 adults with facts on energy conservation, safety and environmental awareness. FFWC was responsible for providing an in-service training video for teachers. A state-wide hotline, staffed daily, handled over 2,300 calls in one year.

An environmental supplement to the above programs was designed specifically for Florida under the direction of FFWC. This supplement assisted schools in complying with the 1988 legislative mandate that environmental education must be a part of the curriculum. The Florida Legislature provided $100,000.00 to FFWC to design, produce and distribute these materials.

A task force made up of governmental, university, community college and FFWC personnel revised the OFFALOT/BRIGHTLAND program to include oil recycling. The Governor's Energy Office provided office space in the state capitol to assist FFWC in coordinating these school related activities. FFWC received awards from the Commissioner of Education and the Florida Wildlife Federation because of the OFFALOT/BRIGHTLAND programs and other environmental activities. Total grants of $1,228,000.00 were received by FFWC to fund these projects. The Florida Federation continued to give generously as a list of donations at the end of the 1988-1990 administration showed.

$1,500.00 to the Audubon Society

$5,210.00 to the Nature Conservancy

$1,500.00 to Lowry Park Zoo Manatee Hospital

$5,000.00 to Care

$10,000.00 to Special Olympics

$1,000.00 to Devereaux (A facility for the treatment of autistic patients)

$30,000.00 to Hope Lodge ($10,000.00 to Gainesville, $20,000.00 to Miami)

$4,000.00 to AIDS Research

$33,132.57 to Hacienda (Cookbook proceeds over $25,000.00, donations of materials, gifts, and income from three estates resulted in a total of $93,212.76.)

$43,813.00 to HOBY

General membership was 19,694, juniors 2,046 and juniorettes 652 making a total of 22,392. Nineteen new clubs joined FFWC during the 1988-1990 period. Although the population of Florida increased, membership in FFWC continued to decrease from the alltime high of almost 33,000 members, due mostly to women joining the work force. Clubs found it difficult to recruit 50 to 65 year old members who had the responsibility of their own homes, jobs and sometimes aging parents who occupied both their time and energy. A surprising number of women active in their clubs were 65 to 80. After 80, many members had given years of service and no longer had the energy to do more than attend meetings. A longer life span was a phenomenon that had far- reaching consequences particularly for Florida, a state attractive to more and more retirees.

13 – The Nineties

INSTALLED at the 95th Convention in Tampa, 1990, were Tammerson Duggan, President; Marcia Bright, First Vice President; Bert Alberti, Second Vice President; Ramona Thompson, Third Vice President; Gloria James, Recording Secretary; Pat Crisp, Treasurer and Nancy Crawford, Director of Junior Clubs. A post-convention meeting elected Connie Locke, Member-at-Large. Appointed to serve for the 1990-1992 administration were: Bunny Sandlin, Corresponding Secretary; Judy Martin, Finance Chairman and Mary Bearss, Parliamentarian.

Fall Board met at Twin Towers, Orlando, September 28 – October 1, 1990. Workshops on almost every phase of club work kept registrants busy taking notes, and gathering handouts. Club presidents and chairmen got handbooks consisting of over 200 pages of material written by officers and chairmen. Each fall at the Board of Directors' meeting, new presidents and state chairmen received so many pages of material that they had to be reminded that no club could do everything in every department and division.

The 96th Convention was May 17-20, 1991, at Twin Towers, Orlando. While membership was down, attendance at Fall Boards and Conventions remained around 1000 registrants. To eliminate extended travel from Key West or the Panhandle, meetings were held more often at hotels in Orlando or Tampa. Meetings were planned two to three years in advance to get suitable dates in a hotel with facilities for delegate assemblies, luncheons and banquets as well as enough break-away rooms to allow several workshops to be held simultaneously. There were only five or six hotels in the price range that delegates could afford and in those, a room, tips, and parking cost delegates about $100 a day. Often three or four delegates shared a room. Meals cost from $15 for breakfast to $25 for banquets. To help meet the cost of attending state meetings, some clubs had fund raisers called "Dollars for Delegates". Banquets were usually gala affairs with speakers whose aim was to enlighten, inspire, entertain and motivate their listeners. Luncheons tended to be working meetings with reports from committee chairmen and awards given to clubs for outstanding work in various departments and divisions.

Much of the business of the federation was customarily done by the executive committee previous to the general meetings. For example, the executive committee made the following recommendations to the Board of Directors for the Pre-Convention meeting May 18, 1991.

 1. That a fund entitled "Endowment Operating Fund" be established.

 2. That the Board of Directors recommend to the Convention the endorsement of Jeannine Faubion for President-Elect of GFWC.

 3. That NCNB be ratified as a depository of funds.

 4. Designate Sun Bank, First Florida Bank and C and S Bank as depositories for FFWC funds.

 5. Adopted the 1991-92 budget and authorized the treasurer to pay all bills designated by the budget.

The Board of Directors adopted the recommendations, accepted resignations, ratified appointments, accepted new clubs into membership and elected a member to serve on the nominating committee. This was the type of business that had to be done for an organization handling hundreds of thousands of dollars for over twenty thousand members.

The 96th Convention increased the dues to FFWC to $3.00 per capita plus GFWC dues except for Juniorettes whose per capita dues were $1.00. One dollar of dues was allocated to furnish the member with *The Florida Clubwoman* except for juniorette members.

Resolutions adopted by delegates at the 1991 Convention concerned:

 1. United States-Mexico Free Trade Agreement

 2. Safety for Bicyclists

3. Bicycle, Pedestrian and Passenger Safety

4. Energy Policy

5. State's Reauthorization and Funding of the "Historic Tallahassee Preservation."

The delegates also reaffirmed the resolution on Literacy and Learning Disabilities.

The Fall Board of Directors met at Hyatt Westshore in Tampa, September 27-30, 1991. Workshops for Juniorettes, Juniors and Generals, club presidents, treasurers, department chairmen and divisions were held. Meetings started early in the mornings and continued until late at night. Funds transfers, ratification of appointments and adoption of executive committee recommendations occupied business meetings.

The 97th Convention met at the Clarion Plaza Hotel in Orlando, May 1-4, 1992. In addition to workshops, business, resolutions, inspiring speeches, music, visiting among old friends, skits and awards a major feature of each convention was always the Arts and Crafts exhibit. Each article that was exhibited at the state convention had already been judged at its local club and then had won a blue ribbon at the district level. The chairman and the judges of these exhibits did an incredible job in a very short time. For many years, each convention had a style show — dresses or outfits made and modeled by members. Article II of the Articles Of Incorporation states "The object of the corporation shall be educational, literary, scientific and charitable." Those words traditionally covered a wide field of endeavor.

Wetlands Preservation and Global Warming

The 1992 Convention reaffirmed previous resolutions on the preservation of wetlands and also firmly insisted that the arts be included in school curriculums for a complete education. Another resolution asked that "the state of Florida limit and define liability of volunteers to diminish their concern with regard to personal liability associated with volunteer work, that a Florida Volunteer Immunity Act be enacted by the Legislature of the State of Florida."

An emergency resolution stated:

The Florida Federation of Women's Clubs urges the President of the United States to give full and energetic support by attending and signing the International Treaty on Global Warming in Rio de Janeiro, Brazil, June 1, 1992.

The United States was one of the few industrialized nations that did not sign the International Treaty on Global Warming in 1992.

The 97th Convention changed the bylaws raising registration fees at state meetings from $5.00 to $7.00 and more clearly defined the Juniorette program:

> Juniorette clubs whose membership is composed of young women fourteen (14) through high school — such clubs shall undertake one or more projects of civic, educational or cultural interest. A Juniorette Club must have ten (10) members to be eligible to affiliate membership in FFWC.

The office of State Director of Juniorette Clubs was created and eligibility for the office defined. Term of the office was for one year and representation for clubs was allowed at Fall Board and Annual Conventions.

Black Club Welcomed

Among the new clubs accepted for membership since the last convention was the Electralyte Charity Club with 24 members from District 6 and most of them were present at the 97th Convention. This club's admittance to FFWC marked a change in that its members were black. These women sought to work through a larger organization than their local club would allow. They were unanimously welcomed into the Florida Federation.

Judy Lutz, president of GFWC Southern Region, installed 1992-1994 officers: Marcia Bright, President; Bert Alberti, First Vice President; Ramona Thompson, Second Vice President; Connie Locke, Third Vice President; Bunny Sandlin, Recording Secretary; Judy Martin, Corresponding Secretary; Sandy Townsley, Treasurer; Joyce Johnston, Director of Junior Clubs. Pat Crisp, Finance Chairman and Carl Ann "Jimmy" Stickeler, Parliamentarian. Ann James was elected Member-at-Large at the post convention meeting.

President Marcia Bright chose as her theme, "Children Are The Heart Of It All" and her projects were "Have a Heart for Children" and "Reach Out to Cancer Kids" (R.O.C.K. Camp).

Leading the Way: A Century of Service

    The Florida Federation of Women's Clubs functions through individual clubs and its 14 districts. Each district elects a director who helps the clubs of her district carry out the goals of FFWC. Much of the success of FFWC programs and individual clubs rests on her leadership. She conducts district meetings keeping the clubs in her district well-informed about FFWC. Each fall two state officers attend a meeting in each district. For example, in the fall of 1992, President Marcia Bright and Second Vice President Ramona Thompson visited Districts 8 through 14. First Vice President Bert Alberti and FFWC Director of Junior Clubs Joyce Johnston visited districts 1 through 7.

    These "fall tours" enable club members to get acquainted with their officers and allow the officers to learn more about the clubs and districts. Occasionally, officers reared in one of Florida's urban areas are surprised while visiting the "Other Florida." One Director of Junior Clubs was amazed to learn that there was no K-mart close by where she could buy a pair of tennis shoes for a boat ride on the Suwannee which was part of the hospitality extended by the district club hostessing that fall tour. She was also heard to say, "And you know those women up there drive on those two lane roads at night and there are no street lights." Many of "those women up there" would have thought long and hard before tackling the streets of Tampa, Miami or Jacksonville at night. Florida had long been much more urban than rural, but toward the end of the twentieth century, there were still some club members who canned vegetables from their own gardens and their children were members of 4-H Clubs which FFWC members of an earlier time had sponsored and encouraged.

    The president of the Florida Federation of Women's Clubs had multiple responsibilities in addition to leading her state organization. There were regional meetings of GFWC to attend as well as the meetings of this large international organization. Because of her position as the leader of the Florida Federation, she was named to various boards of other organizations and Governor's committees. These appointments offered her opportunities not only to broaden her knowledge but also to make contacts with other leaders so that her influence and that of the Florida Federation could have a stronger voice when its members took a stand for certain principles or for legislation which the women of FFWC thought necessary. Being president of the Florida Federation demanded skills in communication, efficient use of time, ability to mediate differences and, above all, leadership. Women elected to the presidency of FFWC had served a long apprenticeship in other offices and knew when elected that their two years in that office would be hard work and a tremendous responsibility. No woman agreed to be a candidate for the presidency of FFWC without knowledge of what the office would mean to both her and her family.

Hurricane Andrew

The Fall Board of Directors met at the Clarion Plaza, September 25-28, 1992. Leaders were concerned about poor attendance at district meetings, so President Marcia Bright formed a Membership Action Team (MAT) to study the problem.

Meanwhile, delegates waited anxiously for their friends to arrive from South Florida. Telephone and mail service had been disrupted by Hurricane Andrew on August 24th and a month later Andrew's devastation was still being assessed. Andrew was the worst natural disaster ever to hit the United States, killing people in both Florida and Louisiana. In Florida alone, at least 250,000 people were left homeless and thousands of others were living in homes partially destroyed. Entire sections of cities were gone. Lei McElveen, historian for the Woman's Club of Hialeah, wrote:

> On August 24, at 4:00 a.m. Hurricane Andrew made landfall in Dade County and forever changed the lives of our residents. Those most severely affected, living in Homestead, Florida City, Cutler Ridge and Country Walk, had devastating damage and Dade County became a war zone for many months. Those living north of the worst hit areas felt hard-hit as well, with power outages, spoiled food and a need to get food and water for ourselves as well for those less fortunate down south. Military planes flying over our houses, curfew hours and tree and plant clean-up made this a nightmare for some and a time of sharing for all of us. We learned

to put things in perspective and began to realize how small our problems had been before the hurricane. With the help of the military, the government and our caring for each other, we have begun to put our lives back together again, but the process is very slow and will be ongoing for some time. Our club ached for our sister clubs in the south end of Dade County that lost both their club houses and their homes.

Telethons raised hundreds of thousands of dollars; practically every organization in the state collected food and money; Florida Federation and General Federation members sent money to FFWC headquarters for emergency relief; many FFWC clubs sent aid directly to schools, churches and people in addition to contributing through relief organizations such as the Red Cross and the Salvation Army; tent cities were set up by the Federal Government and military units were stationed in the area both to assure order and to help with food and supplies distribution. Club houses and homes of many members were gone. Businesses and jobs disappeared. As insurance claims were made, estimates of damage rose to $30 billion and several insurance companies failed. Others were reluctant to renew policies on property located in Florida's coastal communities. Rebuilding and recouping losses would take years.

Everglades National Park Threatened

In addition to concern over friends and club members, there was reason to wonder how Everglades National Park would recover because the storm had cut a 25 mile swath through the park, snapping forty year old pine trees like match sticks and uprooting mature mahogany and gumbo limbo trees. The park was closed to the public. Only scientists, park rangers and a few reporters were admitted. The wisdom of replacing the destroyed park buildings was questioned. The Florida Federation was interested, but Friends of the Everglades was an organization that worked specifically to keep the park as it was. When Marjory Stoneman Douglas wrote *River of Grass*, published about the same time that FFWC gave its Royal Palm Park to the national park service to become a part of the Everglades National Park, her book interested people in the Everglades area as nothing else had done and resulted in many environmental groups taking on welfare of the park as a major concern.

Club members from South Florida who had responsibilities at the Fall Board came to the meeting at the Clarion Hotel in Orlando. Their friends were relieved that they were able to come and naturally asked how they were. Often the answer was, "Wonderful, now, I've just had my first hot bath in a month." Before the 98th Annual Convention in 1993 met, it was obvious that destroyed club houses and disrupted lives would not stop the women's clubs of South Florida. All of the clubs located in the most devastated part of the state sent their dues to headquarters on time.

When delegates met at Convention in April 1993 at Twin Towers, Orlando, women from Crystal River and Yankeetown clubs had their own disaster stories to tell. With little warning, what became known as "the no-name storm" had come in off the Gulf during the night of March 12th and 13th pushing a nine foot surge of water before it, which inundated homes, streets and highways. Sliding glass doors popped out of their tracks when rising water hit them, washing debris, sea weed and even boats into living rooms. When water reached six feet in depth, members said they learned that refrigerators float. Airboats patrolled streets rescuing people from their flooded homes. No club houses were entirely lost but club members had severely damaged homes.

Centennial Planned for 1995

In spite of all the natural disasters of 1992 and '93, committees were busy planning for two major events — Jeannine Faubion's installation as President of the General Federation of Women's Clubs in 1994 and the FFWC Centennial celebration of FFWC in 1995. The departments of arts, conservation, education, home life, international affairs and public affairs kept to their schedules. Individual clubs working through their various departments supported with volunteer hours and funds dozens of other organizations such as Literacy Volunteers of America, March of Dimes, Salvation Army, Rescue Mission, Special Olympics, United Way, Save Our Species, community libraries, American Cancer Society, CARE, Hope

Lodges, Hospice, HOBY, Habitat for Humanity, American Heart Association, rest homes, humane societies, Adopt a Teacher, A GIFT— A Life Donors, girls clubs, museums, drug free graduation parties, science fairs, Audubon, scholarships, senior citizen centers and more, depending on the community's needs.

Rose Appenzeller concluded her 1990-1992 history of the Woman's Club of Panama City with this statement which could describe most of the clubs of FFWC:

> We have a synergetic relationship with our community for as we strive to serve and better our causes so do we reap the benefits of living in a progressive and welcoming city.

Since the Florida Federation of Woman's Clubs was first organized members had approached improvement in many areas and as a result groups which had specific interests had spun off. Many garden clubs had their beginnings in women's clubs. PTAs often had their origins in a local woman's club as did music organizations. Each group had the blessing of the local woman's club and often women were active in the new club that was formed as well as remaining in their woman's club. However, a woman with limited time tended to belong only to the club where she had a specific interest. To some extent the nurturing of these spin-off clubs eroded the membership potential of the women's clubs. But there remained more than enough volunteer work to be done and as Florida's population increased so did the prospective member pool. Recruiting new members and retaining old members was one of the goals of the 1992-1994 administration of FFWC.

A Polluted Paradise

The quality of life in Florida was declining in areas where communities had reached their growth capacities. However, for most people, the advantages of living in Florida continued to outweigh the disadvantages. Florida's population had been doubling every 19 years since 1830 but water consumption had doubled every fifteen years. In planning for the future, conservationists had to educate the citizenry on prudent use of energy and water. The Florida Federation with its OFFALOT and BRIGHTLAND programs for kindergartners and first graders took a significant step toward educating a new generation to save energy. Delegates also adopted resolutions imploring the legislature to preserve wetlands. They supported Friends of the Everglades and other environmental groups that were interested in restoring the water flow through the Everglades' "river of grass." Drainage canals had diverted much of the water that once flowed through the Everglades and water which continued to filter through the park had become polluted from the cattle ranches, vegetable farms and sugar cane fields that flourished on the drained land. Subdivisions, paved streets, golf courses and shopping malls extended westward from the east coast of South Florida into previous swampland. Citrus groves moved farther south as agriculturists learned that swamps could be drained into a retaining lake and when needed the lake water could be used to irrigate the trees. Computers allowed measured amounts of nutrients to be added to the water resulting in the citrus groves being "fertigated" rather than irrigated. Fertigated citrus trees produced earlier, more prolifically and more profitably. The tension between trying to preserve the natural beauty of Florida in such places as the Everglades National Park and providing housing, food, jobs, education, transportation and health services for Florida's ever increasing population was frustrating. Overcrowding, homelessness, traffic jams, increase in crime and environmental degradation demanded the attention of the citizens of Florida.

Runaway Crime

Stopping the increase in crime had long been a priority of FFWC members. A resolution adopted by delegates to the 98th Convention asked that:

> Florida Federation of Women's Clubs pursue all avenues to effect change in the Florida statutes regarding provisional gain time which results in early release of prisoners sentenced for violent crimes. FFWC clubs and their members should contact their state representatives urging them to change this law to protect the citizens of Florida and to see that these criminals serve their full sentence.

However, if the legislation were passed, it would be difficult to implement because Florida's prison beds and jail space did not meet legal requirements against overcrowding sufficiently to permit all of the criminals sentenced to serve their full time. For some, prison was preferable to life outside because it provided shelter, food, clothes, and health care. There was a high percentage of repeat offenders among early released prisoners.

Taking money from school budgets to build prisons has been counter-productive but people generally are against higher taxes. Florida has no state income tax, which has made it an attractive place for retirees who have little interest in improving schools, but who want health services and crime-free neighborhoods. Florida has relied chiefly on a sales tax for funds and when there is an economic downturn such as that experienced in the early 1990s funding for schools, parks, prisons, universities and social services is often cut.

Causes for the ever increasing rate of crime are multiple. Club women have tried unsuccessfully to withhold from children movies and comic books that depict extreme violence, believing that crime has increased because television programs have become more and more violent. Certainly, movies no longer exercise any internal or external control on violence and horror. Gun control is a panacea extolled by others. Schools are blamed as harassed teachers must deal with children of drug addicted mothers, pregnant teen age girls with no parenting skills, abusive parents and homes where disrespect for any authority is the normal adult attitude. In the early 90s there were more than three million children in Florida under the age of 18 and instances of deprivation, abuse, juvenile crime, educational failures, teen pregnancy and poverty filled the news and overwhelmed teachers and social workers. Florida's future depended on giving its children a chance to live up to their potential through appropriate health care, adequate nutrition, a safe environment, education and nurturing adults. Florida Federation women had been volunteering in their communities for a hundred years and it was clear that the decades of FFWC's second century would demand dedicated volunteers to solve problems more complex than any that faced FFWC members during their first hundred years.

Take Back Your Poor, Your Huddled Masses...

Another resolution adopted at the 98th Convention was a response to large numbers of immigrants coming to the state from Central and South America and from Haiti. Some of these people were sick and became an economic burden. Many of them asked for political asylum but they came as economic refugees, too. South Florida especially had experienced a change in language and culture with the influx of Hispanics and Haitians. Immigrants with the AIDS virus required expensive treatment. Health authorities had considered tuberculosis a conquered disease, but it reappeared in a form highly resistant to antibiotics. The resolution that spoke to health requirements for immigrants said:

> WHEREAS, The United States Government's first responsibility and obligation is to protect the health and welfare of its citizens.
>
> WHEREAS, The United States of America cannot afford to support more unhealthy and financially dependent immigrants, and this has affected funds for education, safety and the general welfare of our citizens.
>
> RESOLVED, The Florida Federation of Women's Clubs expresses its belief that everyone immigrating to the United States of America for any reason shall be tested for venereal diseases, hepatitis, AIDS and tuberculosis. Positive results on any of the above mentioned shall deny admittance to the United States of America.

The United States as a haven for the "world's troubled masses yearning to be free" was a dream no longer sustainable in the opinion of many citizens of the United States.

Community beautification remained a high priority with clubs doing their part on the "Adopt a Highway" program which helped recycle discarded containers and removed trash from highway right-of-ways. Town parks and playgrounds were improved. An outstanding example of a community improvement program was the Panama City Junior Woman's Club that raised, through cash donations and work, the equivalent of $100,000.00 and completed a park in three days.

Name recognition for the General Federation of Women's Clubs, the largest women's volunteer organization in the world, was a problem because each state organization was

Leading the Way: A Century of Service

JEANNINE FAUBION (Mrs. Raymond A.)
President of FFWC, 1978-1980; President of GFWC, 1994-1996

Jessie Hamm Meyer

Fig. 37. Entrance to FFWC Headquarters, 4444 Florida National Drive, Lakeland, Florida. Dedicated May 6, 1990.

Leading the Way: A Century of Service

"BERT" ALBERTI (Mrs. Patrick)
President of FFWC during its Centennial Year (1994) and the first year of its second century (1995). Editor of *Leading the Way.*

Jessie Hamm Meyer

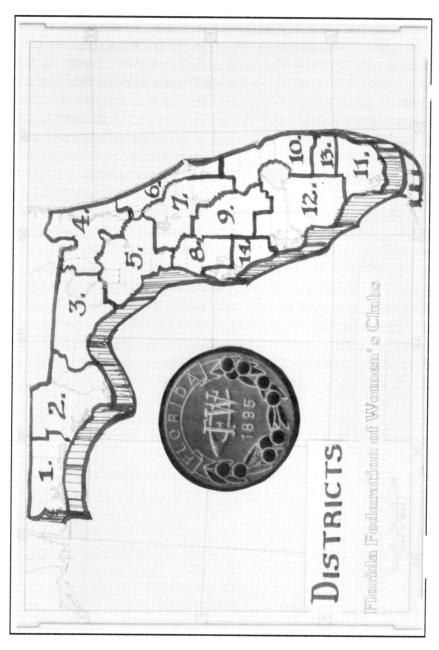

Fig. 39. Outline map of the fourteen districts of the GFWC Florida Federation of Women's Clubs.

Leading the Way: A Century of Service

federated under its state's name. At the 98th Convention delegates voted to change the name of the Florida Federation of Women's Clubs to GFWC Florida Federation of Women's Clubs giving more prominence to the international federation. This name change was made at an appropriate time as Jeannine Faubion of the Florida Federation was President Elect of the General Federation and would be installed as president in 1994.

The Fall Board of FFWC met September 17-20, 1993, at the Omni Hotel in Jacksonville with workshops to help each club enhance its image on the local level by letting its community know that service to the schools and to the community was its priority.

The 99th Convention was to meet at Twin Towers in Orlando April 22-25, 1994. Plans for their Centennial celebration were foremost as delegates looked forward to their 100th year under the leadership of President-elect Mrs. Patrick Alberti (Bert). The Centennial Celebration was the plan for the 100th Convention at the Clarion Plaza Hotel, Orlando, May 5-9, 1995. Delegates dressed in costumes of a century ago, should look back at what their organization had accomplished and strengthen their determination to continue their service to their communities in their second century.

Jessie Hamm Meyer

14 – Conclusion

THIS history has recorded what Florida Federation women did and is not intended to overlook their human weaknesses. Goals were high and visions clear but club members did not agree at all times about how they should get things done. Their accomplishments were heroic but they often stumbled along the way.

When Mary Stewart wrote *The Collect For Clubwomen* in 1904, she knew exactly what she was saying when she wrote, "Grant that we may realize it is the little things that create differences, that in the big things of life we are as one." Women have difficulty internalizing Mary Stewart's words even though they repeat them at every meeting.

An updated warning — not nearly so elegant would be:

"Don't sweat the small stuff."

Women have an infinite capacity for details and sometimes lose sight of their goals while they decide whether to stuff the tomatoes at the luncheon with chicken salad or tuna. They have strayed down the path of elegant teas, boresome book reviews, endless discussions over clubhouse decor and "the way we've always done it." A club can lose half its membership in disagreement whether to serve lunch, just have punch and cookies or nothing at all at its business meetings. Yet those same women can unite on a project and raise hundreds of dollars to give a high school graduate a scholarship. They will make lasting friendships while planting trees and flowers to beautify their town but nurse hurt feelings over an imagined wrong. During the many achievements recorded in these pages, there have also been private struggles when strong personalities clashed, when politics of administrations diminished their expressed goals and when a power structure developed that shut out rising talent. When this has occurred, clubs have often stagnated and declined.

While the population of Florida has increased, membership in FFWC has decreased, particularly during the last twenty years. A reason often given is that women now hold jobs and have little time for volunteer work. That is true for many women who have full time jobs and are caring for their families and also aging parents. But there are thousands of women who have retired in their sixties and have no responsibilities. Many of them are volunteering and making their contributions, but there are too many who feel that they have done their share. Women live longer at the end of the twentieth century than at the end of the nineteenth century and it would appear that health permitting, they need "to justify the space they occupy." The needs for caring, helping and nurturing those less fortunate have never been greater. Women's clubs are a service organization and requirements for membership make no demands as to religion, financial condition, race or degree of education. Clubs should reach out and enlist retired women, many of whom have recently moved to Florida. A local FFWC club can offer these new Florida citizens friendship and an opportunity to enrich their lives with meaningful service.

Any woman who is elected to an office of her local club, the Florida Federation or the General Federation of Women's Clubs, understands that she is going to sacrifice much of her personal time and energy to the organization which she has agreed to serve. Praise, respect and honor are due each of those women who have served in any official capacity. Very few club members who have not held office know how many hours their officers spend planning meetings, keeping records, communicating with clubs and trying to solve problems that arise when dealing with many members.

However, a tribute should be given to the thousands of members of FFWC who have contributed to their state and community in ways which never get their names on plaques, in histories or even in the minutes of their own clubs. An example of a person who epitomized the best of this kind of club woman was a member of what was the Twentieth Century Club of Gainesville, later the Woman's Club of Gainesville. Her name was Adelaide Nieland. She was active in her church, the American Association of University Women, the Garden Club, the University Woman's Club and the Woman's Club of Gainesville. She never sought office and shied away from chairing committees but her work was thorough, organized, driven by high intelligence and wisdom. She guided young and experienced members to become leaders. Equally skilled at keeping records, working in the kitchen, making travel arrangements for delegates, pricing articles for rummage sales, explaining needed legislation, or doing the detail work to establish a loan or scholarship fund, Mrs. Nieland worked with modesty and grace, allowing others to sit in the limelight and take the credit. Adelaide Nieland influenced all whom she touched to become better than they thought they could be. There are such women in almost every club and, without them, there would be no history of the Florida Federation of Women's Clubs.

Bibliography

Primary Sources

Florida Federation of Women's Clubs Archives, containing minutes, scrapbooks, treasurers' reports, yearbooks, manuals, bylaws, officers reports and correspondence.

The Florida Federation Of Women's Clubs Year Book, 1903-1904

The Florida Federation Of Women's Clubs, 1904, 1905, 1906
Beginning with the 1908 publication, the yearbooks are titled:

Florida State Federation Of Women's Clubs Manual, 1908-1913

Florida Federation of Women's Clubs, 1913-1924 (State and Manual omitted from titles)

Year Book of the Florida Federation of Women's Clubs, 1924-1940.

Florida Federation of Women's Clubs Reports, 1940-1942; *Manual*, 1942-1944 (published in one volume).

Florida Federation of Women's Clubs Reports, 1942-1944; *Manual*, 1944-1946 (Golden Jubilee Issue).

Florida Federation of Women's Clubs Reports, 1944-1946; *Manual*, 1946-1948.

Florida Federation of Women's Clubs Reports, 1948-1950; *Manual*, 1950-1952.

Florida Federation of Women's Clubs Manuals and Reports, 1952-1980.

Florida Federation of Women's Clubs Handbook, 1980-1994.

Florida Federation of Women's Clubs Manual, 1980-1994.

Florida Federation of Women's Clubs Directory, 1929, 1931-1932, 1933-1934.

The Florida Bulletin, published by the Florida Federation of Women's Clubs (September 1921 through December 1926)

The Florida Clubwoman, published by Florida Federation of Women's Clubs (January 1927-June 1993)

Histories of FFWC Clubs by Club historians (manuscripts, see below).

History of the Florida Federation of Women's Clubs 1895-1960, by Mabel Meadows Staats (unpublished)

History of the Florida Federation of Women's Clubs 1948-1956, by Mary Newell Eaton (unpublished)

History of the Florida Federation of Women's Clubs 1960-1980, by Jeannine Collier Faubion (unpublished)

General Federation of Women's Clubs, First Triennial Convention, Detroit, Michigan, June 4-12, 1935, compiled and edited by Grace Morrison Poole and Vella Alberta Winner, Editor and Manager, *The Clubwoman*, GFWC NEWS SERVICE, Washington, D.C.

Other Sources

Adler, Mortimer J., Editor-in-chief, *The Annals of America*, Volumes from 1895 to 1968, Encyclopedia Britannica, Inc.

Blackman, Lucy Worthington, *The Florida Federation of Women's Clubs, 1895-1939*, Southern Historical Publishing Associates, Jacksonville, 1939.

Burt, Al, *Becalmed in the Mullet Latitudes — Al Burt's Florida*, *Tropic Magazine*, *Miami Herald* and *Florida Classics Library*, 1983.

Douglas, Marjory Stoneman, *River of Grass*, Rinehart and Company, Inc., New York, 1947.

Douglas, Marjory Stoneman, *Florida, The Long Frontier*, Harper and Row, New York, 1967.

Hanna, Alfred Jackson and Katherine Abbey, *Flori da's Golden Sands*, Bobbs-Merrill, 1950.

Hoffman, Mark S., Editor, *The World Almanac and Book of Facts, 1993*, Pharos Books, Scripps Howard Company, 1992.

Houde, Mary Jean, *Reaching Out,*, Mobium Press, Chicago, 1989

Jahoda, Gloria, *The Other Florida*, Charles Scribner and Sons,

New York, 1967.

Morrison, Samuel Elliot, *The Oxford History of the American People,* Oxford University Press, New York, 1965.

Oppel, Frank and Tony Meisel, Editors, *Tales of Old Florida,* Castle, Secaucus, N.J., 1987.

Parks, Pat, *The Railroad That Died At Sea,* The Stephen Greene Press, Brattleboro, Vermont, 1968.

Smiley, Nixon, *Yesterday's Florida,* E. E. Seemann Publishing, Inc., Miami, 1974.

Tebeau, Charlton W., *A History Of Florida,* University of Miami Press, Coral Gables, FL. 1971

Wells, Mildred White, *Unity In Diversity - The History of the General Federation of Women's Clubs,* Diamond Jubilee Edition, General Federation of Women's Clubs, Washington, D.C., 1965.

Wood, Mary I., *General Federation Of Women's Clubs, The History of the First Twenty-two Years of Its Organization,* Norwood Press, Norwood, Mass., 1912.

Jessie Hamm Meyer

FFWC CLUB HISTORIES

(Submitted to FFWC historians, Jessie Meyer and Lee Nees)
(Dates indicate years for which history was submitted.)

DISTRICT 1

Woman's Club of Crestview	1917-1976
Fort Walton Beach Woman's Club, Inc.	1920-1992
Milton Woman's Club	1913-1991
Myrtle Grove Woman's Club, Inc., Pensacola	1991-1992
Woman's Club of Pensacola, Inc.	1920-1992
Santa Rosa Woman's Club	1961-1992
Twin Cities Woman's Club, Niceville	1983-1992

DISTRICT 2

Blountstown Woman's Club	1986-1992
Chattahoochee Woman's Club, Inc.	1915-1975
Woman's Club of Chipley, Inc.	1921-1989
GFWC Gulf Coast Woman's Club, Inc	1991-1992
Marianna Woman's Club, Inc.	1919-1982
Woman's Club of Panama City, Inc.	1913-1988
Philaco Woman's Club of Appalachicola	1896-1990
Wewahitchka Woman's Club	1933-1988

DISTRICT 3

Branford Woman's Club, Inc	1946-1979
Perry Woman's Club	1989- — —
The Woman's Club of Tallahassee, Inc.	1903-1990

DISTRICT 4

Crescent City Woman's Club, Inc.	1890-1988
The Woman's Club of Fernandina Beach, Inc.	1920-1964
Jacksonville Beaches Woman's Club, Inc.	1907-1992
The Woman's Club of Lake City	1990-1991
Lakewood-San Jose Woman's Club, Inc.	1947-1990
Orange Park Woman's Club	1910-1992
The Woman's Club of St. Augustine	1990-1991
Southside Woman's Club, Jacksonville, Inc.	1912-1991
V.I. A., Inc., Green Cove Springs	1890-1988
The Woman's Club of Welaka	1959-1992

DISTRICT 5

Beverly Hills Woman's Club	1987-1992
Crystal River Woman's Club, Inc.	1907-1989
The Gainesville Woman's Club, Inc.	1903-1991
Greater Ocala Woman's Club, Inc.	1989-1992
Hawthorne Woman's Club	1912-1992
High Springs New Century Woman's Club	1899-1992
The Inverness Woman's Club	1917-1974
The Woman's Club of Keystone Heights, Inc.	1924-1992
Melrose Woman's Club, Inc.	1890-1992
The Woman's Club of Ocala	1909-1991
Woman's Club of Trenton	1929-1989
Williston Woman's Club	1914-1992

DISTRICT 6

Cocoa Beach Woman's Club, Inc.	1965-1982
Community Woman's Club, Inc. Cocoa	1922-1989
DeBary Woman's Club	1955-1989
The Woman's Club of Deland	1906-1991
Deltona Woman's Club, Inc.	1964-1988
Flagler Woman's Club, Inc.	1946-1992
GFWC Melbourne Woman's Club, Inc.	1912-1990
Merritt Island Woman's Club	1966-1990
The Woman's Club of New Smyrna, Inc.	1911-1992
Palm Coast Woman's Club	1974-1991
The Palmetto Club, Inc., Daytona Beach	1894-1992
Satellite Beach Woman's Club, Inc.	1964-1992
Woman's Club of Titusville, Inc.	1900-1967
Village I. A. of Orange City, Inc.	1894-1960

DISTRICT 7

Central Civic Council, Kissimmee	1970-1992
Clermont Woman's Civic, Inc.	1921-1989
College Park Woman's Civic Club, Orlando	1949-1992
Oviedo Woman's Club, Inc.	1989-1990
Woman's Club of St. Cloud, Inc.	1910-1991
Sorosis of Orlando	1893-1991
Suburban Woman's Club, Orlando	1956-1992
Umatilla Woman's Club	1920-1988
Wekiva Woman's Club, Apopka	1981-1991

DISTRICT 8

Brooksville Woman's Club,Inc.	1910-1992
Lutz-Land O'Lakes Woman's Club,Inc.	1960-1991
Federated Woman's Club of New Port Richey	1923-1992
Woman's Club of Plant City,Inc.	1984-1992
Ruskin Woman's Club,Inc.	1912-1992
Sun City Center Woman's Club,Inc.	1962-1991
Tampa Woman's Club,Inc.	1900-1988
Tampa Civic Association	1989-1992
Temple Terrace Woman's Club,Inc.	1959-1992
Woman's Club of Zephyrhills	1915-1992

DISTRICT 9

Woman's Club of Auburndale, Inc.	1914-1990
The Woman's Club of Avon Park,Inc.	1919-1989
Woman's Club of Bartow, Inc.	1910-1990
Fort Meade Woman's Club	1924-1989
Frostproof Woman's Club,Inc.	1924-1989
Lake Hamilton Woman's Club	1965-1989
Lake Placid Woman's Club,Inc.	1923-1989
The Woman's Club of Lake Wales	1928-1989
The Woman's Club of Mulberry	1948-1990
Polk City Woman's Club,Inc.	1929-1989
Woman's Club of Sebring, Inc.	1919-1989
Sorosis Woman's Club of Auburndale,Inc	1946-1989
The United Women's Club of Lakeland	1912-1992
Wauchula Woman's Club	1906-1992
Woman's Club of Winter Haven,Inc.	1913-1990

DISTRICT 10

Casaurina Club of Lantana	‒ ‒-1991
Coterie Club of Palm Beaches	1960-1989
Woman's Club of Delray Beach	1902-1982
Woman's Club of Fort Pierce,Inc.	1913-1992
Woman's Club of Jupiter/Tequesta,Inc.	1911-1990
Woman's Club of Lake Worth, Inc.	1914-1989
The Lantana Woman's Club	1940-1989
Palm Beach Gardens Woman's Club	1967-1992
Port St. Lucie Woman's Club,Inc.	1975-1991
Royale Woman's Club of Boca Raton,Inc.	1964-1991

Leading the Way: A Century of Service

St. Lucie Shores Woman's Club,Inc.	1987-1990
Vero Beach Woman's Club,Inc.	1915-1983
Woman's Club of West Palm Beach,Inc.	1910-1977

DISTRICT 11

Bayshore Woman's Club	1955-1963
Woman's Club of Hialeah,Inc.	1922-1991
Woman's Club of Homestead, Inc.	1914-1991
Key West Woman's Club, Inc.	1915-1992
Miami Woman's Club	1900-1955
Miami Springs Woman's Club	1939-1991
Palm Springs Woman's Club,Inc.	1960-1989
Whispering Pines Woman's Club,Inc.	1965-1992

DISTRICT 12

Moore Haven Woman's Club	1916-1991
Naples Woman's Club,Inc.	1932-1992 (oral history)
Woman's Club of Port Charlotte,Inc	1968-1992

DISTRICT 13

Coral Springs Woman's Club	1970-1982
Woman's Club of Deerfield Beach,Inc.	1917-1989
Fort Lauderdale Woman's Club,Inc.	1911-1991
Oakland Park Woman's Club	1916-1954
The Plantation Woman's Club,Inc.	1949-1992
Pompano Beach Woman's Club,Inc.	1910-1984
Woman's Club of West Broward,Inc.	1990-1992

DISTRICT 14

Anna Maria Island Woman's Club,Inc.	1941-1992
Beta Woman's Club, St. Petersburg	— — -1991
GFWC Clearwater Com. Woman's Club	1971-1992
Woman's Club of Gulfport	— — -1991
Gulfport Coterie	1953-1991
Pinellas Park Woman's Club, Inc.	1965-1982
Pinellas Seminole Woman's Club	1960-1991
St. Petersburg Woman's Club,Inc.	1913-1989
GFWC Suncoast Com. Woman's Club,Largo	1979- — —
Woman's Club of Tarpon Springs,Inc.	1882-1967

Jessie Hamm Meyer

Appendix — List of Past Presidents, and Junior Directors

PRESIDENTS, 1895-1995

1895-1897	Mrs. P.A. Borden Hamilton	V.I.A. Green Cove Springs
1897-1899	Mrs. N. C. Wamboldt	Town I.A Fair field, Jacksonville
1899	Mrs. William Ruger (resigned)	Palmetto Club, Daytona Bch
1899-1901	Mrs. J.C. Beekman	W.T.I. & C.A, Tarpon Springs
1901-1903	Mrs. W. W. Cummer	Woman's Club, Jacksonville
1903-1905	Mrs. Lawrence Haynes	Woman's Club, Jacksonville
1905-1906	Mrs. Richard F. Adams	Woman's Club, Palatka
1906-1908	Mrs. Charles H. Raynor	Palmetto Club, Daytona Bch
1908-1910	Mrs. Thomas M. Shackleford	Woman's Club, Tallahassee
1910-1912	Mrs. A. E. Frederick	Woman's Club, Miami
1912-1914	Mrs. William Hocker	Woman's Club, Ocala
1914-1917	Mrs. W.S. Jennings	Springfield I.A., Jacksonville
1917-1919	Mrs. Edgar Lewis	Woman's Club, Fort Pierce
1919-1921	Mrs. J.W. McCollum Palmer	Twentieth Cent.C , Gainesville
1921-1923	Mrs. Elizabeth S. Jackson	Woman's Club, Dunedin
1923-1926	Mrs. William F. Blackman	Sorosis, Orlando
1926-1928	Mrs. Katherine B. Tippets	Woman's Club, St. Petersburg
1928-1930	Mrs. Murray L. Stanley	Palmetto Club, Daytona Bch.
1930-1932	Mrs. William L. Wilson	Woman's Club, Panama City
1932-1934	Mrs. Meade A. Love	Woman's Club, Quincy
1934-1934	Mrs. Robert Shearer	Sorosis, Orlando
1934-1936	Mrs. T. V. Moore	Woman's Club, Miami
1936-1938	Mrs. John G. Kellum	Woman's Club, Tallahassee
1938-1940	Mrs. Mildred White Wells	Palmetto Club, Daytona Bch.
1940-1942	Mrs. Thurston Roberts	Woman's Club, Jacksonville
1942-1944	Mrs. Ralph Austin Smith	Woman's Club, Sanford
1944-1946	Mrs. Joseph L. Gray	Woman's Club, Lake City

Leading the Way: A Century of Service

1946-1948	Mrs. L.J. McCaffrey	North Miami Woman's Club
1948-1950	Mrs. A.T. MacKay	Sorosis, Orlando
1950-1952	Mrs. Raeburn C. Horne	Woman's Club, Madison
1952-1954	Mrs. Walter S. Jones	Woman's Club, Jacksonville
1954-1956	Mrs. E.D. Pearce	Woman's Club, Miami
1956-1958	Mrs. C.M. Washburn	Woman's Club, Tampa
1958-1960	Mrs. C.L. Menser (Mrs. Leslie Schweitzer)	Woman's Club, Vero Beach
1960-1962	Mrs. M. Lewis Hall	Woman's Club, Coral Gables
1962-1964	Mrs. J.R. Glover	Woman's Club, Lakeland
1964-1966	Mrs. Mark W. Emmel	Woman's Club, Gainesville
1966-1968	Mrs. Henry H. Carleton	Woman's Club, St. Petersburg
1968-1970	Mrs. Thomas Harrison	Woman's Club, Fort Lauderdale
1970-1972	Mrs. J. C. Pratt	Woman's Club, Tallahassee
1972-1974	Mrs. Karl J. King	Woman's Club, Tampa
1974-1976	Mrs. E. Ross Harris	Woman's Club, Jacksonville
1976-1978	Mrs. Elmer M. Norton (Mrs. Lester Wofford)	Southside W. C., Jacksonville
1978-1980	Mrs. Raymond A. Faubion (Jeannine)	Woman's Club, Fort Myers
1980-1982	Mrs. John W. Mace (Mary)	Cocoa Beach Woman's Club
1982-1984	Mrs. Kenneth Perkins (Lois)	Wilton Manors Woman's Club
1984-1986	Mrs. Louis Lutz (Judy)	Clearwater Com. Woman's Club
1986-1988	Mrs. Lee A. Thornburg (Vi)	Auburndale Woman's Club
1988-1990	Mrs. Eugene Smith (Jimmie)	Melbourne Woman's Club
1990-1992	Mrs. Malcolm Duggan (Tam)	Woman's Club, Ocala
1992-1994	Mrs. Braxton Bright (Marcia)	Woman's Club, Lakeland
1994-1996	Mrs. Patrick J. Alberti (Bert)	North Miami Woman's Club

JUNIORS

Mrs. W.S. Jennings, President FFWC (1914- 1917), appointed Mrs. G. O. Palmer of Lake City as Vice Chairman to direct the work of the Junior Civic League.

Mrs. William F. Blackman, President FFWC (1923-1926), appointed Mrs. E. M. Galloway of Sanford as first chairman of junior membership. Other appointees to that office were:

1926-1928	Miss Daisy Belle Johns	St. Petersburg
1928-1930	Mrs. W. L. Robinson	Coral Gables

In 1930, Juniors became a department of FFWC with an age limit of 25 years and Mrs. R.J. Greene was named vice chairman of juniors for

Jessie Hamm Meyer

1930-1932.

CHAIRMAN OF JUNIORS

1932-1934	Mrs. R.J. Greene	Perry
1934-1938	Mrs. Joseph Gray	Lake City
1938-1940	Mrs. Mary Stewart McLeod*	Bartow
1940-1942	Mrs. Malcolm McDonald	Coral Gables
1942-1943	Mrs. George D. Hore	Jacksonville
1943-1946	Mrs. A.W. Bloodworth	Lake City
1946-1948	Mrs. C. Russell Morgan	Miami

*First Chairman who had been a junior member.

Revision of FFWC Bylaws in 1948 changed title Chairman of Juniors to Director of Juniors.

STATE DIRECTORS OF JUNIOR CLUBS

1948-1950	Mrs. Neil Bitting	Ocala
1950-1952	Mrs. N.A. Benevento	West Palm Beach
1952-1954	Mrs. Lawton Swann, Jr.	St. Petersburg
1954-1956	Mrs. Ben Rich, Jr.	Ocala
1956-1957	Mrs. Charles Campbell	Zephyrhills
1957-1958	Mrs. Judd Chapman	Tampa
1958-1960	Mrs. Joseph Clark	Jacksonville
1960-1962	Mrs. John G. Mahon	Jacksonville
1962-1964	Mrs. Herbert Savage	Northeast Miami
1964-1966	Mrs. J. Frank Johnson, Jr.	Tampa
1966-1968	Mrs. Charles F. Hunt	Tampa
1968-1970	Ginny Winsemann	Hollywood
1970-1972	Jo Conibear	Lakeland
1972-1974	Jeannine Faubion	Fort Myers
1974-1976	Lois Perkins	Wilton Manors
1976-1978	Lynne Blount	Temple Terrace
1978-1980	D. Judith Lutz	Largo
1980-1982	Julie Babcock	Lakewood-San Jose
1982-1984	Dianne Foerster	Brandon
1984-1986	Marcia Bright	Lakeland
1986-1988	Karen-Lee Donohue	Tamarac
1988-1990	Pat Warbritton	Brandon
1990-1992	Nancy Crawford	Sanford
1992-1994	Joyce Johnston	Temple Terrace

About the Author

JESSIE IRENE HAMM MEYER was born in Kentucky and has lived most of her life in Florida. With a bachelor of arts degree from Berea College and a master of arts degree from the University of Florida, Meyer has taught in two Kentucky high schools and three Florida high schools, as well as the American school of Managua, Nicaragua.

She has lived in Ocala, Hollywood, Jacksonville, Pensacola, Gainesville, and Boca Raton, and is now retired at the Meyer lake home near Melrose, Florida.

Meyer served as president of the Gainesville Chapter of the American Association of University Women, Alachua County Teachers, Florida Moravian Women's Fellowship and the Woman's Club of Keystone Heights. She also served on the state board of the Florida Education Association and in several state positions with the Florida Federation of Women's Clubs. Meyer is a member of Phi Kappa Phi, Delta Kappa Gamma, Daughters of the American Revolution and is a Kentucky Colonel! She has been named Distinguished Alumna of Berea College.

Meyer has traveled in 48 states, more than 50 countries in five continents, has been involved in international meetings and consultantships in Sweden, Denmark, Luxemburg, Colombia, and Guatemala and lived in Central America for two and a half years.

She is the author of historical materials on education of the American Indian, on the Republic of Honduras, and collaborated in a national study for the trustees of the Moravian Theological Seminary.

She has been married to Harvey K. Meyer for almost 60 years, is the mother of three, grandmother of three and great-grandmother of two. Meyer has been acquainted personally with many of the federated leaders about whom she wrote.